AF262980

CANCEL ME IF YOU CAN

CANCEL ME IF YOU CAN

DAVE PORTNOY

GALLERY BOOKS

New York Amsterdam/Antwerp London
Toronto Sydney/Melbourne New Delhi

Gallery Books
An Imprint of Simon & Schuster, LLC
1230 Avenue of the Americas
New York, NY 10020

First Gallery Books hardcover edition June 2026

Interior design by Jaime Putorti

Manufactured in the United States of America

10 9 8 7 6 5 4 3 2 1

Library of Congress Control Number: 2026939157

ISBN 978-1-6682-2202-7
ISBN 978-1-6682-2204-1 (ebook)

Contents

Author's Note

Before I begin the process of writing my first-ever book, I'd like to take a second and blame this entire thing on not giving a shit about Future Dave. Because back when I was first pitched the idea to write the Barstool story, it sounded great. I was infatuated with the idea of walking through airports all across America and seeing my book on newsstands everywhere. I just thought that would be supercool. Plus I know how incredible and improbable this journey has been: from hawking newspapers in the streets of Boston to the media behemoth it has become today, the story of Barstool Sports is insane. I mean Barstool was literally just named one of the top 250 most iconic companies in the history of America by *Time* magazine. Pretty insane stuff. So like I said, when I was offered seven figures to write our story last year, it was all sunshine, rainbows, and gumdrops. As far as writing the book went, that would be a problem for Future Dave to handle, not Present-Day Dave. Well, guess what? The future has arrived. Now I have to sit down and write this thing. I have to somehow capture two decades of madness in a couple hundred pages. If Present-Day Dave could go back in time and give back the advance and undo all the commitments I made a year ago, I'd do it in a heartbeat. But alas, here we are, and one thing I've always done in the twenty years of Barstool is honor my commitments. So here we go. Here is my best attempt to tell the Barstool Sports journey through my eyes.

CANCEL ME IF YOU CAN

1

The Beginning

As long as I can remember, I always wanted to work for myself. To try my own thing. The motivation was simple: I didn't want to wake up every day and dread going to work. If I could have found a job that I enjoyed doing more than working for myself, it wouldn't have mattered; in fact, Barstool Sports probably wouldn't exist. But I couldn't find that dream job.

It probably didn't help that the only two things I liked were sports and gambling—not exactly the easiest fields to break into. By the time I was looking for jobs, I was essentially like every other white middle-class dude in the world who graduated with a liberal arts degree. I had no real skills, so I did what everybody like me does: I took a sales job out of college.

When I graduated from Michigan in 1999, the economy was booming. It was the height of the dot-com era, and any idiot could get a sales job. I moved back to Boston and landed at a place called Yankee Group. Every day I woke up and dragged myself to this job that I was good at but didn't care about. I was making $80K a year out of college, which seemed like an ungodly amount of money at the time. But I was bored out of my mind.

I was living with five of my high school buddies crammed into a tiny apartment in Allston-Brighton. If you are unfamiliar with Boston, Allston-Brighton was pretty much where every single young college graduate lived because it was relatively cheap and you could take the subway to work. Every night we'd sit around and brainstorm different business ideas that we could all start together. And every night kinda went the same way: we'd be watching whatever Boston team was in season, scheming up some cockamamie business idea in extreme detail with everybody ready to quit their jobs and go all in on this new company, only to never discuss it again by the next morning. Reflecting back, I don't think any of my buddies grasped how serious I was about these brainstorming sessions. In my head, I knew I was fully committed to trying one of them. It was just a matter of which one would get the green light.

After a year of long-shot brainstorming fueled by cheap beer and ramen, I narrowed down the list to the three best concepts. My three ideas:

1. A COLLEGE USED FURNITURE BUSINESS

You know how, at the end of every semester of college, kids dump all their old furniture onto the sidewalk? My idea was simple: drive around in trucks and take this free, used furniture, store it in warehouses, and then sell it online to new incoming students who could buy it way cheaper than if they bought it new. One hundred percent profit margin. Brilliant.

2. NEXTSTEP SCOUTING

I actually wrote a business plan for this idea and paid a couple grand to have the software built for it. The idea for this concept was to connect kids who wanted to play Division II or Division III athletics in college with college coaches who didn't have the budget to recruit. The theory is that lots of kids want to play sports in college but aren't Division I–type players. But playing sports is still an important part of where they go to school. Figuring out how to match these players with the right coach and program seemed like a win for everybody. Parents would pay to enter their kids into our database. We'd have regional scouts (townies who go to all the games anyway) scout the players and report back if they were worth a shot. Coaches could then search our database for players in their area that fit their criteria and find when they play, watch tape, contact them, and ultimately give a look to these kids who otherwise might never have been seen.

3. A SPORTS GAMBLING NEWSPAPER

I loved gambling. I had even started a website in college called thegamblingman .com. (I wonder if the person who owns that domain now knows that I once owned it.) It was basically a mini-blog where I offered my picks for the week to a pretty small group of friends who read it. Little did I know that it would be the precursor to what the world would come to know as Barstool Sports, media giant. But back then, I just wanted to talk and write about gambling.

* * *

My first memory of gambling is when my dad took me to Rockingham Park as a kid. This is a now-defunct horse track in New Hampshire. Even though I was only ten years old, I would dress up like I was in the movie *Goodfellas* to go to the track. I wore little suspenders, a fedora . . . the works. Seeing the horses up close was magical to me, and the thought of turning two bucks into ten or more was exhilarating. I was hooked instantly.

Once I was old enough to go to the track without my parents, I became a regular at Suffolk Downs—another dumpy track a few miles from my hometown. In high school, I'd head over after baseball practice or after games some nights just to bet on the ponies. My dad and I would take annual trips to Saratoga in the summers. That was my idea of a dream vacation: going to a racetrack and betting on horses. I loved it. And it wasn't just the ponies either.

I loved all forms of gambling. In middle school, I became the school bookie of sorts. I started passing out white cards in seventh grade. To be honest, I'm not even sure if I knew that what I was doing back then was illegal. For the uninitiated, a white card was a card that listed all the NFL games, and you could just check off your picks. The more picks you made, the higher the odds. I charged two dollars per white card, and you had to hit all your picks to win. (These were the international white card rules.) Anyway, this lasted halfway through the NFL season before word made its way up to the principal's office that I was running a bookmaking operation, and he put a kibosh on it. I ended up with a week's detention.

So it was no surprise to anyone that after college, I flew out to Vegas and interviewed with casinos, hoping to break into the big gambling business. But at each place, I was told the same thing: you start as a dealer and work your way up from there.

No thanks. I wasn't exactly interested in having cigarette smoke blown in my face at 9 a.m. I'd find another way in.

Anyway, I called up the offshore casinos and sportsbooks that I gambled with throughout college and asked if they were hiring. Again I was told no by just about everyone I spoke to, with the exception of a place called BetJamaica. They told me they weren't hiring BUT if, for some reason, I ever decided to start a gambling and fantasy sports newspaper, they'd be interested in advertising with me. At this time in the internet's evolution, gambling sites were all filled with infinity pop-up ads and other malware that made you terrified that your credit card info was being stolen. BetJamaica was apparently looking for ways to get off the internet so they could differentiate themselves. So even though starting a gambling newsletter was the furthest thing from my mind when I started the call, by the time I hung up, I was officially in the newspaper business.

In 2003, traditional newspapers were dying left and right. The magazine industry was heading off a cliff. People were increasingly choosing SportsCenter as their one-stop shop for all sports news, and print media was limping to the glue factory. Was this the ideal time to start a newspaper? Absolutely not. Did I realize this in real time? No. Did I research this? No. Did anybody call me a moron for starting a newspaper during this time? I honestly can't remember. Would I have cared even if they did? Probably not.

One thing I've always been blessed or cursed with, depending on how you look at it, is I truly don't care what other people say about me, or for their opinions on what I should do. It's just the way my brain has always worked. I'm not doing it to be an asshole; I just trust my instincts.

I had a directive from a potential revenue stream, and I set to work envisioning how I wanted my newspaper to look and sound. Naturally, I didn't have a journalism background. I hadn't taken a single writing course in college and I hadn't read too many books. I knew nothing about actually printing a newspaper, distributing it, how many copies I'd need, layout, editing, etc. But I'm a quick learner and was motivated by the pure, blinding hatred I had for my sales job. So I dove in, gathering all the information I could find to get my paper off the ground.

Let's start with the name. Where did it come from? I honestly don't remember the other names I kicked around, but Barstool Sports was the first name that had a URL that was available and that I liked. Barstool Sports was supposed to encompass anything that guys would discuss sitting around at a bar watching sports. It was supposed to have the tone of a real sports fan, which was the direct opposite of how the Boston sports media was at the time. Even though it was the dot-com era, this was still internet 1.0, before anybody really knew what a blogger or influencer was. The only social media company that existed was Myspace. Traditional newspapers and sports talk radio had a monopoly on sports media. And it seemed that all the sports reporters who covered the local teams weren't actually fans of the teams. Dan Shaughnessy of the *Boston Globe* openly rooted against the Red Sox. Ron Borges hated Bill Belichick and the Patriots. It was infuriating that the only media outlets covering your favorite teams were seemingly run by crusty old men who rooted and probably profited from their demise.

Barstool Sports would be the exact opposite. Sure, we'd criticize, but we were actual fans of our teams and would celebrate with their wins and lick our wounds with their losses.

The first two paragraphs from the first edition of the Barstool Sports newspaper reflected this sentiment:

> Welcome to the world of *Barstool Sports*, the only newspaper in Boston written by the common man, for the common man.
>
> Quite simply, the people at *Barstool Sports* are a bunch of average Joes, who like most guys, love sports, gambling, golfing and chasing short skirts. We spend our NFL Sundays worrying about our fantasy football teams, and our summers worrying about the Sox. Our writers are the type of guys you'll bump into at a sports bar skipping work on the first and second days of March Madness.

In other words . . . I am one of you. I wanted Barstool Sports to be the antithesis to the current state of media in Boston.

Once the name and general ethos of Barstool Sports were determined, there were two things I spent my time maniacally doing in the months leading up to launch week. The first was cold-calling advertisers. I'd always heard that story about Bill Gates pitching IBM his operating system before Microsoft had even invented one. He basically sold them a dream. Then, once he sold it, he set out to build it. At least that's how I envisioned the story in my head. (I'm not a Bill Gates fan and I think he's a super weirdo, but I digress.) Anyway, that's what I was doing with Barstool. Anybody I could get on the phone, I would sell the dream of this new sports newspaper that was about to launch and take over the city of Boston.

How do you sell ads for a newspaper that doesn't exist? On promises. I went to Hooters and some of those gambling companies I'd spoken to, explained the idea, and maybe fudged my projections a bit. The bottom line was that I was making a newspaper that would hit their target audience—twenty-five- to thirty-five-year-old men. I promised that my paper would find its way into the hands of the exact consumers Hooters was trying to coax through their doors, and I felt confident my method was more direct and convertible than the promise of slathered wings and orange booty shorts.

BetJamaica was true to their word and committed to advertising for an entire year of the first issue. Hooters was in. As crazy as it sounds, my sales experience and background finally paid dividends. I was able to essentially sell out the first few months of Barstool Sports before we ever went to print or I even knew what the paper looked like.

(Funny little anecdote with BetJamaica. For some reason, once I solidified the ad deal with them, they sent me boxes and boxes of little cocktail napkins and matches with their logo on it. My parents' basement became filled with this stuff. We had so many of them that we didn't know what to do with them all. Still to this day, when we are lighting candles for Hanukkah, my mom will whip out the BetJamaica matches. Or if she is hosting Thanksgiving, we'll have little BetJamaica napkins underneath our drinks—a small little reminder of the early days of Barstool. It's also a good reflection on my mom that nothing is ever worth throwing out if she can save it to use at a later date.)

Now that this thing was starting to become very real, the next step was figuring out exactly how I was going to publish it and get it into the streets. I had a grand total of $50,000 to get me started: $30K that I had managed to save from my sales job and $20K my dad loaned me that I'm sure he thought he'd never see again.

The biggest chunk of my startup money went toward buying newsracks.

We've all passed these things hundreds of times on the street, and you probably never thought about how expensive they are. They were about a hundred bucks a pop, which was a fortune to me back then. And of course Boston requires permits for every newsrack you want to put out on the street, so I had to pay for those too. I bought a hundred newsracks to start because that's all I could afford.

I'll never forget the day they arrived. Not because I was overjoyed that they finally came, but rather because the truck driver called me when he was about an hour away and said that he refused to drop them off to the delivery address he had on file because it wasn't a commercial address and he didn't think his truck would fit on my street (I had moved back home to Swampscott at the time to save money and didn't really give it much thought). Anyway, there was no negotiating with this dude. He stopped on the Lynnway in the Building 19 parking lot and just dropped all the cargo there without me to receive it. If you're unfamiliar with Building 19, which I'm pretty sure is out of business now, just picture the driver pulling into a random Walmart parking lot and dropping a hundred newsracks off in the middle of it. I obviously panicked. I had some irrational fear that somebody was going to steal them all. Kinda funny looking back. Like who the fuck wants a bunch of Barstool Sports newsracks? But if I had lost them, I would have been dead on arrival. So I ran out and rented a U-Haul and made about twenty trips back and forth to the Building 19 parking lot picking up my newsracks. I then dropped them in my high school parking lot until I could deploy them throughout the streets of Boston. Somehow my high school parking lot felt like a safer pasture for my precious racks.

Deploying them around the city was another absolute shit show. My mother and I drove the same rented U-Haul all throughout metro Boston, planting our newsracks throughout the city and beyond. Every single newsrack needed about a hundred pounds of sand in it so it wouldn't blow over. I probably emptied out ten local Home Depots of all the sand they had. I'm pretty sure each bag of sand weighed forty-five pounds, and I'd fill each rack with two bags. I don't think I could lift one of those bags right now if my life depended on it. But back then I had the strength and hunger of desperation, and I was tossing those bags around like a bodybuilder. There were definitely moments when I thought, *What the fuck did I get myself into here?* But I kept my head down and saw each phase to completion.

The entire process of setting up the newsracks took a week or so. Every time we'd stop at a new subway station, my mother would be screaming at me to be careful because hanging out at subway stations at 3 a.m. didn't seem like the safest thing to do. Fun times indeed.

The last major expense was the delivery vehicle I needed. I went straight to Craigslist to find an Astrovan. I found one that looked decent, drove over to the guy's house to pick it up, paid him his cash, shook his hand, and started out the driveway. As I turned onto the street, I heard a deathly rattle followed by a pop, and then the gas pedal stopped responding. The van wheezed to a shuddering halt not a hundred feet from the house. I walked straight back and knocked on the guy's door. He wasn't even surprised to see me again; he just handed me back the money without saying a word.

I went back to trawling Craigslist and managed to get a working Astro-van for $1,800. It was a little more than I paid for the first one, but this one had the goods and held steady. The family was in a rush to sell it because they had to leave for a Mormon mission the next week. Provo Dave had done it again.

(Sidenote: this is an ongoing battle in how I write this book. That little "Provo Dave" joke I just slid in is very much an inside joke. You have to be fully aware of my life to understand it. My editor thinks I should omit those jokes. She thinks it makes it confusing for people who don't know me. I think they are little easter eggs for my hardcore fans and don't take away from the book if you don't get it. Regardless, if you are reading this right now, that means I got my way on this one. And for the newbies, long story short, last year I was on *Big Noon Kickoff*, which is the Fox college football kickoff show, and I fell in love with BYU and Provo and they fell in love with me. Who would have thunk it, right? Anyway, I developed the nickname Provo Dave, and it's kinda funny looking back on it that my trusty steed, the Astrovan, was given to me by Mormons.)

In fact, looking back on it now, maybe it was the Church of Ladderdy Sakes watching out for me in the early days of the company—when I was doing my paper route and my front right tire exploded going sixty mph down the Mass Pike, causing me to lose control and suddenly swerve across three lanes of highway into the divider. It happened so fast I didn't even have time to be scared. But in hindsight, if any other cars were near me as I pinwheeled out of control, that could have been deadly. It was probably my one and only near-death experience I've ever had. Somebody was looking out for me that day. God's plan indeed.

(This picture is from when I found a boot on my Astrovan mid–paper route. I literally jumped out of my car to drop papers off, and when I ran back to my car fifteen minutes later, I was booted. Luckily, I was parked near City Hall. I took the ticket, ran to the parking clerk office, paid it, and was back on the road in forty-five minutes. The show [paper route] must go on.)

By the end of summer 2003, I had my initial advertisers lined up. I had my newsracks laid out throughout the city. I had bought a trusty Astrovan to deliver the newspapers. I was a one-man show, wearing ten hats and playing five roles just to get this thing off the ground. And now it was showtime; time to introduce the world to Barstool Sports. I knew I couldn't just rely on people taking the newspapers out of the newsracks at subway stations. Who would pick up something they'd never heard of before? Sure, a few guys might have been intrigued by the name alone, but I had to physically get the newspaper into people's hands.

I needed a workforce to hand out the papers that didn't go into the racks. If you strolled through Boston in the early 2000s, you might have passed by a guy trying to sell you the *Spare Change* newspaper. It was a nonprofit newspaper distributed by homeless people, and they seemed to do a pretty good job of it. Far be it from me to reinvent the wheel.

Through some research I learned that there was a staffing agency. It managed job opportunities for the homeless and jobless in Boston. I contracted them for week one. I would have an army of homeless drunks handing out the inaugural issue of Barstool Sports at subway stations throughout the city. What could go wrong? I even printed out roughly a hundred T-shirts emblazoned with "Barstool Sports" in big block red letters for my homeless to wear, to drive the point home that Barstool had arrived. I was seventy-two hours out and cautiously optimistic that things were rounding into shape.

There was only one last thing I had to do before issue #1 of Barstool dropped: I had an in-person meeting with my printer, Gannett Publishing, the Monday before we were ready to go live. This was just a formality to make sure I understood delivery timeframes, how to get the paper to print, and make sure there would be no surprises come print day. Surprise, there were. Maybe a better way to say it is, a quick slap in the face of reality that I truly didn't know what the fuck I was doing.

There were two major issues I learned about in this meeting. The first had to do with my logo. I had a buddy of mine draw the original logo for Barstool Sports. It was a pretty intricate design of a guy sitting at a crowded bar watching sports with his buddies.

The printer took one look at it and shook his head.

"There is no chance we can print this on newspaper ink. It's too detailed and will just blur into an unreadable ink spot."

"Okay, so what do you suggest since we go to print in forty-eight hours?"

He opened his clip art (yes, clip art) and picked out the most generic "barstool" you'd ever seen. Okay, done and done. That piece of clipart, to which we would eventually add a few basic stars, remains the official logo of Barstool Sports to this day.

The second issue was a technology problem. I know what I'm about to say sounds so stupid and ignorant that it's laughable, but when the printer asked how I planned on delivering the content for the newspaper to them, I told them I was planning on sending all the articles as individual Microsoft Word documents and all our ads as PDFs (or however BetJamaica or Hooters had sent them to me).

I think there was about a five-second moment of awkward silence while he stared at me, trying to decipher if I was serious. Uh, yes, I was dead serious. Longtime Stoolies who have seen my battles with technology over the years can attest that this type of technological ineptitude is par for the course with me. (I am writing this book on HP Desktop, not on a Mac, because I still don't know how to use a Mac computer. And the only reason I got rid of my BlackBerry and got an iPhone is because they stopped making BlackBerrys. I did invent the world's first iBerry, when I duct taped an iPhone and a BlackBerry together. But the point is that technology has never been my forte.)

After my mini-staredown with my printer, he realized that the guy starting a newspaper had absolutely no clue how newspapers are printed. He told me that I needed a very specific program in order for them to be able to print it. For a guy who can't figure out how to use a MacBook, I was so out of my element that I thought there was a pretty decent chance I was done before I had even started. Honestly, I left that meeting truly thinking I was fucked and had wasted all my startup capital on nothing.

But then I caught an unbelievably lucky break. Remember that apartment I lived in after college with five high school buddies? The one where we brainstormed ideas together? When I told them that they probably made the right choice by not getting involved in this disaster business with me and that I didn't even know how to print Barstool Sports, I was thrown a lifeline. One of my best friends, Brian Hayes, had a buddy whose wife was in the newspaper business and actually worked at Gannett. He said, "If you want to give her a call, maybe she can help?"

Enter Erin Boyce. It wasn't just that Erin worked in the newspaper business; she actually did graphic design for Gannett. In other words, she did exactly what I needed. Furthermore, she had just quit her job and was looking for some freelance work. Well, freelance work she would have.

Starting that Wednesday, and for the next *nine* years, I would send all those unformatted articles and ads to her, and she would format it in the language the printer needed. The process would start Tuesday night around 6 p.m., and we'd stay up until around 4 a.m. every single print week putting together the latest and greatest issue of Barstool Sports.

Throughout the course of Barstool Sports, I've been asked a million times what made it successful. I always say right person, right time, hard work, and a lot of luck. Take out any of those ingredients and you've probably never heard of me and I'm definitely not writing this book. Instead I'd probably be living on some island being a beach bum, following my other life passion, which is Jimmy Buffett, except I'd be doing it on a budget. Instead, luck has always shined down on me and Barstool. Whenever I've needed someone or something to break our way, it seemingly has. I'm not saying that to be humble. I truly believe almost every successful business has benefited from extreme luck, and we are no different. Lots of smart, hardworking people have failed through no fault of their own. (It's probably the reason why, years down the road and in the midst of COVID, the Barstool Fund became so important to me. I know firsthand how hard it is to build a business and how fickle it can be. I was lucky enough to be able to help entrepreneurs who were about to lose their life's work through no fault of their own, and I wanted to pay back some of that luck the universe had granted me in tough moments. But we'll get to that later.)

With those two printing crises solved, I went from dead on arrival to ready to rock and roll in the span of a few short hours. And on Wednesday, August 27, 2003, the first official issue of Barstool Sports hit the streets.

Barstool Sports

August 27, 2003 "By the common man, for the common man" FREE — Take One!

Welcome to the First Issue of Barstool Sports!

To say the release of the first issue was an unmitigated disaster would be an absolute insult to the phrase "unmitigated disaster." There is a famous expression that I'm sure you've heard of: you get what you pay for. My primary distribution method for the first issue of Barstool was the homeless drunks contracted by the staffing agency. I'd say 90 percent of these people didn't show up to work that day. Oh, you mean the homeless drunk getting a couple bucks to hand out newspapers didn't make it? Gee, you don't say. And those who did clock in didn't seem overly interested in handing out the newspaper. The papers were flying everywhere. Entire stacks were dumped onto the subway tracks. More than a few were still drunk, picking fights, and if anyone was wondering who might have been responsible for this mess, my company's name was front and center on their chests in bright red.

Suffice it to say the homeless experiment ended that day. It was a gigantic waste of money and I was right back to square one, staring down the reality that issue #2 needed to be turned around in a couple days.

So week one wasn't the smoothest launch of all time, but it could have been worse. I did manage to publish, and deliver, a newspaper. I'd written almost all the articles myself, with the exception of a couple submitted from friends of mine. I sold all the ads myself. I delivered it myself. I'd actually done it. Even if this thing never made it to week two, I had a sense of pride from having done what I'd said I would do for years. I stopped talking about starting a business and did it. So what now?

There wasn't a lot of time to harp on what had gone wrong in week one. Week two was staring me in the face. I was in it. It was sink-or-swim time now.

Clearly the most pressing issue was figuring out my homeless distribution problem. How do I get people to take the newspaper? Then it hit me: if some strange homeless guy were to offer a newspaper to me, would I take it from him? No shot. Or if I did, I'd toss it immediately. But what about if a pretty girl handed it to me? Duh. Not exactly rocket science, to be honest.

I contracted a modeling/promo agency in Boston called Candy Ford to supply me with some attractive local girls looking to make a few bucks on the side. I bought youth-sized Boston sports jerseys from Foot Locker and dressed the girls in them. So for issue #2 of Barstool Sports, instead of local commuters being met by drunk homeless guys trying to force-feed a newspaper down their throats, they were met with young, pretty college girls dressed in sexy sports attire handing out the newspaper.

Guess what? If week one was a distribution disaster, week two was a smashing success. Thanks to the models, every single copy of issue #2 was gobbled up by a willing reader. But quickly, I was forced to ask myself how long I could afford to do this. Because homeless people are a lot cheaper to hire than hot girls. Like I said earlier, you get what you pay for. I reasoned that there was no point in saving for a future I might not have; no point in saving money for a rainy day. I decided to empty the Barstool bank account for as long as I could afford because the exposure the girls were bringing me was worth the risk. I used the models for the next month, and by the end of it, guys across Boston came to look for the girls each week. And by association, they came to look forward to their new issue of Barstool Sports.

This experiment was where I met Renee. She was a BU student at the time and happened to be one of the girls in the original group assigned to this project by Candy Ford. I remember driving her to her designated subway station the first time I met her, and she was peppering me with questions about the business that she had no business asking, to be frank. But I was polite and tried to answer them the best I could. She then got out of the front seat, looked at me, and said, "Good luck, but I don't think this is going to work," before descending to her designated subway station.

I thought, *Who is this girl? Does she think she's me with these snarky one-liners?*

Renee would later become known to the Stoolies as "The First Lady," aka my wife. She remains my best friend to this day.

While the girls had clearly gotten Boston's attention, they had also cleaned out my bank account. I mean I was out of money. Truly. Between the Astrovan, the newsracks, printing costs, and paying the models, I had emptied every last dollar out of the vault. There was now a magic number that ran my life: $3,400. That was my biweekly all-in carry nut to publish Barstool Sports. I was able to trim it down to that number after I discontinued using the models.

At this point the business model was pretty simple: if I could sell $3,400 worth of ads in the newspaper, I would break even. I didn't have any real expenses beyond that. I had moved home to save money. It's not like I cared about living in Boston anyway. I was working 24/7 on this newspaper, so I had no time for a life outside it. My weeks consisted of three things at this time: writing articles for the newspaper, delivering the newspaper, and most importantly, sourcing revenue any way I could. The original gambling ads I'd sold provided me a bit of a cushion, but that wasn't enough. Now that the paper was in circulation, I needed more revenue. I was cold-calling and knocking on doors constantly. I'd sift through all my competitors' publications in Boston and call every single one of their advertisers every single week to poach them to Barstool. I was relentless, calling them over and over again. Nothing was too small. I literally couldn't have been more persistent.

I also made up a ton of fake aliases for the newspaper to make Barstool seem bigger than a one-man operation. But I was just one man doing ten jobs like one of those guys who play all those stupid instruments strapped to their bodies, trying to make it all sound good together. I created a bunch of fake ads (using real companies) to fill those early pages. Fleming's Steakhouse "won" a giant spread, which allowed me to call Morton's to warn them that their competitor was gaining a major marketing edge thanks to the hottest newspaper they hadn't heard of (yet). Of course, Fleming's saw the ad and called me in a rage to figure out why their ad was in my paper—which is baffling to think about now. Umm, it's free ad space, morons. Why are you upset? No wonder Ruth's Chris has more than double your locations now. So shortsighted. So dumb.

I was able to scrounge up a ragtag group of clients in the early days: from Jack Diamond DUI lawyer to local bars to porn sites. I needed every cent they paid to stay afloat.

And it wasn't just advertising—I was willing to do or try anything to drive revenue. For example, my mother makes a spectacular dessert called Sour Cream Cake. Bad name, but it really is a spectacular cake. So I tried to sell my mom's cake through the newspaper. All my close friends ordered the cake because they loved it. Unfortunately, but rather predictably, my mother refused to charge them for it but still sent the cake, so I took a bath on that project. Many years down the road, and long after I had "made it," I tweeted out a picture of this ad to show people how far Barstool had come from the early days. I forgot to redact my mom's cell phone number in the picture. Needless to say, she was quite confused when her phone rang for forty-eight hours straight with random Stoolies trying to buy her Sour Cream Cake, from Alaska to Africa.

Move Over Finale, here comes
My Mom's Cake

"Simply the best cake on the planet"

- a friend of mine

$14.00 per Cake
Always baked fresh and shipped fresh
To Order Call My Mom at [redacted] or
email orders to cake@barstoolsports.com

Remember those Barstool Sports T-shirts I bought for the homeless guys to wear as they handed out the first issue? I still had like fifty or sixty of them lying around because half the guys didn't show up. I decided to sell them, and I kept the readers updated on how many we sold each week. In every new issue of Barstool Sports there would be a little box counting how many "Ugly Shirts" we'd sold.

This would serve as the forerunner of the Barstool Sports merch business—a vital revenue stream that would sustain the company for the next twenty years. I had no idea then that you wouldn't even be able to walk

The Rise of the Ugly Shirt - Version 2.0

After weeks or rumor and speculation, the Ugly Shirts are back! They are brighter, bolder and uglier than ever. For all those Barstool Sports rookies out there, the legend of the Ugly Shirt began many, many moons ago. Basically when Barstool Sports limped out of the gate and onto the local scene 15 weeks ago, we hired a group of bearded men, some would say drunken, homeless, bearded men, to hand out our newspaper at local T-stations. We ordered the cheapest T-shirts we could find for these guys to wear while handing out the paper. The result was the birth of the Ugly Shirt. As most of you know who have been following the maturation of Barstool Sports, the bearded guys only worked for us once, before we switched to using models. The result was that the majority of the original Ugly Shirts faded into Bolivia. However, a few shirts did survive the genocide and the staff of Barstool Sports regularly wears them when handing out newspapers or trying to track down stolen newsracks. Much to our surprise, something very strange happened whenever we wore the Ugly shirts. People seemed to really like them. Therefore, we decided to sell them for 10 bucks a pop, hoping it would serve as a sneaky way to get our readers to help market the newspaper by having them wear our ugly shirts around town. The resulting Ugly Shirt sale was a complete success. Shockingly we sold out of all the original Ugly Shirts and were asked by readers to develop another model of the Ugly Shirt and that's exactly what we did. Hence, today we continue the legacy of the Ugly Shirt by introducing Ugly Shirt V.2.0, which can be yours for $13.00. Version 2.0 is a radical departure from its predecessor, which was white with red lettering. The newer, bolder version of the shirt is now red with white lettering and a special surprise on the sleeve.

For all those who can't wait to get their hands on Ugly Shirt Version 2.0 please email your address for shipping to shirts@barstoolsports.com.
Send checks to [redacted]

And as always, thanks for your support!

in my apartment over the years because it would be littered with T-shirts and mailing supplies that I'd pack and ship myself; that I'd do five runs to the post office per day and do all the customer service myself. That is, until it became too big to manage and we had to outsource what by then was a multimillion-dollar, high-eight-figure revenue stream. And it all started with the Ugly Shirts, left behind by a bunch of homeless people who skipped work that day.

It was all-hands-on-deck for myself and whatever aliases I created. I did whatever I had to do to meet the $3,400-per-week nut and stay afloat.

I don't know how many water analogies I'm allowed to use in this book, but here is another one: the key to staying afloat is keeping your oars in the water at all times. In other words, as long as you are in the game and have a pulse, you never know what can happen. What I did know was that my current business structure was unsustainable. My daily routine consisted of waking up at 4 a.m., driving to a T station in Boston, and handing out the newspaper myself during the morning commute. Then, after the morning commute died down, I'd try to sell ads. Then I'd reappear at a different T station during the evening commute to hand out more newspapers. Then I'd drive back to Swampscott and write articles for the newspaper. I was literally writing all the content for the paper, sometimes under a few different fake names to make it seem like we had different writers. On publication weeks, I would drive in loops around the city in what equated to a forty-eight-hour paper route, delivering the latest and greatest issue of Barstool. Like I said, it was unsustainable for one man to keep this up. I could handle the waking up early, the sales calls, and delivering the paper. But all that took its toll on creating a quality product that people enjoyed, and it became too tough to balance. I knew I needed help.

I put an ad in an early issue announcing that I was looking for writers. I believe the exact verbiage was: "Barstool is looking to hire writers. We don't pay at all, but we make up for it by offering zero benefits."

That's literally what it said. You had to be in it for the love of the game. I'm not going to sit here and say I was inundated with submissions. A few trickled in here and there, and among them were three guys who stood out from the rest, and who would be absolutely pivotal to the newspaper era and growth of Barstool Sports.

Introducing Pete Manzo, Jamie Chisholm, and Jerry Thornton. Along

Manzo, me, Chisholm, Uncle Buck, Jerry Thornton

with myself, we comprised the original Core 4. As a sidenote, Jerry Thornton still writes for us today, which seems impossible since I'm pretty sure I hired him on the eve of his eightieth birthday. His nickname back then was "Old Balls," and that was twenty years ago.

These guys weren't just page fillers; they were legit great writers. I'm talking guys I still would hire today even with the thousands of job applications we get. That's how talented they were. It was just another example of lady luck shining down on Barstool Sports. I've seen so many horrible applications and bad résumés in my time that it's insane to think that three of the first people who ever offered to work for me, for free, were three of the most gifted writers I'd employ in twenty years. Who knows what would have happened if I had never found those guys. But with them by my side, Barstool Sports began to find its sea legs.

In addition to the regular staff pieces, I started receiving full articles to my email address from readers—the best of which I actually published. "Talkin' State Street Blues" was a reader submission that detailed the voluntary severance package offered by State Street Bank, which had sent a mass email to their employees announcing that a big round of layoffs was coming. They had offered employees the option to voluntarily resign in exchange for a cushy severance package. Problem was, they expected only about 1,500 people to pack their bags, but over three thousand walked out. Then they tried to walk it back, only to get sued by the employees who were now on Caribbean beaches and cruise ships, sipping piña coladas as they claimed their severance checks bounced. The article caught fire. It was the newspaper equivalent of a viral video, and everybody in Boston was talking about it. It was so well written and funny that I immediately understood the value of avoiding any one path or genre in our pages. I didn't want to confine Barstool Sports to just sports because you never knew what might catch people's attention or get them arguing over an issue. These were the exact types of stories that so deeply wove us into the Boston subculture.

Our free little twice-monthly newspaper was turning into must-read material for citizens of Boston. The topics in the paper ranged from those layoffs at State Street Bank to an ode to a stereotypical Softball Dude to Pete Manzo's night with the Playboy Bunnies to Sales 101. You just never knew what you might read in any particular issue of Barstool. And slowly but surely, every time I would drop the newspaper off at T stations and bars around Boston, a few more people would comment, "Finally Barstool is here! We've been waiting for it."

Still, I wasn't making a dime. Each week was a war to hit the $3,400 break-even point. But in my bones, I could tell something was brewing. Something was building. It was easy for me to imagine that in my old life, working my nine-to-five sales job in Boston, I would have found Barstool Sports and become a fan. That's a method I've often used to determine whether something at Barstool seemed like a good idea: Would I like this if I were just a regular person, with no connection to this place?

Despite my cautious optimism, I wasn't thinking we'd ever be anywhere like where we are today. But maybe, just maybe, I thought I'd be able to eke out a living on $60K a year, doing something I loved.

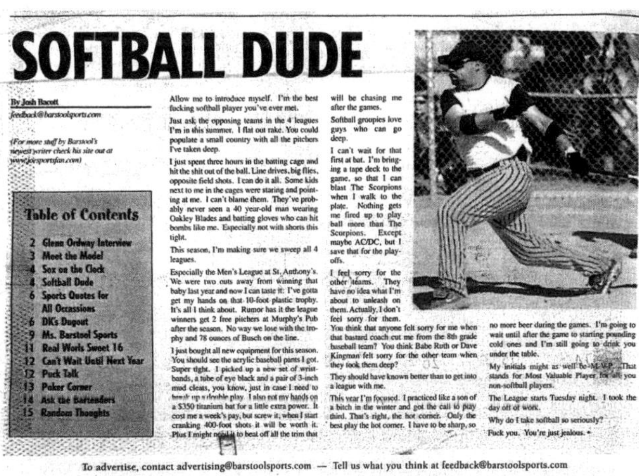

SOFTBALL DUDE

By Josh Bacott
feedback@barstoolsports.com

(For more stuff by Barstool's newest writer check his site out at www.joesportsfan.com)

Table of Contents

Allow me to introduce myself. I'm the best fucking softball player you've ever met.

Just ask the opposing teams in the 4 leagues I'm in this summer. I flat out rake. You could populate a small country with all the pitchers I've taken deep.

I just spent three hours in the batting cage and hit the shit out of the ball. Line drives, big flies, opposite field shots. I can do it all. Some kids next to me in the cages were staring and pointing at me. I can't blame them. They've probably never seen a 40 year-old man wearing Oakley Blades and batting gloves who can hit bombs like me. Especially not with shorts this tight.

This season, I'm making sure we sweep all 4 leagues.

Especially the Men's League at St. Anthony's. We were two outs away from winning that baby last year and now I can taste it: I've gotta get my hands on that 10-foot plastic trophy. It's all I think about. Rumor has it the league winners get 2 free pitchers at Murphy's Pub after the season. No way we lose with the trophy and 78 ounces of Busch on the line.

I just bought all new equipment for this season. You should see the acrylic baseball pants I got. Super tight. I picked up a new set of wristbands, a tube of eye black and a pair of 3-inch mud cleats, you know, just in case I need to break up a double play. I also got my hands on a $350 titanium bat for a little extra power. It cost me a week's pay, but screw it, when I start cranking 400-foot shots it will be worth it. Plus I might need it to beat off all the trim that will be chasing me after the games.

Softball groupies love guys who can go deep.

I can't wait for that first at bat. I'm bringing a tape deck to the game, so that I can blast The Scorpions when I walk to the plate. Nothing gets me fired up to play ball more than The Scorpions. Except maybe AC/DC, but I save that for the playoffs.

I feel sorry for the other teams. They have no idea what I'm about to unleash on them. Actually, I don't feel sorry for them. You think that anyone felt sorry for me when that bastard coach cut me from the 8th grade baseball team? You think Babe Ruth or Dave Kingman felt sorry for the other team when they took them deep?

They should have known better than to get into a league with me.

This year I'm focused. I practiced like a son of a bitch in the winter and got the call to play third. That's right, the hot corner. Only the best play the hot corner. I have to be sharp, so no more beer during the games. I'm going to wait until after the game to starting pounding cold ones and I'm still going to drink you under the table.

My initials might as well be M.V.P. That stands for Most Valuable Player, for all you non-softball players.

The League starts Tuesday night. I took the day off of work.

Why do I take softball so seriously?

Fuck you. You're just jealous. •

To advertise, contact advertising@barstoolsports.com — Tell us what you think at feedback@barstoolsports.com

Barstool Sports

September 17, 2003 — September 24, 2003 "By the common man, for the common man" FREE — Take One!

Talkin' State Street Blues

I just took a voluntary layoff from State Street Bank. I was in the wrong line of work, and I hated it. It was boring, monotonous, and full of nitwits suffering from diarrhea of the mouth. State Street planned to lay off 1800 employees, and presumably offered the severance package to soften the public relations damage typically incurred in a downsizing.

Three thousand one hundred employees signed up for the voluntary layoff, which should tell you something about the joys of working there. The higher-ups claim that they never expected that many people to take the package. This means they never bothered to take a short stroll around one of their offices. Sneaker, t-shirts and all-around slobbishness have worked their way into the SSB employee's definition of "business casual." Some of the dumbest people you would ever not want to talk to said some of the dumbest things that you would ever not want to hear. All day long, at very high volumes. Ninety percent of SSB's employees would openly tell you that they were suckers who hated every second of it, living an office life of quiet desperation. Anybody, except, apparently, for SSB executives, could have plainly seen that there would be a stampede for the severance.

State Street decided to involuntarily lay another 150 people off anyway, which was awfully nice of them. And if that's not enough, SSB isn't even just moving forward with the streamlined workforce, which they easily could, they're hiring to replace the laid off workers at a cheaper salary.

Making a statement that says nothing, the always creepily smiling State Street CEO David Spina said, "We acted decisively to position State Street for improved profitability."

On a more enlightening and enjoyable note (for me, at least), an analyst told the Boston Globe, "They misgauged the sentiment of their employees, number one, and they probably made the severance package too generous, number two, and, three, do you really want to train 800 new employees?"

"It doesn't make sense," he said.

Meanwhile, the company's doing fine; it's just the difference between a gigantic pile of money and an even more gigantic pile of money for Spina to roll around naked in. Incidentally, he made 34 million dollars last year, according to the Boston Herald.

Two little things convinced me that the company pretty much had to be making money in spite of itself. The rank and file chain of management has a uniquely ass-backwards way of doing things. Two spectacularly, unbelievably, mind-bendingly dumb sequences of events that almost gave me an aneurysm:

1. Two days before Opening Day at Fenway, we get a mass email from a higher-up. We can wear Sox gear and jeans the day of the game, and there'll be peanuts. Hot damn, right?

The next day, we get another email from the same guy saying that the aforementioned best-party-ever was cancelled, due to State Street's recent poor performance. The higher-up adds that he doesn't want to appear to be rewarding us in this particular climate. Mind you, this is the first time we actually heard anything from anyone about poor performance, but I have to say, dangling that kick-ass peanut party and then yanking it away inspired me to work harder. Good work, management.

2. When I went out to lunch the other day, I passed a friend of mine who was waiting in the lobby for an interview. After lunch I

Continued on page 5...

EXCERPT FROM "TALKIN' STATE STREET BLUES"

By Brendan Walton

I just took a voluntary layoff from State Street Bank. I was in the wrong line of work, and I hated it. It was boring, monotonous, and full of nitwits suffering from diarrhea of the mouth. State Street planned to lay off 1800 employees, and presumably offered the severance package to soften the public relations damage typically incurred in a downsizing.

Three thousand one hundred employees signed up for the voluntary layoff, which should tell you something about the joys of working there.

The higher-ups claim that they never expected that many people to take the package. This means they never bothered to take a short stroll around one of their offices. Sneakers, T-shirts and all-around slobbishness have worked their way into SSB employee's definition of "business casual." Some of the dumbest people you would ever not want to talk to said some of the dumbest things that you would ever not want to hear. All day long, at very high volumes. 90% of SSB's employees would openly tell you that they were suckers who hated every second of it, living an office life of quiet desperation. Anybody, except, apparently, for SSB executives, could have plainly seen that there would be a stampede for the severance.

SOFTBALL DUDE

Allow me to introduce myself. I'm the best fucking softball player you've ever met. Just ask the 4 teams in the opposing leagues I'm in this summer. I flat out rake. You could populate a small country with all the pitchers I've taken deep.

I just spent three hours in the batting cage and hit the shit out of the ball. Line drives, big flies, opposite field shots. I can do it all. Some kids next to me in the cages were staring and pointing at me. I don't blame them. They've probably never seen a 40 year-old man wearing Oakley Blades and batting gloves who can hit bombs like me. Especially not with shorts this tight.

This season, I'm making sure we sweep all 4 leagues.

Especially the Men's League at St. Anthony's. We were two outs away from winning that baby last year and now I can taste it. I've gotta get my hands on that 10-foot plastic trophy. It's all I think about. Rumor has it the league winners get 2 free pitchers at Murphy's Pub after the seasons. No way we lose with the trophy and 78 ounces of Busch on the line.

I just bought all new equipment for this season. You should see the acrylic baseball pants I got. Super tight. I picked up a new set of wristbands, a tube of eye black and a pair of 3-inch mud cleats, you know, just in case I need to break up a double play. I also got my hands on a $350 titanium bat for a little extra power. It cost me a week's pay, but screw it, when I start cranking 400-foot shots it will be worth it. Plus I might need to beat off all the trim that will be chasing me after the games.

Softball groupies love guys who can go deep.

I can't wait for that first at bat. I'm bringing a tape deck to the game, so that I can blast The Scorpions when I walk to the plate. Nothing gets me fired up to play ball more than The Scorpions. Except maybe AC/DC, but I save that for the playoffs.

I feel sorry for the other teams. They have no idea what I'm about to unleash on them. Actually, I don't feel sorry for them. You think that anyone felt sorry for me when that bastard coach cut me from the 8th grade baseball team? You think Babe Ruth or Dave Kingman felt sorry for the other team when they took them deep? They should have known better than to get into a league with me. This year I'm focused. I practiced like a son of a bitch in the winter and got the call to play third. That's right, the hot corner. Only the best play the hot corner. I have to be sharp, so no more beer during the games. I'm going to wait until after the game to start pounding cold ones and I'm still going to drink you under the table.

My initials might as well be M.V.P. That stands for Most Valuable Player for all you non-softball players.

The league starts Tuesday night. I took a day off of work.

Why do I take softball so seriously? Fuck you. You're just jealous.

Once I was through a few of these early months, I found that I was actually semi-proud of what Barstool Sports had become. It had morphed from a four-page, black-and-white sports and gambling newsletter into more of a men's entertainment/comedy magazine with a solid core of writers. I was fairly confident that if I could get the paper into people's hands, I'd hook them. But how do you get the person who keeps brushing past you, who refuses to take a newspaper, to finally cave in and take it? And then *actually* read it? I wish I could say I sat in a room and concocted some master plan to solve this, but like almost everything at Barstool, it occurred organically and without much thought.

I wrote an article in the April 2004 issue of Barstool Sports called "My 10

Hottest Chicks Alive." Again, not rocket science. After all, everybody from *People* to *GQ* to *Maxim* had their own version of a sexiest humans list, so here was ours. The next thing I did I believe legal experts might frown upon and refer to as "blatant copyright infringement." I took a photo of Lindsay Lohan in a bikini and stuck it on the front page next to the article. It was a little square picture of her that I found somewhere on the internet. I really didn't give it much thought or comprehend what I was doing at the time. Back in those days, I'm not even sure I knew what copyright infringement was, nor did I care. Luckily, nothing ever came of it in a legal sense. No lawyers, no cease and desists, nothing—a far cry from today's world, where you can't sneeze without some ambulance chaser trying to shake you down for cash. The Lohan photo did, however, lead to an email that would forever change the course of Barstool Sports. Eric Levin was a local photographer in Boston with an eye for talent and opportunity. He'd seen the Lohan cover and I guess a flashbulb went off in his brain, because he reached out to ask if I'd consider featuring local girls on the cover. Given the success I'd had utilizing the Boston models to hand out the paper, and given that Barstool was, at its core, a local newspaper, it immediately clicked for me that homing in on a "girl next door" motif might move the needle.

If I could find them, Levin offered to shoot the girls professionally, in the style of *Maxim*, in a proper studio with lighting and makeup and all the bells and whistles.

Naturally, I had to solve the question of where to find the girls. By this time, I had hung out with Renee a few times. If you are wondering how she went from handing out newspapers, telling me I was doomed to fail, to us hanging out a few times, it was because when my buddies found out that I had hired models to hand out Barstool they were like, "Hey asshole, why don't you ask these girls if they want to go out sometime?" So that's exactly what I did, and Renee and I hit it off. Things were progressing nicely, or as nicely as they could considering I was broke and working 24/7.

Renee was following along with the progress of the newspaper, and I think she was somewhat surprised and impressed that not only was Barstool still in business, it was seemingly growing. That's when I told her about the email I received from Eric. We both thought it was a great idea and, more importantly, Renee had a short-term solution for me. She volunteered two of her friends as tribute to be the first-ever cover models for Barstool Sports (shout-out Jillian and Luba, still two of Renee's best friends to this day). Looking back, I don't know what she said to get them to agree, or if they even knew what they agreed to, but it didn't matter. I had sourced the girls, and Eric Levin lived up to his word and produced a professional photoshoot. Starting with that photoshoot, for the next six years every single issue of Barstool Sports would feature local girls on the cover.

By the common man, for the common man

Barst Sports

CELEBRATION 101

How did Red Sox Nation celebrate?

MS. BARSTOOL SPORTS

New champion is crowned

1918 SWEPT AWAY

YOU PATHETIC BASTARDS

Yankee fans deal with the choke

GLORY DAYS

Boston doesn't get better than this!

Photo By: Eric Levin

Volume 2 · Issue 25 November 3 – November 10, 2004 FREE

There's no doubt that this was yet another defining moment in our history. Barstool was introducing these girls to the entire city, which had the effect of introducing Barstool to more and more people. All of a sudden, I'd added another key ingredient to an ever-growing and changing men's interest newspaper. What made these covers work wasn't just the fact that these were professional photoshoots unlike anything Boston had seen. The key was that our cover models weren't celebrities living across the country who only came out for red carpets; these were sports medicine majors at Boston University, bartenders at Lansdowne Pub, nurses at Boston Children's Hospital, girls who lived down the street from you. They were sorority sisters you might run into at your next formal. In other words, they were real people.

With each step, Barstool continued to evolve from just a newspaper to a brand. It started to become something people talked about, and not just in person. College bros would ask each other if they'd seen the latest cover or read a certain article. I was getting inundated with submissions for cover girls.

The paper started moving around college campuses, which opened Barstool up to a younger audience in addition to the postgrad professionals I'd been targeting downtown. Boston is a *college* town, with over 118 colleges—the fourth most of any city in America, despite not even cracking the top twenty cities in terms of population. Breaking into the college demographic was gigantic.

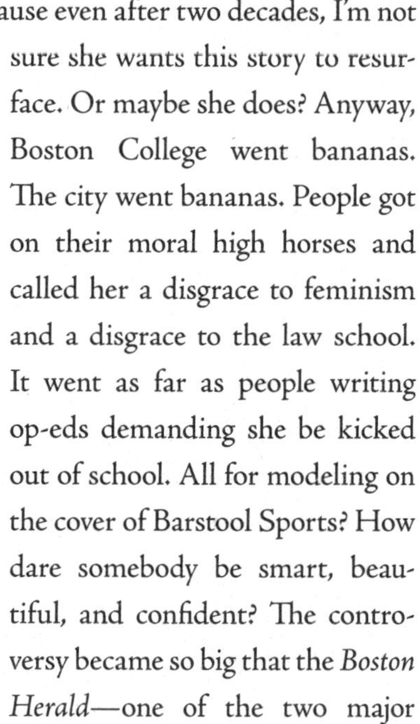

The onset of the cover model era also gave birth to our first (but certainly not our last) full-fledged controversy. In March 2007, in preparation for March Madness, we featured a Boston College law student covering her chest with a BC pennant.

The caption said "Let's Dance" as a nod to the NCAA tournament, aka the "Big Dance." For people who say I'm mean or rude, I didn't include her last name here because even after two decades, I'm not sure she wants this story to resurface. Or maybe she does? Anyway, Boston College went bananas. The city went bananas. People got on their moral high horses and called her a disgrace to feminism and a disgrace to the law school. It went as far as people writing op-eds demanding she be kicked out of school. All for modeling on the cover of Barstool Sports? How dare somebody be smart, beautiful, and confident? The controversy became so big that the *Boston Herald*—one of the two major

ERIN GO BLAH!

BOSTON Herald

Storm wreaks havoc . . .

. . . but that won't stop St. Pat's revelers

EAGLE EYE CANDY

HERALD EXCLUSIVE: P. 3

BC law student's racy photos spark outrage

'Idol' Ayla's dad did it too, and he backs risque display!

SHAKY DICE HITS THE SHOWERS

DUDLEY READY FOR SOUTHERN COOKING

Courtesy of the *Boston Herald*

daily newspapers in Boston at the time—printed the cover of Barstool Sports on the cover of their newspaper. I vigorously defended her and my company. It was none of anybody else's business the decision that Adrienne made. Nobody told you to read it, look at it, or be offended by it. There is nothing I hate more than people who pretend to have the moral high ground when they don't. I don't tell you how to live your life and you better not tell me how to live mine.

This would be the first of many times that critics of mine or of Barstool would learn that I will not back down from what I believe. If you come at me with a feather, just know I'm coming back at you with a sledgehammer. Did I feel bad that Adrienne found herself in the middle of this mess? Of course I did. Was I thanking my lucky stars for the free publicity we were gaining from it? You better believe it. *Oh hey, look at this new newspaper that features local, scantily clad, beautiful women and also has hilarious articles inside it . . . What a bunch of jerks.*

As the early newspaper years passed, I began to find my rhythm. I wasn't making any real money, but I was starting to eke out a living—just enough to afford an $800 month-to-month studio in Boston. On nights when I felt like getting crazy, Renee and I would order takeout from the Cheesecake Factory, which was across the street from my apartment.

(By the way, I consider myself a food snob, and the richer I've gotten the more I've been able to eat at some of the best restaurants in the world. But I will tolerate zero Cheesecake Factory slander. The bread and Cajun Chicken Littles can go toe-to-toe with anybody. Don't ask me how a restaurant that has a menu the size of the Yellow Pages can make everything good, but they somehow do.)

I had the rhythm of creating, publishing, and delivering the newspaper down cold. I became omnipresent in Boston during those years. You could spot my Astrovan driving around the city or see me handing out newspapers outside the Garden.

(Funny sidenote: Last year I went to a Celtics playoff game, and I bumped into a ticket scalper out front. I didn't recognize him at first, but he said, "Hey

Dave, we're all proud of you for your success." Then I remembered him: he was one of the guys I used to stand next to every week, hawking newspapers while he was scalping tickets.

By the way, did you know that all the scalpers are like part of one big group? That they aren't actually competing against each other, but are in cahoots with each other? I think the name of the group is affectionately known as the Mob, but don't quote me on it. I never knew this till I spent hours and hours and hours hanging out with these guys while I was slinging my newspapers and they were slinging their tickets. Comrades in battle.)

If you were really lucky, you might have seen me cleaning shit out of my newsracks. Yes, I mean literal shit. To this day, I don't know how someone managed to poop *inside* the thing. Either way, I had to clean it because nobody else was going to. As gross as that sounds, it didn't faze me in real time because I had become immune to being disgusted. Everywhere I went I had news ink on me and papers everywhere. I had cleaning solution on me at all times so that if I saw graffiti, stickers, poop, or God knows what else, I would pull over and clean it. I had to. If I didn't keep the racks clean the city stole them and threw them into the impound lot. And then I'd have to drive around hunting them down and paying fines to get them back.

Barstool started hosting trivia nights at local bars.

We threw theme parties ranging from March Madness parties to Ski parties to Halloween parties and Cover Model parties. We held a name tag party where our most die-hard fans, who regularly left comments under blogs on the website, had to write their commenter names on their name tags—Dana Bible, Lugnutz, Soog . . . all the major players showed up. But not every party was a hit.

We were everywhere. We became part of the fabric of the city. I knew everybody in the bar industry and beer business. I still stay in touch with lots of these guys today. Jason Medeiros from Miller/Coors, Steve Shaughnessy, Scotty Diamond, Michael Glenn, Dessie, Harry Conforti . . . These names obviously mean nothing to you, but these were our early advertisers and advocates, people who vouched for Barstool and without whom we never would have made it.

But without a shadow of a doubt, our biggest reason for survival and success was our early fans and readers. Barstool Sports was an underdog story that really had no business succeeding, and I wanted to impress that upon people. From day one, I was always brutally honest with our readers. Even in the early issues, I gave them consistent updates on the health of the business—whether we'd make it another month or whether I was gonna run out of money. Whatever was on my mind I shared with people in a column called "Random Thoughts." This was basically my version of an editor's note brain dump, and it was where I expressed just how much I needed the readers' help. In other words, if you enjoyed the newspaper, we needed your support. If you wanted to root for this underdog, buy a T-shirt, write a guest article, do something to help us survive.

Our readers, the Stoolies, always delivered. I think a lot of that was due to the city in which Barstool was born: Boston. It's a fiercely loyal, tribalistic, hardworking city that respects hard work. I mean people saw the grind. They watched the rise of Barstool and started rooting for us like we were the fifth major sports team in the city. They became part of the movement. I always say that during those days, if you wanted to pretend like you knew about Boston, you talked about Ben Affleck, Matt Damon, or maybe Bill Simmons. But if you were really from Boston, you talked about Barstool.

(Author's note: Weirdly enough, I've never met with or spoken to Matt Damon or Ben Affleck. However, I did have a well-documented feud with Bill Simmons. And when I say well-documented, it's because I documented it. When I launched Barstool Sports, Bill Simmons was the man; the best writer I had ever read. His writing style certainly influenced the early days of Barstool. I eventually reached out to interview him for the paper and he blew me off a few times. And by a few times I mean like probably ten times. Finally he got back to me and said to send over the questions, which I did. He then replied that he didn't want to do any additional media, so the interview was canceled. I wouldn't say it hurt my feelings, but it definitely pissed me off. He had just moved from Jimmy Kimmel to ESPN. What do you mean you don't want media attention? *Fuck this guy then,* I thought. In hindsight, maybe I was a bit harsh. He didn't live in Boston anymore and maybe he had no clue who we were. Either way, it knocked him down a few pegs in my book. The one thing that I always said about Simmons back then and still maintain now is that he is definitely a far better writer than I am. But there is nobody on earth who would rather have a beer with him than have a beer with me. Of course, I've never met the guy, but I'm pretty sure I'm right.)

Earning a living throughout the newspaper days was a struggle. Yes, readership was growing. Yes, we had taken hold of Boston. But it wasn't necessarily translating into revenue. And the more I made, the more I poured back into the business. More newsracks meant bigger circulation, bigger circulation meant greater printing costs, etc.

Renee and I had been dating for a couple years at this point, and we wanted to move in together. But there was no chance this tiny apartment would suffice. And we couldn't afford anything else, so we moved to Abington, Massachusetts, and lived with her mother to save money. That's how tight our finances were. To

Renee's credit, she never once complained. Well, maybe one time she did when she gently suggested that I get a job to augment our nonexistent income. And because I felt bad, I actually did. I interviewed for and accepted a sales job that paid six figures. However, at lunch break on the first day, I walked out the front door, drove my Astrovan home, and never went back. I didn't even make it through the first day. I knew that in my heart of hearts, I had something big brewing, but I just didn't know what it was yet. And more importantly, I knew that to have any chance of success, it needed my full attention.

Once again to Renee's credit, she never said a word about it; she just buckled in for the ride.

At last year's Super Bowl, I did Shannon Sharpe's podcast. A clip went crazy viral when I said that my ex-wife Renee still had access to my bank accounts and could literally buy anything she wanted without my approval. I didn't see what the big deal was. Loyalty is a two-way street with me. If you are loyal to me, I will be loyal to you. Renee was quite literally with me from day one of Barstool Sports. She never doubted me, never flinched, never asked that I change. She was just a true ride-or-die teammate. She had access to our bank account when it had one zero in it, and she still has access to it now that it has eight zeroes in it (classic humble brag/straight brag) and that will never change. She has every right to enjoy the success of Barstool with me because without her, it probably would not have happened. I feel like most people who know me well would probably describe me as fiercely loyal. It takes a lot to get into my inner circle and gain my trust. I don't have a ton of friends. I don't want a ton. But if you stand by me and do right by me, I will die for you.

2

Internet 1.0

The newspaper years were exhilarating but a grind. Every cent I made was a war. That's the nature of the print business. That's probably why, in hindsight, it was the dumbest possible startup idea I could have had. Like the more popular the newspaper became, the more issues I had to print, which meant the more expensive the publication costs became, which meant I needed more newsracks throughout the city, which meant the paper route took longer, which cost more gas, and on and on and on. There was no easy way to scale. Every step forward felt like two steps back monetarily. I was still doing the same routine year after year: publishing the newspaper, doing my paper route, cold-calling for ads, doing events in Boston, and handing out the newspaper every single day throughout the city. Yes, we were growing, but the business model wasn't improving. I wasn't thinking about quitting, but at the same time I had no clue how to evolve to the next step. I just kept my oars in the water, hoping I'd catch a break. And then I finally did.

One evening while I was planted outside South Station, handing out the newspaper to the evening commuters who were heading home from work, a guy took a paper from me and struck up a conversation. This wasn't unusual by the way. I had become friendly with lots of the people I'd seen over the years. It was kind of like seeing your local barista you start to get to know after seeing them every day. You just naturally start saying hello.

Anyway, this person was Ian White, and he would forever change the future of Barstool Sports.

Ian was a Bostonian who was about to move to New York City and had become a fan of ours, dutifully taking the paper directly from me every week. At this point we were still strictly a print publication. If you didn't live or work in metro Boston you couldn't get Barstool. Ian matter-of-factly said, "I'm going to miss reading this thing. If I build you a website for free, will you upload the paper to it so I can still feel connected to the city?" *Oh, you're going to build me a website for free? Say less. Yup, I'm happy to do that, Ian.* And boom—just like that, www.barstoolsports.com was born.

Needless to say, the advent of the website was a game-changer. I'm sure at some point along the way I would have eventually decided we needed to move the newspaper online, but I'm also the most stubborn, worst technology guy in the world. It certainly wasn't a pressing issue for me at the time. Going online was never part of any grand business plan I'd conceived. Instead, once again, Barstool had been struck by a lightning bolt of good fortune. The right guy came along at the exact right moment, and I was the right guy to take advantage of it.

At first, I just uploaded the PDF to the website.

Then slowly and organically, I asked Ian to modify the website he had built for free. *Hey, can you make it so I can start writing just my random thoughts on it? Can I upload pictures? Can I upload videos?* Even after Ian moved to New York around 2008, he continued to modify, adjust, and maintain the website. I no longer had to wait every two weeks to get my thoughts out; I could offer them instantly and whenever I had them. Barstool Sports would never be the same. Readership was no longer confined by physical distribution. Content could be updated instantly. Barstool Sports became one of the first blogs to ever exist. I'd watch the Red Sox every night and rate Heidi Watney's outfit. She was the gorgeous blond sideline reporter for the Red Sox. I'd upload videos of Dennis Drinkwater, who sat behind home plate for the Red Sox every single game, sprinting out of his seat the second the final out was recorded to beat traffic. We'd talk about a guy throwing a pizza off another guy's face in the crowd.

Nobody else had ever done this. It was revolutionary for the time. That's why the timing of Ian White was so important. He gave me a huge head start on the rest of the internet. In the early online days of Barstool, I could sit on stories for weeks and nobody else would blog them. There just weren't many sites like ours. People didn't even know what a blog meant yet. I was sitting on a powder keg, all thanks to Ian White moving to New York City.

Barstool Sports™

"By the common man, for the common man"

Barstool Sports Radio Show
Every Wednesday Night at 7pm
on 1510 the Zone

Welcome to the world of Barstool Sports, the only newspaper in Boston written by the common man for the common man. Quite simply, Barstool Sports consists of a bunch of average Joes, who like most guys, love sports, gambling, golfing and chasing short skirts. We spend our NFL Sunday's worrying about our fantasy football teams and our summers worrying about the Sox. Our writers are the type of guys you'll bump into at a sports bar skipping work on the first and second days of March Madness. We are the type of guys who rent a small 3 bedroom house in Newport RI with 14 friends every summer. We are the guys who wait in line for Pats playoffs tickets from midnight until 1pm the next day in sub artic temperatures and honestly think we deserved a shot at being the Sox GM. In other words, the staff of Barstool Sports consists of a bunch of slobs, who think and care about what the average guy thinks and cares about.

While we realize that there are already tons of free newspapers in Metro Boston, our goal in creating Barstool Sports was to create a paper that appeals to the large group of men like ourselves, who would rather watch SportsCenter than the local news when they get home from work. It is meant to give average Bostonians something to read while either suffering on the Green Line, getting a coffee at Dunkin Donuts or in preparation for making a friendly wager with a buddy on a football game. Barstool Sports will be published once a week and cover an endless range of topics from fantasy football, to local sports teams, to pop culture, to dating ideas in Boston, to great guy vacation spots. Basically, anything that could be a topic of conversation between buddies at local pub is a potential topic for Barstool Sports.

The most important thing for us at Barstool Sports is that our newspaper is fun to read and discusses things that are of interest and importance to most men 18-45 years old in this city. We don't take ourselves very seriously and view working at Barstool Sports as a way to avoid becoming slaves to cubicle life. All of our stories will be written from the heart and we can assure you that there will be no hidden agendas or politics involved in anything we discuss. We always encourage feedback from our readers on what you like and don't like about our newspaper and will try and make this thing as entertaining and fun to read as humanly possible. We truly look forward to becoming part of this city and hope that you have as much fun reading the paper as we do putting it together.

BUY AN UGLY T-SHIRT
BARSTOOL SPORTS
FRONT BACK
Email your shipping address to:
shirts@barstoolsports.com

SIGN UP
Entertainment News Email List
entertainment@
Free Pick Email List
freepicks@

VIEW THIS WEEK'S ISSUE
June 2 - 16, 2004

FEATURED ARTICLE
Tuesday's Baseball Bets
Tuesday Random Thoughts
June 7th Weekend Random Thoughts

» Send this page to a friend

Back Issues

May 19- June 2, 2004
May 5 - 19, 2004
April 21 - May 5, 2004
April 7 - 21, 2004
March 24 - April 7, 2004
March 10 - 24, 2004
February 25 - March 10, 2004
February 11 - 25, 2004
January 28 - February 11, 2004
January 14 - 28, 2004
January 7 - 14, 2004
December 24, 2003 - January 7, 2004
December 17 - 24, 2003
December 10 - 17, 2003
December 3 - 10, 2003
November 26 - December 3, 2003
November 19 - 26, 2003
November 12 - 19, 2003
November 5 - 12, 2003
October 22 - 29, 2003

Pre Website Hall of Fame Articles

Talkin State Street Blues
I hate BC
The New MBTA
Sales 101
Down With Wellesley
In Search of the White Buffalo
CT: Masshole in Paris
10 Best Public Golf Courses
The Unbearable Lightness of John Mayer
Gambling God: Fact or Fiction?
Searching for Chris Moneymaker
The Seven Faces of No
Barstool Sports Gets Invited to Peking Tom's Launch Party
A Dream Realized- NCAA Football 2004

(Sidenote: When Barstool Sports moved to NYC a decade later, we were looking to hire our first CTO [chief technology officer for the idiots out there]. Well, guess who we almost hired? Ian White. Talk about a full-circle moment. Turns out Ian wasn't just some part-time tech hobbyist. He was actually the CTO of Business Insider. [Yes, that same Business Insider, but long before they would become one of my mortal enemies.] I don't think we were able to pay enough for somebody of his stature at the time, but again, it just showed how lucky I was to have found him when I did.)

Anyway, the website changed everything instantly. I had already built up a rabid loyal fan base in Boston with the newspaper. Now these people could consume Barstool daily. They didn't have to wait for their morning commute and be done with the entire paper before they reached work. Now they could sit in their office and refresh all day long.

My schedule changed too. Instead of worrying about increasing the size of the newspaper or looking for new advertisers, I just wrote and wrote and wrote. Ten to fifteen blogs per day, every thirty or forty-five minutes, seven days a week. People stopped seeing me handing out the newspapers in the streets of Boston because I'd be blogging till 1 a.m. Then I'd wake up and be ready to go again at 9 a.m.

My blogs could literally be on anything: sports, girls, gambling, entertainment, comedy etc. I'd scour the internet looking for anything to joke or comment on; anything guys would talk about at a bar watching a game could land on the website. There was no editor. No thought really given. I'd find something funny or interesting, post it, and move on to the next. Bostonians would send links to their friends in other cities. People would send me funny videos they took from around the city, videos that only existed on Barstool. There was no other social media at the time. If your friend fell down a flight of stairs at a party, you didn't have Instagram or TikTok to upload it to. So they sent it to us, hoping we'd post it. As I wrote and wrote, Barstool grew and grew. I imagine it's how a band feels when they start to explode. Like . . . *what the fuck is going on here?*

The transition from a newspaper publication to a website was not the only transition that was going on at this time. Blogging was a different type of writing from the long-form articles in the newspaper. Blogging was an insatiable, relentless beast. You had to write fast, concisely, and be on top of everything. My original crew of writers had been writing religiously for six or seven years just for the love of the game. We had all started in our mid-twenties with the exception of Old Balls Thornton, who was like a hundred when he started. Prior to the website, I don't really think any of us thought there was a light at the end of the tunnel. If I could have made a modest living for myself, that would have been a huge win at the time. I was living at my girlfriend's mom's place, broke as can be, six years into this venture. There was no budget for anything. These guys had been with me for years but it was time for them to move on, and the website was kind of the perfect breaking point for them. They all had full-time jobs and couldn't be chained to the computer, blogging 24/7. Plus, the newspaper clearly wasn't my priority anymore. So the original Core 4 slowly faded away . . . just as Barstool was ready to explode.

3

The Lessons of the Newspaper

The early blog days were the absolute Wild Wild West. You could literally say or write anything and nobody blinked. Nothing was out-of-bounds. Facebook was just taking off. YouTube was just invented. Nobody even really knew what going viral meant. But I took what worked with the newspaper, and I morphed it into the blog. I knew people loved the local cover models from the newspaper, so in between all the random blogs, I would feature a local pretty girl at 5:30 p.m. every single day. The segment was called "Local Smokeshow of the Day." To put it mildly, it was a big hit.

The process was fairly simple: I would introduce the girl—"Here is Rebecca from Framingham State," say a couple words, and then we would post pictures from the girl's Facebook profile. To find a girl for the next day, I'd ask for submissions from our readers. We would reach out to new girls and tell them they had been nominated and ask if they were cool with us featuring them. I'd say 95 percent of the girls who were nominated gladly agreed, and it absolutely took off like wildfire. Both girls and guys nominated their friends, coworkers, and classmates. *Maxim* had a feature called "Hometown Hotties," but Local Smokeshow of the Day shit all over it.

In fact, "smokeshow" became part of the vernacular and is still used to this day to describe a pretty girl.

Whenever I tell people I invented the word "smokeshow," they look at me like I'm crazy. Do not be confused. I invented that. I used to root for the Miami Hurricanes when I was a kid and always loved the way they came out of the tunnel and through the smoke at the Orange Bowl. I imagined a pretty girl coming out of smoke the same way. Hence, Local Smokeshow of the Day.

Like I said, I invented the word.

One day, an angry dad showed up to my in-laws' house in Abington. Thankfully I wasn't home because, as it was described to me, "he was so angry that if he had had a gun, he would have put it in my mouth." This dad was not pleased that his daughter was featured as a Local Smokeshow of the Day. He didn't love the fact that all his friends at work read Barstool and were gawking at his daughter. Fair point, I suppose. When I found out about it, I messaged the girl and was like, "Umm, your dad showed up at my house today ready to kill me. Did you tell him you gave us permission?" To her credit she said, "Better he kill you than me. I had to lie to him." I respected her honesty.

This raises a point that I would consistently make throughout the years when feminists would call us sexist. People always acted like we were stealing photos or exploiting girls with our Smokeshow of the Day feature. That's just not true. We always asked their permission and were only posting pictures they had already uploaded themselves to the internet. All we were doing was saying they were pretty. That's it. That's a compliment where I come from. We weren't saying they weren't talented, intelligent, or whatever; just that they were attractive. It's science.

As the website continued to grow, I found two new revenue streams. Technology was slowly but surely catching up with the internet, and I discovered a new company called Blogads. Can you guess what it did? It sold ads for blogs that didn't know how to sell online ads themselves. Basically, a marketplace to connect the buyer and seller. Advertisers could go onto this site and buy banner ads on Barstool Sports without ever having to talk to me. I simply set the price and companies could buy space. It was all automated in the backend so the ads would just show up when they were purchased. Which meant no heavy lifting by me, no time spent selling. The more traffic we got, the more I could charge. It didn't make me rich, but it was something.

The second revenue stream was much more work but much more profitable: the T-shirt business. Warren Buffett once said the most valuable thing a business can have is eyeballs or attention. (At least I think he said that. If not I'll take credit for it.) Basically, as long as you have eyeballs on you, you can figure out a way to monetize those eyeballs. As the website continued to grow and more and more eyeballs came to Barstool, I took advantage of it by selling T-shirts about anything and everything. I mean I truly created some of the ugliest T-shirts ever made. If there was a viral internet moment, I made a shirt about it. If an athlete had a funny quote in a postgame interview, I made a shirt about it. What I learned was that even if a shirt wasn't successful, so long as we sold even *one* shirt, I knew you could sell a shirt about *anything*.

In 2007, the Red Sox won the World Series again and the Patriots had an undefeated regular season. In 2008, the Celtics won the NBA championship. Around the success of our teams, we made T-shirts that the leagues wouldn't have come within a hundred miles of selling. We had a Kevin Garnett "Bar Fight" tee after he described a game as a bar fight in a postgame interview; a Dustin Pedroia "Laser Show, Relax" tee. If a Boston athlete said something catchy in a postgame interview, we made a T-shirt. And Boston fans bought them by the bushel.

Just like our content, we didn't confine our shirts to sports. We made a Charlie Sheen "Winning" shirt to capitalize on the virality of his crack-addict interviews. When Tiger Woods's many affairs with different women, including waitresses and porn stars, were revealed to the world, we made a "Nailing Putts Banging Sluts" T-shirt. We had a shirt that said "Who Else Seen the Leprechaun?" to trade on one of the internet's most famous viral videos, where a small town was profiled on a local news segment because everyone in the town thought they had . . . seen a leprechaun. There were shirts for famous movie quotes: "Vaya con Dios" from *Point Break*, "We're Gonna Need a Bigger Boat" from *Jaws*, etc. Anything I could sell, I did. I'd be on my hands and knees with Renee and my parents, packing and shipping shirts for days on end. And for the first time, my bank account began to grow.

Not that I was putting that money into a Roth IRA. Although my mother did try to steal money from me and put it into a retirement fund because she was convinced Barstool would eventually fail and I'd be dead broke when it did. I remember getting into a fight with her and my dad and yelling, "YOU'RE STEALING FROM ME! YOU COULD GO TO JAIL FOR THAT!" I'm not sure if it's really theft when they are taking money from one account and putting it into your own retirement account, but I was not happy. And yes, my mom had access to the Barstool accounts because she was still helping me pay bills and rotate credit cards that had business expenses on them.

Thanks to Blogads and T-shirt revenue, for the first time I was able to look for paid help growing the company. When I say help, let me be clear: I'm not talking about Gaz. Aka Stool Sales Guy. Aka Bald Paul. Aka Ogazzumforu. Aka Employee #1 at Barstool Sports.

Employee #1 Paul "Gaz" Gulczynski had grown up with Renee, and they were close friends. It was through her that I met him in 2004, and he sort of just started hanging around and helping me out with random stuff. I told him that we had no money to hire anybody, but I was happy to give him money if he could make *us* money. So he concocted a plan to take our T-shirts and sell them outside Fenway Park, and we'd split the profit, which seemed straightforward to me. I bought three thousand T-shirts—a huge investment at the time—for Gaz to sell, and he set off on his mission only to return less than an hour later saying he got kicked out because you needed a permit to do that. Oh sweet. So not only was I stuck with these three thousand "ARoid" T-shirts; I was also stuck with Gaz for life. Yup, he never left, or took his hat off for that matter, and is still chewing gum as loudly as ever. He became our first sales guy who sold nothing until he eventually morphed into our social media guy even though he knew nothing about that either. But in the same way that I learned everything, he learned social media on the fly, and he is still the head of our social media today, overseeing one of the most powerful marketing engines in the United States. Oh, and he's a millionaire a couple times over. The Barstool Difference indeed.

What is the Barstool Difference, by the way? Well, it's had a lot of connotations over the years. But to me, it essentially means when the stupidity of Barstool is fully on display but somehow ends up benefiting us. While lots of other companies shy away from their shortcomings, we lean into them. Like in no other world should an idiot like Bald Paul be running the social media of a media giant like ours, yet here he is. In no other media company should a squirrel be living in the walls, literally eating the wires so your internet keeps going out, but that was us. None of us had done this before. None of us knew what we were doing. Chaos and morons followed us around, but that was part of the charm, I think.

While our first full-time employee, Stool Sales Guy, would only be known in Barstool circles, our second full-time employee would become known worldwide. I'm talking about Jenna Mourey, otherwise known as Jenna Marbles.

When I met Jenna, nobody knew who she was. I remember that she and Gaz used to work at my kitchen table in Dorchester before we had an office. Kermit, her Italian greyhound, would be pooping all over the place while her other little dog, Mr. Marbles, just gave you an evil glare. How did I find Jenna? Well, as Barstool continued to grow in Boston, we continued to do all sorts of events, promos, and parties across the city. Because of our cover models and our Smokeshow of the Day feature, we had connections with the prettiest girls in town. We'd get all sorts of calls to staff promo events with the girls we had featured.

(Sidenote: Renee and I briefly started a promotion company called R+S Promotions—her initials—because so many companies were calling me to book models. It seemed like a legit new revenue stream, but Renee and I fought constantly because I wanted everything done instantly and she took more of a "chill out" approach. For the sake of the relationship we shuttered that company pretty fast.)

Back to Jenna Marbles. We got booked to do a two-month campaign around Boston for Dr. McGillicuddy's. It's like a peppermint shot, adoringly referred to as Southie Mouthwash. Surprisingly it's pretty decent, and that's coming from a guy who doesn't like shots. They had retrofitted this old *Ghostbusters*-looking car into an ambulance. Gaz and I would drive it around Boston going bar to bar with promo girls dressed as nurses who provided shot samples to customers. This was kind of the early advertising magic of Barstool. We could advertise your company, your event, provide the promo girls, and execute it. Then we'd follow up with pictures on the website to recap it all. I used to call it 180 advertising. Nobody ever corrected me to say I meant 360 advertising, but that's what it was. Well, Jenna Marbles had been on the cover of Barstool and was featured as a Smokeshow of the Day. She was one of the girls we hired for this campaign. At the time, she was working in a tanning salon and go-go dancing in Boston. Those days would soon be over for her.

Jenna was awesome at the promos. Sexy, outgoing, funny, easy to talk to. Guys and girls loved her. Barstool was getting more and more requests for this type of shit, so I offered Jenna a full-time job. She could help with the promos, managing the girls, and we'd try to figure other shit out for her to do around the office.

That other shit turned into the launch of Stoolala. Yes, Stoolala—the girl version of Barstool Sports. I didn't necessarily have some grand vision of starting a female version of our site. But on the days that Jenna had nothing to do she started writing blogs, and they were very good. The only problem was that Jenna's content was geared more toward women, so we had nowhere to put it. Hence Stoolala was born. Where Barstool had Local Smokeshow of the Day, Stoolala had Local Smokebro of the Day. The website started to gain a loyal following in Boston, just as the male version did. I think we even hired an intern for her. I'd constantly be giving her content ideas and telling her what I thought she should do like she was my little sister, and she was down for anything.

Then, on a Friday afternoon in July 2010—right after the Fourth of July, typically a super-low-key week for site traffic and breaking stories—an explosion occurred. Jenna posted a simple two-minute tutorial to YouTube titled "How to trick people into thinking you're good looking."

She made a funny tutorial of doing her makeup and hair where she transformed herself from an unattractive goblin to a bombshell blonde in a matter of minutes.

By Saturday afternoon, it was the number one trending video on YouTube—the most viral piece of content ever released by an employee of Barstool Sports.

Not that you'd know it. Jenna had not put the Barstool logo or any reference to Barstool anywhere. I was furious. I mean this thing went absolutely ballistic, and it would have driven people to our website if they'd had any idea whatsoever about how to get there.

I called Jenna to explain, and she truly felt awful about it and quickly retrofitted the Barstool logo into the video. She explained that she had just made it for fun and had no clue it would go nuclear.

I thought Jenna's meteor of a video would be a one-off. I didn't know how the YouTube algorithm really worked, or how virality tends to feed upon itself. Because she followed that video up with another . . . and another . . . and they all went to the absolute moon. Her videos were burying anything and everything I, or any of my guys, had tried to toss up to catch the interest of the internet. She had found a winning formula, and I told her to just put all her effort into focusing on creating her videos.

As Jenna blew up, her attitude changed dramatically. She went from being the hungry rookie who was up to do anything and everything for the brand to, overnight, it felt to me like anything and everything she did was a favor, an obligation, to the brand.

In 2010, we didn't have contracts. I was never and really am still not a contract guy. I mean we need them but I hate them. I hate agents. I hate all of it. I'd prefer an unwritten contract, an understanding of "You do right by me and I'll do right by you." And because Jenna was *the* "It Girl," it was only a matter of time before she decided to bounce for bigger and better things. Less than a year later, she'd been offered an entertainment contract out in Los Angeles. I honestly wasn't bitter at all. The writing was on the wall. People probably think I'm lying, but I'm not. I had no idea how to capitalize on her newfound fame. I'm not sure anybody did. After all, like I said, she was literally like YouTube's first megastar. She has a wax statue in Madame Tussauds for Christ's sake. That's how big she was. With all the stars we've had, from Alex Cooper to Pat McAfee to Caleb Pressley to me to Big Cat, all the biggest names who have walked through our doors, I think at the height of her power Jenna may have been the biggest. There was nothing I could offer her at that point in Barstool that would have made sense for her to stay. I read over her entertainment contract, gave it to my dad (who plays an attorney at night) to make sure she wasn't getting screwed, and wished her well. But any warm fuzzy feeling we had didn't last long.

The next day, Jenna wrote a blog announcing her departure from Barstool. In it, she said something to the tune of wishing she could keep blogging, how it wasn't up to her, and she thanked the readers—and only the readers—for getting her to where she was.

This infuriated me. Even if she had said nothing I think I would have been okay with it. But I believed she was just flat-out lying about wanting to keep Stoolala going. I gave her the IP. I had no use for it without her. I'm not sure if she just wanted to create sympathy by leaving, or not to feel guilty, but it pissed me off. She had every right to chase her dreams in LA, and I encouraged her to do it. But don't make Barstool the bad guy. And it wasn't just her readers who blew her up; those were our readers as well—the readers and community that I spent almost a decade working my ass off to build. I mean I blogged her "How to trick people" video when it had zero views on the site. Then a Barstool commenter took her video and posted it to Reddit, where it exploded. Would she have been found without us platforming her? Without our community behind her as a launching pad? I have no clue, but there is no doubt we gave her a gigantic leg up. And as soon as she had scaled the wall, as soon as she was being interviewed in the biggest publications about where the hell she'd come from, her story curiously lost any memory or trace of her Barstool Sports roots.

It really rubbed me the wrong way. I wasn't jealous of her success. I was mad at her perceived lack of loyalty and what I felt was her spitting in my face. She was a full-time employee for her first ten videos or something. You can't tell the story of Jenna Marbles without Barstool Sports. A few years later, and now a full-fledged superstar, Jenna posted a video where she traced the journey of her life on a whiteboard. In it, she did thank Barstool and me for the important role we had played in launching her career. I think her quote was something like this:

"I hated my life and that all changed when I met Dave Portnoy and he hired me at Barstool Sports and taught me the internet."

It was the first time she had mentioned us since she left. That was all I needed, and it squashed whatever grudge I had held toward Jenna.

Despite Jenna's tumultuous career at Barstool, her time taught me a valuable lesson. For months, I had tried to guide, nudge, and suggest what Jenna should do for content. The work that came from those efforts was okay . . . nothing great or memorable. But when she started making those quirky videos on her own, she exploded. They were videos and content ideas that I could never have dreamed up in a billion years, and the lesson here was simple: hire great, talented people and let them run wild.

In 2008, right around the time I hired Jenna and Gaz, Barstool was exploding, and not just in Boston. Thanks to the website, we were building a cult following up and down the Northeast Corridor. So the next move seemed like a no-brainer. What if I could replicate what I had going on in Boston in NYC? I put an ad out that I was looking for NYC writers who would cover the world in the same Barstool tone but from a New York perspective, and this ad yielded KFC.

Meet Kevin Clancy, aka KFC. (KFC originally wanted to be known as the Colonel on the blog, like KFC's "The Colonel." I vetoed it and almost didn't hire him because I thought the name was so stupid. That veto is probably the nicest thing I've done for him.) Anyway in 2008, Kevin was a twenty-five-year-old kid working for Deloitte, crunching numbers and moving manila folders from the "open" pile to the "closed" pile. To round out his dismal life, he was a die-hard Mets, Jets, and Knicks fan. I had a perpetual loser on my hands whose tormented, fatalistic complaining would come to translate as a strong voice that absolutely jumped off the blogging page.

Kevin's day job was to audit collateralized debt obligations. This was 2008, when the entire world was learning that CDOs were the poison pills that had flatlined the U.S. economy. As if Kevin needed any other reason to hate his job, he was poring over hundreds of pages of numbers that all simplified to the same sum: CDOs were shit, and a lot of people had lost their homes as a result.

His story rings familiar to the stories of so many people who have come through the hallowed halls of Barstool Sports: guy hates his cube job and starts a side project to cope with the dissatisfaction of his life.

Kevin was reading every blog we posted on the website from his desk. Thanks to some extremely lax oversight of his actual job, he decided to start his own blog on the side, ForSureNot.com. I guess this was a saying that he and his buddies would toss around (cool!), but he was diligent in writing and posting blogs every day. At its peak, Kevin said his blog was getting about five hundred readers a day. It wasn't much, but it was enough for someone to pass the blog my way. I liked his tone and especially liked the fact that he could keep up the cadence of our new world of blogging that I knew was critical to our success.

The other real contender for the NYC position was a young guy named Keith Markovich (alias KMarko). Kevin and Keith wrote guest blogs for the website for weeks. They were both great. Problem was, I only had enough money to pay one person, and I could not make up my mind who to hire between them. I was so torn that I eventually just told them I'd hire them both if they were willing to split the one salary of $50,000. Against all odds, they agreed and NewYork.Barstoolsports.com was born. Now, Kevin agreed to the terms in part because I was willing to let him continue his accounting job so long as he hit his blogging marks. Somehow, Kevin managed to blog from his desk at Deloitte for TWO YEARS without them finding out that the acerbic "KFC" of Barstool New York was their very own CDO auditor.

I don't know how he did it, honestly. Kevin tells me that on the second day of blogging from his desk, Deloitte's internet firewall shut down his access to the backend of our WordPress site. But Keith told him to simply send him his blogs via Gmail, whereupon Keith would format them and post them to our website. This was the setup for two years. It was like some sort of Cold War underground countergovernment newsletter shit.

Of course, Kevin's growing contributions and preference for his side job came at the cost of his . . . actual job. His work began to slide as he tanked his deliverables for Deloitte. But corporate America can often be quite forgiving to employees who fall behind, and his bosses tried to transfer him to a different department with more lenient quotas. Smartly, Kevin refused. Then they offered to put him on a performance plan, which he also refused. He wanted to get fired, because it would mean severance and continued healthcare benefits through their COBRA plan. After another year, they were sad to tell him his day had come. I guess he did so little work they were left with no other choice.

For months, Kevin had been taking stacks of manila folders and papers from open CDO cases and hiding them in locked filing cabinets. This kept his case pile low, giving the appearance of a man entirely on top of his assignments. By the time his bosses realized he was not, in fact, closing out those cases, Kevin was out the door with a cushy severance package and on to his new life as a full-time blogger at Barstool.

In Kevin and Keith, I had found two people who could match my pace and output on the blog. From the start, they both understood the importance of being on top of stories. Yes, we were reacting to breaking internet news. But we were also trying to break it ourselves. This meant never leaving your house, or if you did, bringing your laptop everywhere you went. We were on call 24/7, 365.

4

Stoolapalooza

The fact that KFC was able to hang on for two years at Deloitte while blogging was huge—and surprising. Because during those years, Barstool took off like a rocket ship. Now, not to hit the rewind button on you, but a couple months prior to Jenna hitting the big time and packing up her shit for the West Coast, she was part of something called Stoolapalooza. This was 2010, and I would say it was a seminal moment in Barstool history. To this day when people ask me, "Hey Dave, when was the first time you knew Barstool was big enough that you wouldn't have to worry about getting a traditional job again?" my answer is always the same: Stoolapalooza.

In 2010, I decided that it was time for Barstool Sports to spread its wings. The company was operating reliably and comfortably in Boston. Until then, we had hosted all our live events within the safe and familiar playground of city limits. If we threw an event anywhere in the city, I knew there would be a line around the corner. I still didn't entirely know what I had created, what shape it was taking, or just how popular we were elsewhere, but I knew it was time to find out.

I wanted to do a college tour. But we had a presenting sponsor in Southern Comfort, and they were nervous about sponsoring a college tour with us because so many of those kids would be under twenty-one years old and not legal to drink. But somehow, we worked through it by deciding it would be a music tour that just happened to take place near colleges. We picked six venues within a short distance of each college that we wanted to target: Providence (for the URI kids), New Haven, UMass Amherst, Boston, and UNH.

Next up, I had to find a headliner for said music tour. In one of my blogs, I asked our readers who they wanted to see in concert or who they were currently listening to. The name that kept coming up was Sammy Adams.

He was a young rapper from Boston who rapped about college, partying, and his love for Boston. His debut album, *Boston's Boy*, was rocketing up the iTunes charts. I agreed to pay him $20,000 for six shows. It was a lot to me at the time, but it would prove to be some of the best money I ever spent. Also, booking Sammy Adams thrust me into rap beefs long before the days of my now-famous diss tracks, "Rise Pageviews Rise" and "Smallest Man Alive." (At some point along the timeline of Barstool lore, KFC wrote that the singer Ariana Grande was too good for rapper Big Sean after they broke up. This enraged a rapper named Tiko Texas, which led to them recording diss tracks against each other, which led to me recording my own diss track . . . There aren't enough pages in this book for me to tell that story, so just google it, trust me.)

Anyway, other rappers started accusing Sammy Adams of buying his own iTunes songs to inflate his numbers. One guy, Chris Webby (who I think eventually dated Halle Berry), banned me from coming to Connecticut, whatever that means. He also included me in a diss track (again, google it). It was wild. I was out in the streets defending Sammy like he was one of my own, even though I didn't know the first thing about any of this. But you come at one of my guys, I come at you. Shoot first, ask questions later. Also I think it's safe to say that all Sam Adams's iTunes numbers were real. Every spot we went to was filled with students who knew every lyric to every song.

I guess I should also briefly mention this is when I met Dante the Don (sick name, Dante). Dante was a local guy who reached out to me and asked if we could meet. I have no idea why I said yes, but I did. He pitched me the idea of being Sammy Adams's DJ for the tour. I didn't even know Sammy needed a

DJ, and to be honest I'm not sure Sam knew he needed one either. How could Sam not know that? Well, had I mentioned that Sam Adams had never performed live before Stoolapalooza? And now he had a sold-out tour with tens of thousands of people waiting for him. No pressure.

As for Dante, he got the gig and has been the resident Barstool DJ ever since. He's DJ'd everything from the Blackout Tour to Pizza Fest (the giant pizza festival I created) to Sales Upfronts, when our sales team presents our best shows to potential advertisers. I've seen him so drunk onstage that he played the same song five times in a row. I've taken a piss next to him at a urinal when he should have been onstage performing in front of five thousand people. Needless to say, we've had our ups and downs, but he has been with us in some fashion since 2010. And for as much grief as I've given him, he is part of Barstool lore. A legit looney tune character. There is no conspiracy theory he doesn't believe in. He's convinced that I'm part of the illuminati. I don't even know what that means. He's truly just one of those weird-brain dudes who somehow entered our universe and never left. That has always been a calling card of Barstool: finding these weird brains and implementing them into the circus. Some could even argue that Barstool's natural gravitational pull for weirdos has been our secret sauce throughout the years. We're the best there is at finding people who have no business existing in real life anywhere but with us.

Back to the tour. The original plan was just to go to local bars or small venues around the college. First come, first served. But then something strange happened: the day after announcing the tour on the blog, I got a call from the Mullins Center at UMass. This is where they play their home basketball games—their big arena. The guy running the venue asked me if I was in charge of Stoolapalooza. When I said yes, he said he was fielding a ton of calls from students trying to buy tickets. He then asked if I'd ever throw Stoolapalooza at the Mullins Center instead of the little bar down the road, where we were originally planning to hold it. I told him I couldn't afford to rent out the venue, to which he replied he'd structure the deal so there was little risk on my end. UMass would cover the up-front costs and put three thousand tickets on sale. That was the maximum capacity they could have on the floor. If it was a dud, no harm no foul. If we sold over two thousand tickets, we'd start making money. I agreed to give it a shot.

Tickets went on sale one week later. I was on the phone with the Mullins Center when they officially went up. That same guy told me they were live and I could promote it. We hung up, but he called me back one minute later. All three thousand tickets had sold in less than a minute.

Umm, what the fuck just happened?

Needless to say, I rescheduled the entire tour for the biggest locations we could find around each school. The demand was through the roof. The entire tour ended up selling out within minutes. It honestly couldn't have gone better, with the exception of one place that I'll get to later.

At Quinnipiac we held our show at Toad's Place, which is a relatively famous concert venue. Our show happened to coincide with the major spring concert put on by the school. We didn't do that on purpose; it just landed that way. Their headliner was The Fray. But when we showed up on campus, kids were wearing "The Fray is Soft, the Stool is Hard" homemade T-shirts. Because of the scheduling conflict, the school had a hard time selling tickets. They simply couldn't compete with us. Stoolapalooza, with our $3,300 headliner, had toppled a $100,000 act booked by the university itself.

(A quick funny story about the Quinnipiac show: Before each concert, we had a pregame party at the college we were at. Well, I was playing beer pong in the rain before this show against a cripple. He was a legit cripple. Like he needed a cane to stand.

There was a crowd watching us. I showed him no mercy. On one of the last shots, he slipped and fell in the mud. I got right in his face: "What's the matter, you gonna cry little man?!" He fucking loved it and so did I. We both had a good laugh. I still remember it to this day. The cripple had a great sense of humor and was a Stoolie. For me, that's really what Barstool has always been about—making people laugh and not taking life too seriously. Almost twenty years later, I still remember that dude. I googled Stoolapalooza as I was writing this and, lo and behold, there was the picture of me with the crippled kid. What are the odds! I bet he's killing it in whatever he's doing right now.)

I think this is something that sometimes gets lost when talking about Barstool and our fans. All you hear is the negative shit. How we're just a bunch of asshole bros. It's a lazy narrative and always has been. We're always pretty good at knowing when to bust balls and when to help out if we can.

For example, do people remember the viral Ice Bucket Challenge? Well, the guy who started it was Pete Frates. Pete was from my neck of the woods in Boston. One day, a high school buddy of mine called me out of the blue and told me he had a friend named Pete Frates who was early in his ALS diagnosis. Pete was a huge Barstool fan and was doing a polar plunge in Beverly to raise money and awareness for the cause. He wanted us to come jump into the ocean with him in the dead of winter.

Say less. We all showed up and became instant friends with Pete.

From that day on, we'd go to his events, raise money, and help out however we could.

Just like the crippled kid from QU, Pete was one of us. And that's exactly how we treated him: like he was one of our buddies or brothers. Part of our family. We didn't let diseases or disabilities affect the way we interacted with people. We treated them like normal dudes being normal dudes. The disease could have hit any of us. To this day, his family is one of the most remarkable families I've been fortunate enough to meet through this journey. The amount of awareness and money they've raised is beyond comprehension. I was actually one of the original people Pete challenged to do the Ice Bucket Challenge—literally one of the first three guys in a challenge that became one of the biggest viral causes ever.

We had Pete's back until his passing and he had ours. I remember when then governor of Massachusetts Charlie Baker wore a "Free Brady" shirt during the Ice Bucket Challenge. The only problem was it was a T-shirt that wasn't one of ours. Who was the first person to reprimand Governor Baker for it? Pete Frates. He even got Baker to publicly apologize for the snafu. Just loyal, East Coast guys having each other's backs. That's who Pete and we were at our core.

Back to Stoolapalooza and UMass. This was the school that really opened my eyes to what was possible. It would be the last time that I ever underestimated the power and reach of Barstool Sports. When we rolled onto campus, I quickly saw that my mission to spread the good word of Barstool was too late; these kids were already believers. From every dorm, every student housing complex, every frat balcony, and every set of sorority steps hung a sign welcoming Barstool. The stool-and-stars logo was everywhere.

People came out to bang on the side of our bus like we were the Beatles. We passed throngs of kids chanting "VIVA LA STOOL!" in full voice. It genuinely seemed that they had been waiting for us.

Before Stoolapalooza, I didn't have a clue whether Barstool Sports had traction on college campuses. Within five minutes of arriving on campus at UMass, I realized that Barstool Sports was bigger than I had ever expected.

The next generation had found us. They weren't just reading Barstool; they were gigantic fans. It felt like a movement. Everyone at UMass knew who I was and was happy to see me, happy to see Sammy Adams. It was surreal.

I had organized a pre-party at Hobart, a housing complex where I figured we could meet a few of the students, play some beer pong, and rally some excitement for the concert that night. We made sure to do that everywhere we went: don't just show up in a city and leave; pound the pavement and meet the people.

Now, UMass is a powder keg of a campus. It doesn't take much of a spark for the students to go from controlled fun to an all-out blitz that borders on booze-fueled rioting. They actually take pride in this, affectionately referring to themselves as "ZooMass." When we showed up at Hobart, we didn't bring a spark—we brought a barrel of napalm.

Thousands of kids were going nuts around us. People started throwing bottles, climbing onto roofs, telephone poles, executing daring wrestling moves from tree branches. It was like they wanted to prove to us that we had chosen the right place to build our nascent live concert business, not that I needed any convincing. And as we drew nearer to concert time, it felt like the zoo knew that feeding time was near.

Somehow we managed to herd everyone toward the Mullins Center, leaving behind a battlefield of wounded beer cans, torn T-shirt fragments, and hair extensions. I took one look behind me and felt relieved to know we were moving inside. There was something primal about having all those kids out in the wild.

But things were just getting started.

The concert opened with some local frat stars we'd found. As the crowd filed in, you could feel the heat in the arena ratcheting up. These kids had been partying all afternoon, wanting to show us how they'd earned their nickname and their reputation. By the time Sammy Adams took the stage, the entire floor in front of the stage was moving as one connected mass of bodies. Adams crushed his set, finishing up with his anthem "I Hate College," to which every single student sang along. Then I came out to thank everyone for coming, and the crowd found another gear to greet me. Chants of "Viva La Stool" rang around the arena as I tried to get a word in edgewise, to give Sammy Adams his props and thank UMass for being so receptive to us. Holy shit, we had arrived.

In just three weeks, Stoolapalooza descended upon six of the largest colleges in New England. We were embraced everywhere we went, even when a school tried to stop us. Yes, I'm talking about you, University of New Hampshire.

This was the only concert that didn't have thousands of students in attendance. Instead, we were relegated to the basement of a local bar called Libby's. It probably fit a hundred people down there all crammed together. It wasn't for lack of effort on my end to find a bigger venue or lack of demand from the students. I did everything in my power to rent out the gym just like I had done at the other schools. Unfortunately the only people who could book concerts at UNH were a group called SCOPE (Student Committee on Popular Entertainment).

I patiently tried to explain how popular this concert was. I showed ticket sales numbers. I was willing to do whatever they needed to make it happen. I wasn't asking SCOPE to pay for anything; just rent me the building like every other school was willing to do. SCOPE brushed me off. They told me I didn't know how to throw a proper college concert. It infuriated me. So what did I do? I aired them out on the blog. I posted emails of the back-and-forth of me trying to book the venue. It enraged the student body at UNH. SCOPE became the villain. When we arrived at UNH, there were "FUCK SCOPE" signs everywhere. I didn't feel bad. They had made their bed, so now they had to sleep in it. This was a philosophy I would adopt over the years. Nothing was off-limits. I would showcase the good, the bad, and the ugly of running this business. My openness in every facet of my life both personally and professionally would continue to ingratiate us with our fans, who consequently felt connected to the brand and invested in our success.

By the end of our tour, we were all exhausted. I could barely think. But one thing I knew for sure was that we were far more popular than I had ever dreamed. The new era of Barstool Sports had begun and there was no turning back.

* * *

Coming off the heels of Stoolapalooza, I knew for the first time since I started Barstool Sports that I was never going back to the cubes. I wasn't sure how we'd made it this far, but the little engine that could was starting to show early signs of becoming a freight train. In fact, in 2010 I was featured in *Boston Magazine* with an article titled "Is This Boston's Next Media Mogul?" Clearly, people were starting to take notice.

Photo by Devon Day

(Funny story: the guy who shot this cover also shot the cover photo for this book.)

What's more, I had become even more dangerous now that I had a little money to spend thanks to Sammy Adams. But this was no time for taking my foot off the gas and enjoying the early fruits of my labor. I took the money we made and poured it right back into the business.

This was how I was able to hire both KFC and KMarko full-time. But I wanted more. I put out the Bat-Signal for more cities in which we could replicate the formula. Philadelphia was the next logical target. I actually tried to buy a site called the "700 Level," which was a good local Philly blog, and fold it into Barstool, but they wouldn't sell. But the guy who ran it introduced me to Maurice Peebles, aka Tall Mo. He became the editor of Barstool Philly and did a pretty good job of running the Philly site for a while. Mo left after about three years and has gone on to build an impressive editorial career at places like Complex, Bleacher Report, and ESPN. A guy named Smitty—who freelanced under Tall Mo while constantly complaining about how he was mistreated by the world—would ultimately take over Barstool Philly.

Next, I set my sights on Chicago. To me this was a critical city. Up to this point, we had only landed in Northeastern cities; cities that fit the Barstool mantra perfectly—sarcastic, rude, asshole-type cities. Typical East Coast vibes. I needed to test out the Midwest. Picture me standing over a big game of Risk with my finger planted straight on Chicago. I needed to have that city next. But finding the right guy proved far harder than it had in New York.

5
Finding Talent

A common theme of Barstool through the decades is that we consistently adapt, shift, adjust, and reinvent ourselves in our never-ending quest to create entertaining content. So in that vein, in 2011, I started doing a gambling call-in show with my longtime buddy Elio Imbornone. We called it the *Power Hour.*

(Elio is now known to the world as Mr. Ice for his hockey picks on Barstool, where he just picks the over every single time, and somehow he has created such a devoted following that he hosts an event called "Ice Con" every year where maniacs fly across the country to gather and root for goals. This is almost one of those sentences that are so preposterous that even when I read it back I can't even believe it's true. What do you mean, people fly from all over the world [literally] to watch a hockey game with my idiot buddy Elio, who they revere as some sort of goal-scoring-deity?

That's not to say it's all been smooth sailing for the Ice people recently. All Mr. Ice's merch just says "Ice" on it. He even has it emblazoned on his suitcase. Well, in case you've been living in a cave, now isn't the best time to be loudly and proudly calling yourself Mr. Ice while wearing ice hats and hoodies and carrying ice luggage. He has been confronted everywhere, from airports to hockey rinks, with people screaming in his face for being pro-ICE. Come on, man, he's just rooting for goals, and he had the nickname long before ICE agents became a political hot button. It's so fucking stupid but also so perfectly Barstool.)

Anyway, I hosted the original *Power Hour* on something called BlogTalkRadio. It was a total shit show. I could barely figure out how to use the technology. I'd hang up on people by accident. Nothing worked. And people loved it. All the dropped calls, the complaining about our disastrous technology, the confusion . . . it somehow made for hilarious radio. It was the Barstool Difference on full display again.

Then I decided to take the *Power Hour* to local airwaves. Obviously no radio executives were interested in hiring me or paying us for content, so I bought radio time on 1510 The Zone, which was a fledgling radio station in Boston. Think of it as an hour-long infomercial for Barstool Sports. We added my childhood buddy Todd McShay as our third host for the *Power Hour*.

It wasn't exactly prime-time stuff over at 1510. I think the only guy who was actually collecting a paycheck at that station during those days was some guy nobody had ever heard of named Ryen Russillo. But I'm sure it was peanuts.

So you had a tiny radio station that could barely afford to keep the lights on with me, Russillo, and Todd McShay all essentially working for free. McShay would eventually find success and fame at ESPN and would help bring Ryen Russillo over to their network. Fifteen years later in 2025, I signed Ryen Russillo to a multimillion-dollar contract at Barstool, outbidding Bill Simmons for his talents. (Yes, the same Bill Simmons who refused to grant me an interview back in the early newspaper days.) It's insane when you look back at those days on 1510 The Zone and the talent who were on a radio station that nobody listened to.

What does any of this have to do with Chicago? Well, one of the regular callers on the *Power Hour* was a guy named Dan Katz, aka Big Cat. When he heard that I wanted to expand to Chicago, he applied for the job. He had already started his own Barstool-style blog with a Chicago slant. It took me less than three seconds reading it to know Dan was perfect. He had everything I looked for in those days. I needed to see that prospective hires were consistent over time; that they had been updating and adding to their own blog at a pace and frequency that were within the realm of how we did things at Barstool. Because by now, we were each writing about ten to fifteen blogs a day. I mean, it was constant, competitive, and there was no end in sight. It certainly wasn't for everyone.

I went back and forth with Dan over the phone a few times before convincing him to fly to Boston to meet. The guy was all in: eager, committed, and ready to take the leap of faith that I'd asked of Kevin, Keith, and every other young person who had come aboard. Then I told him the payment schedule, which cooled his feet off real quick.

I can't say I blame him. Dan was fresh out of college with a degree from the University of Wisconsin and, like so many of our twentysomethings, somewhat leery of a long-term future at Barstool Sports. But it was impossible for me not to take it personally when people balked at my invitations to join us, because I believed so heartily in the company.

Quickly, Dan went from all in to all out, and yes, I sort of thought he was a pussy for it. You have to remember that I wasn't just drinking my own Kool-Aid at this point; I was chugging it. Plus, I always looked at it from my unique perspective of how far we had already come. Like sure, I was still paying people with personal checks and sure, I didn't always pay on time, but at least I was paying people. That was a far cry from back when I started this thing and I had no money, no clue, and no reason to think it would ever work. A far cry from when Manzo, Chisholm, and Old Balls Thornton worked purely for the love of the game. But now Barstool had actually become something. What twenty-five-year-old wouldn't want to be part of this revolutionary rocket ship ride that was surely headed for the moon and beyond? What moron on earth wouldn't be willing to risk their future on us?

So yes, I was pissed Dan turned me down because I knew he was perfect for it. But fuck it: if he didn't see the vision at this point, then so be it. I figured I'd never talk to him again.

But just because Dan said no didn't mean I was done pursuing Chicago. I kept on looking for the right guy to run that city. The applications continued to roll in, but I didn't like any of them. I was getting anxious. I felt like time was of the essence. The world was starting to take notice of Barstool and I couldn't afford to be beaten to the punch in this key city. So after months of trying to find the perfect guy, I ended up settling for a guy named Neil. Now, I'm not going to bash Neil. He was perfectly average in every sense of the word. He wrote blogs. He kept up with the pace of it. You didn't puke when you read it. You didn't laugh. You'd never send one of his blogs to your friends. Everything was wallpaper. The best and most important thing you can say about Neil when chronicling the history of Barstool is that without Neil, there is no Big Cat.

Unbeknownst to me, the hiring of Neil reignited Dan's interest in working for Barstool. He reached back out and asked if he could contribute part-time, for free, to the blog, and I said sure—knock yourself out. Far be it from me to turn down free labor.

I didn't know it at this time, but this was one of the qualities that have made Dan a superstar over the years. He is blessed—or cursed, depending on how you look at it—with perpetual FOMO (Fear of Missing Out). There is just something in his DNA that drives him to always be in the mix with everything. He has an insatiable work ethic because of it. Combine that with insane talent, and that's how a superstar is made.

Of course, within a matter of days of Dan starting to blog, he had absolutely inhaled Neil. To the point that the readers created a conspiracy theory that Dan was writing shitty blogs under the fake name of "Neil" to make his own blogs look that much better. There was actually a small but vocal underground group in Chicago (they called themselves Kneel for Neil) who rooted for their inept king. They'd comment on every blog how great Neil was and how bad Dan was. Funny stuff. But the writing was clearly on the wall. The discrepancy was monumental, and it gave Dan the confidence he needed in both himself and in Barstool to take this blogging thing seriously as a career. After a volatile courtship, Dan "Big Cat" Katz was in, Neil was out, and Chicago was not only covered but instantly every bit as strong as Boston and NYC.

The hiring of Dan essentially completed the overhaul of our Core 4 Barstool employees. We had said goodbye to the original newspaper era of me, Chisholm, Manzo, and Jerry to welcome the new blog era of me, KFC, Dan, and KMarko. (Old Balls Thornton would eventually come back to work for the blog.) While there were obvious differences between the two groups (mainly that the first group worked for free with no delusions of this ever becoming a full-time livelihood), there was also one clear similarity: I had once again been insanely lucky with who I hired. Just as our original group of writers were extremely talented, so too was this new group. Over the decades I've sifted through thousands of résumés for Barstool. But somehow, I found some of the most talented people I've had in two decades . . . right at the start.

After expanding to Chicago, I was convinced I was on to something huge. I had to just keep finding the next KFC or the next Big Cat. The next city I wanted was LA. Once again, just like in Chicago, I had a hard time finding the right fit. I eventually decided on this kid "Nick Insider" who had made some funny videos as a baseball character. But he was a video creator and had no ability to churn out the short-form blogs we needed. You can't make a West Coast kid run at an East Coast pace, and I shut down the LA operation quickly. After the LA debacle I shifted my hiring outlook. I was willing to hire people from anywhere, as long as they were good. What city they wrote for or where they lived wasn't important anymore.

For example, there was a guy trying to sell T-shirts about Iowa college sports and he kept getting hit with copyright violations. He reached out to me asking for advice on how to handle it, and I told him to just ignore it until they sent him a proper cease-and-desist letter. I then noticed he had his own blog going, which I liked, so I brought him aboard. Enter Barstool Trent and Barstool Iowa. Just like the other guys I hired, he knew what was expected of him. I expected him to be blogging 24/7. So imagine my surprise when one day, Barstool Iowa went dark. The last words from Trent were "about to black out to the St. Lunatics" and then *poof,* he was gone. Thankfully he had a good excuse: he had been arrested and was in jail for public intoxication.

If you miss a blog day, you had better be in jail . . . and he was. Trent would eventually earn his way to New York by winning a bet against me on a Michigan vs. Iowa football game in which the heavily favored Wolverines were shocked by the Hawkeyes. When Iowa won, he got to come to New York. He wouldn't be the last employee to earn a job or a promotion through betting against me on my favorite teams. Almost ten years later I hired a total idiot (Nicky Smokes) when the Miami Heat somehow beat the Celtics in the playoffs. The stakes were: If I won, Nicky would get a Barstool tattoo on his face. If the Heat won, he would get a job. The Heat won. And now I'm stuck with him.

My guys in New York, Kevin and Keith, found an intern they liked named John Feitelberg. Ironically, he had interviewed with me for the internship but lost out narrowly to Devlin the Intern Slave. I guess Feitelberg reached out to Kevin about coming to work with them in New York, and they brought him on. Devlin is also still with us, by the way.

We had a freelancer in Boston who covered the Bruins. He would electrify audiences with headlines like "Bruins Beat Leafs 3-2" and then proceed to write a recap of the box score straight from the golden age of sports newspapers when people didn't have television or the internet. His name was Brian McGonagle (aka Rear Admiral). If you don't know who Rear Admiral is, close your eyes and picture the most stereotypical Boston caricature of a human, and that is not even close to how stereotypically Boston he is. In fact, he is so perfectly Boston, he has actually been featured as an extra in movies like *The Town* and *The Departed*. He's the type of guy who legit gets mad if you say you are from Boston when you live five minutes outside city limits. Rear Admiral would eventually start a little hockey podcast called *Spittin' Chiclets*, where he'd be joined first by Ryan Whitney and then Paul Bissonnette (Biz Nasty). It would go on to become the number one hockey podcast in the world and even spawn its own liquor drink called Pink Whitney, which yields millions in revenue every year.

Hank Lockwood was hired as an intern, aka Handsome Hank. I gave him the nickname because of his decidedly unhandsome looks. Hank got the intern job because we needed help filming videos for the blog. He promised us that he had access to video equipment we could use from his college. This turned out not to be true because his college didn't exist anymore. In other words, he lied. Somehow that had slid past Stool Sales Guy in the hiring process. Now, it's not like it was all smooth sailing for Hank. He was screamed at and fired (by me) multiple times, but to his credit he just kept showing up. He became my idiotic foil and punching bag of sorts. Anytime I wanted to prove I was smart, I'd bring Hank in to be my slow-witted counterpart. As an example of this, Hank once cut off the top of his finger trying to catch a drone out of the air. As I rushed him to the hospital, his mother was yelling at him on speakerphone: "I told you not to trust that Dave Portnoy! He's gonna be the end of you!"

I think as a way to blow off some steam, Hank created an alter-internet-ego called Frannie Lydon. Frannie Lydon was a notorious troll in the Barstool comment section, but nobody knew who he actually was. He would eviscerate all the bloggers for everything we did. And not in a playful manner either. Like real mean-spirited shit. On the night of Hank's twenty-first birthday, we threw him a party called "Hankapalooza." As we were getting ready to head to the bar, I said, "Hey Hank, I know what you did," referring to something harmless like him drinking the last beer in the fridge or something. But for some reason, Hank thought I had found out that he was Frannie Lydon. Without any pressing from me, he confessed to the entire thing right then and there. It was shocking to say the least. I told him we'd deal with it after his birthday party.

Most bosses would probably fire an employee if they found out that employee had been talking shit about the company online, on the company's website, for a while. But I don't really fire people. I never have. In order for me to fire someone, they need to mess up in a way that is beyond repair. So with Hank, the punishment I came up with was that he had to wear a T-shirt with "I'm an Internet Troll" for an entire summer in Boston, 24/7.

If anybody spotted Hank out anywhere in the city not wearing the shirt, he'd be fired on the spot. He managed to make it through that summer unscathed. Now he is also a millionaire and produces the most successful sports podcast of all time, *Pardon My Take*. As for the alias Frannie Lydon? Well, Frannie took on another form years later, when I used that alias to sneak into Super Bowl Media Day before being escorted out by NFL security.

I hired our first real sales guy, nicknamed "Lightswitch Lou" for his outrageously quick temper and wild mood swings. The first time I met him he didn't stop talking for an hour straight. I didn't get one word in edgewise, but he said he wanted to pack up all his shit, move to Boston, and eat only what he killed (sales talk for commission only). Lou would manage to become one of my closest friends at the company and eventually one of my biggest regrets, but we'll get into that later. Either way, he is one of those weird brains that only Barstool can attract. The team was filling in, and Barstool was spreading across the country.

Picture that scene in the movie *Major League*, when the manager Lou Brown is seeing his players arrive at spring training and is like, "My kinda team, Charlie . . . my kinda team." That's how I felt about the ragtag crew of castoffs and misfits I was assembling.

As with all expanding businesses, the more you grow, the more your costs increase. The more employees you add, the bigger your payroll becomes. Every dime that I made I put right back into the company. All I wanted to do was re-create what was working and keep adding writers, blogs, sponsors, and events. I wanted us to grow in every vertical that had proven popular with our fans and lucrative to our bottom line.

Stoolapalooza had helped finance the first Barstool wave of hiring and was a gigantic success. The next move seemed like a no-brainer to me: come back bigger and better with a second music tour. We started planning the next concert run immediately for the fall. This time, I wanted bigger acts and venues. I wanted to hit more schools, travel farther across the country, and see just how much I could push us forward.

In the fall of 2010, we billed our tour as "Back to Stool." Each show would feature a lineup of the day's hottest musical acts. I reached out to pop stars, rappers, and chart-topping electronic artists, stretching my budget to an uncomfortable multiple of Stoolapalooza's lean operating cost.

The lineup was: Mac Miller, Wale, Chiddy Bang, White Panda, and Mike Posner. I went from paying Sammy Adams $20,000 for the entire spring tour to paying over $100,000 per show just on talent alone. Crazy to think that Mac Miller was by far the least popular of these artists at this time, and by far the cheapest hire. He was $1,500 a show and the easiest, least-demanding guy on tour. Mike Posner was our headliner, given the gigantic success of his hit "Cooler Than Me." He was expensive as hell but he was number one on the charts at the time, so I swung for the fences.

We had proven that the model was successful just five months prior. With bigger acts, bigger venues, more colleges, and real concert experience under our belts, there was simply no way Back to Stool could fail.

It would become the poison pill that nearly shuttered Barstool Sports forever.

In twenty years of doing this shit, I've learned that it is far easier to work with nobodies or people who are on their way up than established stars. These people may need a little molding and platforming to reach the next level. But the more you pay people, the more they feel that they're doing you some kind of favor. Sammy Adams was a delight to work with; negotiating the logistics and deals for our Back to Stool lineup was a nightmare I wouldn't wish on my worst enemies.

For our first shows, I strategically chose to return to the colleges that had already worked for us for Stoolapalooza. The overhead costs for these concerts were about twenty times the cost of the previous tour, so I had to raise our ticket prices just to cover the artists' pay. I conservatively estimated that we would sell 50 percent more tickets this time. After all, there were so many kids left out of Stoolapalooza; surely they'd gobble up tickets to assuage their FOMO. I couldn't have been more wrong about anything. Despite a much stronger lineup on paper, we sold the same exact number of tickets as the year before. The only problem was, I was spending 20× this time around. I had pushed all my chips into the middle and was taking a beating.

To make matters worse, the artists didn't seem to give a fuck at all. I was pouring my heart and soul into this thing to make it work, and Mike Posner and Chiddy Bang seemed to be out there just collecting a paycheck without a care in the world. It drove me insane.

It all came to a head in Providence. Chiddy Bang and his team were in New York, which is only a three-hour drive to the venue. They were supposed to arrive by 4 p.m. for sound check, and I was going back and forth on the phone with his manager, who told me they wanted to take a train, then drive, then fly to Providence. They kept moving their flight later and later, and finally it was too late. The venue, Lupo's, had a curfew due to sound ordinances in town, and Chiddy simply didn't make the cutoff point.

They showed up late and demanded to be paid. I demanded they get out of my face. I got onstage in front of the crowd and told them that Chiddy Bang fucked me and that he wouldn't be performing. I was fuming. On the car ride home I took out my phone and went scorched-earth on them. That video became part of Barstool lore. "Who does Chiddy Bang think they are . . . the fucking Beatles?!"

The entire tour was more of the same. Every night we took a bath. Every night I had to deal with prima donnas who didn't care that I was losing my shirt. It became a matter of whether it made more financial sense to cancel a show altogether or operate it at a loss. As big of a success as Stoolapalooza was, Back to Stool was an equally gigantic failure.

However, two things did come out of Back to Stool: The first was my extreme hatred of agents. To this day, I absolutely fucking despise talking to anyone's agent or manager. Sure, it's a necessary evil for me at this point, and not all agents are bad. But good agents are few and far between. Most are used-car salesmen leeches. World destroyers. They suck all the nutrients out of your planet until the planet dies, and then they move on to the next planet to destroy that one too. That's how I look at them. I was used to a world where everybody I worked with rowed together for a common goal. I can accept failure when I know everybody gave their best effort, everybody cares, and everybody left it all out on the line. But I experienced the opposite with Back to Stool. I had a failing music tour with artists who wouldn't promote it, arrive on time, or give a shit. If I asked the agent for a tweet, they'd ask for more money. I hated them and hated this tour. I swore I'd never do it again.

The other (and more important) thing I learned was that *Barstool* was driving the ticket sales; not the artists. Despite the huge roster of musicians, we sold the same exact number of tickets as the last tour. At the end of every show, the crowd asked to take more photos with me than with Mike Posner, and it wasn't particularly close. *Hmmm . . . maybe it doesn't even matter who we throw up there to play music.* I swore if we ever hit the road again, I wouldn't pay a dime for talent. We'd use our own people to create the entertainment, keep everything in-house, and control our variables as much as possible.

This would serve as the blueprint for a future tour that would launch Barstool into another stratosphere. But I'll get to that later . . .

If Back to Stool had happened a year or two before it did, I wouldn't have been able to withstand the financial setback. But as is always the case with Barstool Sports, when one thing falls, another always seemingly rises.

Bill Belichick had an old quote: "If we're all wrong together, we can still be right." I'm not sure it makes a lick of sense but I love it, and that's how I felt about Barstool. Yes, the music tour was a disaster, but the blog and all my new hires were humming along. In fact, lots of Barstool fans call the era from about 2010 to 2016 the golden era of Barstool Sports. I call it the "Milton Tough" era, named after our first official headquarters, which were located in Milton, Massachusetts.

I found the space by walking around my neighborhood looking for leasing signs. I found an old doctor's office that was in pretty bad shape. The air-conditioning units were hanging haphazardly from the windows, the lighting cast a putrid shade of yellow, and there were squirrels living in the walls (literally). But it was close to my apartment, close to downtown Boston, and most importantly, cost $890 a month.

So now we had a base and a team. You had me, KFC, KMarko, and Dan each churning out ten to fifteen blogs a day. You could refresh Barstool Sports seemingly nonstop all day long and get more content. As I added more employees, the content continued to grow. If something big happened, we were on it before you could blink. All of us were nailing the Barstool tone. Every city had its own local smokeshows. Every city built a cult following. The business model was simple at the time. These guys ran their blogs almost as independent franchisees. Like if they could sell local ads in their city or do events, they kept all the money. National ads and T-shirts sales went to corporate (me). Barstool Sports and our ragtag group of employees were outblogging, outhustling, and outworking the rest of the internet, and the results started to show. There was no time for vacation days, holidays, or excuses. We just worked our asses off and continued to grow.

This era would also birth some of our most famous controversies that my detractors and haters still reference almost two decades later, like clockwork, every time they want to prove what an asshole I am.

First up on that list is Howitzergate.

By 2011, I had been blogging for four years straight. I was writing at least ten blogs a day, and usually a lot more. Just find something I thought I could write a couple funny sentences about, embed a photo or a video, offer my thoughts, hit publish, and move on to the next one.

There were no editors in chief, no spell-checks, no reserve parachutes to pull in case of emergency. It was like the writing equivalent to talking on live radio without a five-second delay button in case a host says something unfit for air. We didn't have time to stop and consider if what we had just written might offend people. If you didn't like what we said, don't read it.

Back in those days, some of my most reliable sources for blogging inspiration were paparazzi sites. Sites like Egotastic, Dlisted, and the Superficial were all popular back in the day. Generally they featured pictures of celebrities out in the wild. Well, one day, in August 2011, one of them posted a photo of Gisele Bündchen, Tom Brady's then wife, walking on the beach with their naked toddler. It landed on every single paparazzi website that I visited. I thought it looked like the kid had a big dick for an infant. So being the official guardian of Patriot Nation, I decided to offer my thoughts on the photo. I titled the blog "Check Out the Howitzer On Brady's Kid."

Here is the blog in its original form:

> That's a big fucking hog for a 2 year old right? Just swinging low like a boss. I guess we shouldn't be surprised though. That's what MVP QB's do. They impregnate chicks and give birth to big dicked kids. Does Peyton Manning have any children? If he does I bet they got pencil dicks.

Even looking back on it all these years later, I feel like it's pretty obvious what I was trying to do. This was the height of the Patriots vs. Colts rivalry. This blog was just another way to say Tom Brady was great and Peyton Manning sucked. Having a big dick is good. Having a pencil dick is bad. It never in a million years crossed my mind that people would say I was promoting kiddie porn. In fact, I believe, to this day, that anybody who would read that and "sexualize" the kid is more fucked-up in the head than I am for making the jokes. In the shitstorm that followed, I even said that you can't sexualize a two-year-old because they're too young; there's nothing sexual about them. To even bring that word into play means that *you* went there in your mind, you sicko. I stand by this 100 percent.

So I pressed publish on the blog and didn't give it a second thought. Just continued with my day looking for my next story to blog and my next story after that. Little did I know that a hurricane was brewing.

It all started with WEEI, which at the time was the biggest sports radio station not only in Boston but in the country. The host of the most popular show on the station, Glenn Ordway, got ahold of the blog and was teeing off on me for it. It was forty-eight straight hours of coverage from WEEI, with topics ranging from how long I should spend in jail to whether somebody should show up at my house and beat me to death with a baseball bat. They set the tone and, I would argue, incited the furious backlash that ensued. They also left out a few facts, such as that I didn't take the picture myself, or the context of the blog. Instead they made it seem like I was a child pornographer hiding in the bushes outside Brady's house just waiting to snap this picture. Now keep in mind, during this same exact timeframe I was a regular guest on WEEI's Friday morning show, *The Dennis and Callahan Show*. I figured at the least I'd be able to defend myself there and mention a couple facts Glenn had omitted. But the exact opposite happened. Their station manager, Jason Wolfe, put out a press release saying that WEEI had "fired" me from their airwaves. No phone call. No nothing. I read it on the internet like everybody else. Glenn Ordway would later say he had planned on giving me a chance to defend myself but couldn't track down my phone number. Again, keep in mind I was working at the station at the time. He would also later say he only spent a few minutes discussing the blog on the airwaves. I asked WEEI for the audio from those two days so that I could play it uncut on Barstool Sports. They said they had a glitch and the tapes were lost forever. Isn't that convenient . . .

Once WEEI lit the fuse, this story went nuclear. It moved from WEEI's airwaves into the national consciousness. Everybody was talking about it. And it was all WEEI's version of events. The morning after WEEI broke the story, I woke up to Renee throwing a giant dildo at me before she left for work. "I hope you're happy, Dave," she said as she stormed out of the apartment. Somebody had attached it to our door. It's funny looking back at it now, but not so funny in real time when the world thinks you're a child-diddler and knows where you live.

For my part, I was willing to defend myself anytime, anywhere, anyplace, and to anybody. The story got so big I ended up appearing on Howard Stern's show. Stern had spent the last twenty-five years breaking every written and unwritten rule of humor and entertainment that existed. I thought he'd be a sympathetic ear. But as soon as I called in, he started spanking me. Stern called it kiddie porn and inferred that I was a total scumbag for posting the photo. I tried to explain myself, but he wouldn't let me get a word in. Later, I saw footage of Howard being prepped for my interview. His assistants handed him the photo of Brady's kid, and he laughed and said, "Kid's cock is bigger than mine, pisses me off." Then later, after he'd scolded me and was back to running his show, on air he said, "I don't understand how a two-year-old can be better hung than me." The hypocrisy was staggering.

If you were wondering if anybody defended me, there are only two people I can recall. The first was Emily Rooney on NPR, who asked me for an interview. Now, unlike Stern, you'd have thought this would be enemy territory. However, *unlike* Stern, Emily let me speak and asked questions. By the end of the interview she said, "I was expecting not to like you, but I think you made a logical case and I understand your point of view." She wasn't saying she would have posted it, but she certainly didn't think I was a criminal.

The second person was Mike Felger. He was another Boston radio personality, and while all of WEEI was hammering me, he was the only person who said, "Umm, guys, this is just a clear joke . . . let's all relax." Even though Felger has preposterous Patriots takes, I'll have his back till the end of time for that.

As the story continued to grow, I waited for an angry mob to arrive at my door. But I got the state police instead. I remember being tipped off that the cops were on their way by a friend, Matt Robitaille, aka "The Bostonian." Matt had started a company in Boston around the same time I did, and he called and said, "Cops are coming, heads up," and that was it. At least it gave me a few minutes—no more than ten—to brace myself. To say I was nervous would be an understatement. I knew I hadn't done anything wrong, but at the same time I had no clue what was about to happen.

So the cops showed up, I invited them in, and they quickly broke into a classic good cop, bad cop routine. I told them I knew that I was within my legal rights to have posted the photo, given that a hundred other websites had already posted the photo before me and nobody seemed to have any issue with them. The good guy cop nodded and assured me it all made sense and they just wanted to talk to me blah blah blah. Then the bad guy cop told me that if I *didn't* take it down, they would start going through my taxes, dig through my gambling transactions, check for unpaid parking tickets, tail me through school zones . . . basically make my life hell. And I could avoid that hell simply by deleting the blog.

This presented a dilemma for me because more than anything, I wanted to delete the photo and be done with this encounter. However, I have something hardwired in me that can't accept the path of least resistance when I know I'm in the right. I can't just apologize for the sake of apologizing. This has been a trait that has enraged my critics and opposition over the years.

So I said no. Not to be an asshole, but because I believed that retreating from my stance at that point was against everything I stood for.

In the end we managed to reach a compromise. I told the cops that I wouldn't delete it because they were threatening me or saying I broke the law. However, if they asked me to delete it as a favor because the blog was causing such a ruckus and preventing them from dealing with more important police work, then yes, I'd be willing to delete it. It was fugazi mental gymnastics on my part. Everybody in the room knew that the reason I agreed to remove it was because they threatened me. To this day I think it's the only blog I've ever written that I deleted.

After that, Martha Coakley, the Massachusetts attorney general, finally weighed in. She determined that the blog did not constitute child pornography, and that my taking the blog down was the right result and the case was closed.

Nobody was happier to have this entire fiasco behind me than I was. I've heard people say over the years that I look for controversy. I promise you that isn't true. There was nothing fun about this experience. But I also don't run from controversy. If you want to get into the mud with me, I will gladly get into the mud with you. This was also the first time I used the phrase "brick by brick" to describe Barstool. It's an important metaphor for how I built the company—one brick at a time, from the ground up, with my bare hands—and speaks to our success and what allows me to stick to my guns.

Barstool Sports had been in existence for almost nine years before Howitzergate. Our fans had been reading and consuming me daily, nonstop, during this time. They knew everything about me, from the newspaper days to the blogging era. They knew who I was inside and out. It was one thing for our readers to make fun of me, but when somebody from outside our world took a shot at me? They treated that as an attack on their own, and they went to war to defend me. Howitzergate proved that Barstool was not going to be blown away by the winds of public opinion. Our foundation had been built brick by brick and could withstand anything that would come our way.

You know how stupid the world is today? How full of shit it is? How much fake news there is? During this entire fiasco when I was defending myself, I tweeted this out:

X.com

wah, wah it's child porn. bro is 2 years old. relax

3:14 PM · 8/11/11

Clearly I was saying the people who defined this picture as child porn are insane. The kid was two years old. He was basically an infant. If you were sexualizing him then you had the problem, not me. There was a reason this picture was everywhere. It was a big nothing burger. In fact, Gisele was so unbothered by the controversy that she was on South Beach the following week, and once again she was photographed the same exact way, with her naked child.

Fast-forward to today and my haters (mostly antisemitic troll pieces of shit) will post that tweet under everything I say, trying to paint me as a pedophile. They'll say I'm on the Epstein list. All because Peyton Manning couldn't beat the Pats in the playoffs.

Speaking of the Brady vs. Manning rivalry, something else happened that coincided with the rise of Barstool Sports that helped us immensely. And that, of course, was the rise of Boston sports teams. Prior to Barstool launching in 2003, the last Boston championship of any kind was thanks to the 1986 Celtics. It had been basically two decades since any Boston sports team had won a championship. The Patriots had never won a Super Bowl. The Red Sox were the most cursed team in professional sports. Boston was perceived as a city of losers, with the local media seemingly relishing our misery.

But then a funny thing happened almost the second Barstool launched in 2003. We instantly went from a city of losers to a city of champions. The Patriots became a dynasty. The Red Sox came back from down 3–0 to beat the Yankees and win their first of four World Series titles. The Bruins won a Stanley Cup. The Celtics beat the Lakers in the Finals. Every single year, a new team was having a parade, and Barstool was at the center of it all.

I mean, look at this run of championships:

2001 Patriots
2003 Patriots
2004 Red Sox
2004 Patriots
2007 Red Sox
2008 Celtics
2011 Bruins
2013 Red Sox
2014 Patriots
2016 Patriots
2018 Red Sox
2018 Patriots
2024 Celtics

I coined the phrase "Cue the Duckboats" to symbolize when the city was getting ready for another Duckboat parade. Whenever a team won, they'd ride through town on our famous Duckboats, greeting fans by the thousands. We made a young Boston fan famous here (and hated everywhere else, in cities whose teams are perennial losers) because every year that Boston won a championship, he would show up with an updated poster showing his age and how many parades he had attended.

Barstool became the face of the Boston fan. We were loved in Boston and reviled throughout the country. There was a mostly friendly rivalry between the Barstool sites and cities; between Chicago and New York and Boston. If any of us were to visit any of those other cities, we'd be greeted warmly and probably given a bit of good-natured ball-busting. But mostly, those other cities hated Boston because of how much we were dominating them.

Looking back on it now, it's unquantifiable to know how much the success of Boston sports impacted the success of Barstool. It wasn't just all the T-shirts and merch we were able to sell; it was all the sheer awareness of the brand their wins brought us. Anytime something big happened in the sports world, Boston was at the center of it. And by extension, so were we. The blog allowed us to react faster than traditional media. Instead of waiting for your newspaper the next day or to watch SportsCenter, fans flocked to us for our commentary. And Barstool Sports continued to grow.

6

The Blackout Tour

Let's do a quick inventory of the various irons Barstool had in the fire in 2011. I had the blog running relentlessly, generating ad revenue based on clicks and pageviews. I had the merch business, which was similar to the blog in its need for speed: if something viral happened in the world, we'd make a shirt, throw it up on the web store, sell as many as we could till the fad died down, and then move on to the next. And finally, the live events. Ever since the trivia nights at the bars in Boston, live events had kept a steady heartbeat going for the Barstool cash reserves. And once Back to Stool had ended (thank God), we had settled into a nice rhythm.

That all changed when Gaz (Stool Sales Guy) came into my office one day in Milton, chomping on his gum, saying he had a potential advertiser who was having a hard time getting in touch with me to spend money with us. That actually wasn't that unusual back then. I was so focused on content that if I didn't recognize the name of your company or think you had a big budget, I didn't have time for you. Ninety-nine percent of our sales were inbound, which is always a great sign for a growing company. Our reputation was outpacing our sales force.

The name of the company was DraftStreet. Apparently they had invented a new type of online fantasy football. Instead of drafting your team for the season, you could draft it every single week and play against people online. If you are thinking this sounds exactly like DraftKings or FanDuel, you'd be correct. In fact, further down the road DraftStreet would be acquired by DraftKings, and the guy who called Gaz to advertise (Jeremy Elbaum) is my current-day contact at DraftKings; a relationship I've now had for over fifteen years.

The problem DraftStreet had at the time was that nobody knew who the hell they were or what daily fantasy football was. Jeremy said he'd pay me $20K to write one blog about it and draft a team for the NFL so people could see what I was talking about. Twenty K for one blog? Say less.

Well, as Barstool was prone to do over the years, this blog broke DraftStreet's website. They couldn't keep up with the traffic or the signups. The next day, Jeremy called me and said he wanted to 10× his budget and sign us to an exclusive advertising deal. He also had a vision for what he wanted to do: he wanted Barstool to get him into the living rooms of frats across the country on Sunday mornings before NFL kickoff so that he could explain DraftStreet in person to these guys. He didn't care how we did it so long as we got him in there.

Introducing the Blackout Tour. The plan was simple: Barstool would throw a party on Saturday night at a frat, free of charge, with the condition that the next morning, these same kids would stumble down to their frat living rooms to listen as a DraftStreet rep espoused the merits of his company's fantasy sports operation. We went to Spencer's Gifts and bought a ton of blacklights to hang in the frat basement. I bought a truck to haul the lights and generator around from frat to frat. I called up Dante the Don and told him we needed a DJ to play a couple parties. I was resolved to keep costs low, having learned the cautionary lesson of working with uncontrollable diva talent in the past. I had another employee/intern who claimed he could figure out how to make the blacklights blink, so he joined the crew. Stool Sales Guy was put in charge of overseeing the entire operation when I wasn't there. It was a skeleton structure that we would add only a few minor bells and whistles to as the tour picked up steam. We created a simple logo that consisted of a plug being inserted into an electrical socket, and off we went.

The Blackout Tour started in a frat basement at Clemson. I believe it was intended to be six stops total. After Clemson, we went to Michigan, Vanderbilt, Indiana, Iowa, and UVA to round it out. The shows went pretty well. They certainly weren't earth-shattering, but it was an excuse to fill the social calendar for whatever frat we landed at. All of it was captured by my camera guy/sales guy Gaz, who stitched together a few highlight reels for a promotional marketing effort. So steadily we rolled along, from college town to college town in our Chevy Avalanche towing a trailer, fulfilling what was essentially an ad deal. I think by the end, both we and DraftStreet were ready for the tour to be over. In what shouldn't come as a shock to anybody, the Sunday morning fantasy football gospel sermon didn't work so great when you are preaching it to fifty absolutely mangled college kids. DraftStreet would continue to spend big dollars with us but would scrap the live-events portion of their ad buy. But Barstool's future would drastically change on the last stop of the tour, Iowa (shout-out Caitlin Clark).

In Iowa, the frat we partnered with decided to rent out a bar for the concert instead of having it at their house. The bar the frat guys chose for us was already equipped for exactly what we brought to the table: blacklights already installed on the ceiling, gigantic speakers, a stage with a nice table for Dante's MacBook, and a big row of cannons that fired out CO_2 at the press of a button.

While the party itself didn't feel much different than any of the others we had already thrown, the souped-up bells and whistles gave it the illusion of being a much bigger party. Gaz, who was tasked throughout the tour with making recap videos, managed to get some great shots of the CO_2 cannons blasting the scantily clad girls with the cold, harmless gas. We posted the Iowa Blackout Tour recap video and went to bed.

The next morning, I woke up to emails from frats across the country asking how to book the party. Initially I ignored most of these emails or just responded that the tour was over. I had no interest in going back on the road, especially since DraftStreet was no longer financing the tour. It didn't make any sense for us. But these frats weren't about to take no for an answer. They started offering money: $10K to bring it to them . . . then $20K, then $30K. Whatever they needed to pay, they would pay. Turns out lots of these southern frats had significant budgets for partying.

If we thought that Iowa was the last stop on the Blackout Tour, it now looked like it had only been the beginning. Because as the Million Dollar Man once famously said, "Everybody has a price." If these frat boys were willing to pay that much, we'd do it. But one thing was very clear to me: we needed to have the same special effects that the Iowa video did. That's what these kids were expecting. I couldn't show up with our rinky-dink setup and keep our reputation intact. More specifically, we needed CO_2 cannons at every stop.

And CO_2 cannons we had. The video recaps Gaz made after each show became raunchier and wilder. Before we knew it, we had a monster on our hands. It wasn't just frats calling us up asking to book the party; it was Live Nation and every other major music venue in the country. As simple as it seems, it all started because of CO_2 cannons in Iowa.

It's hard to overstate how quickly the Blackout Tour exploded onto the scene. It seemed to happen overnight. In classic Barstool fashion, the timing was perfect for us. EDM (electronic dance music) was just becoming mainstream at this point, but it hadn't quite reached its peak, so it wasn't oversaturated. In the early days of the Blackout Tour, we would be the only EDM concert in a city for months. In fact, we actually had Avicii co-headline one of our concerts for a couple thousand bucks. It was super early in his career but he was just starting to explode thanks to his new hit, "Levels." But Barstool was still the main draw.

I couldn't schedule enough concert dates to keep up with demand. Initially, we rented all our equipment. But as ticket sales kept rolling in, I started buying everything. I bought lasers, lights, speakers, all the stuff we needed so we could cut out the middleman. Our venue size went from a hundred people in a frat basement to five-thousand-person arenas almost overnight. I created an entirely new production company called Purple Starfish Productions just to run the tour. At our peak, we were doing three to four events a week, crisscrossing the country.

The formula for these parties wasn't rocket science. We had Dante the Don as our house DJ. He would play the most popular EDM songs in the country. We had tons of lasers and lights and special effects. Girls would dress in skimpy clothes and dance onstage. And as dumb as it sounds, this seemed to be a huge part of the allure for them. We had a rotating policy where we'd allow ten girls up onstage at a time, let them dance for a song or two, then rotate in the next group. Each group would seemingly try to outdo the group before them. We started seeing homemade Barstool shirts and hats popping up everywhere in the crowd.

Kids were taking it upon themselves to spray-paint or embroider their own shirts with "VIVA" lettering in neon. I put Feitelberg and Devlin in mascot outfits and grizzly bear suits, and they would dance off five to ten pounds of water weight a night. And of course we had CO_2 cannons everywhere. And when CO_2 seemed like it was getting stale, we brought in foam.

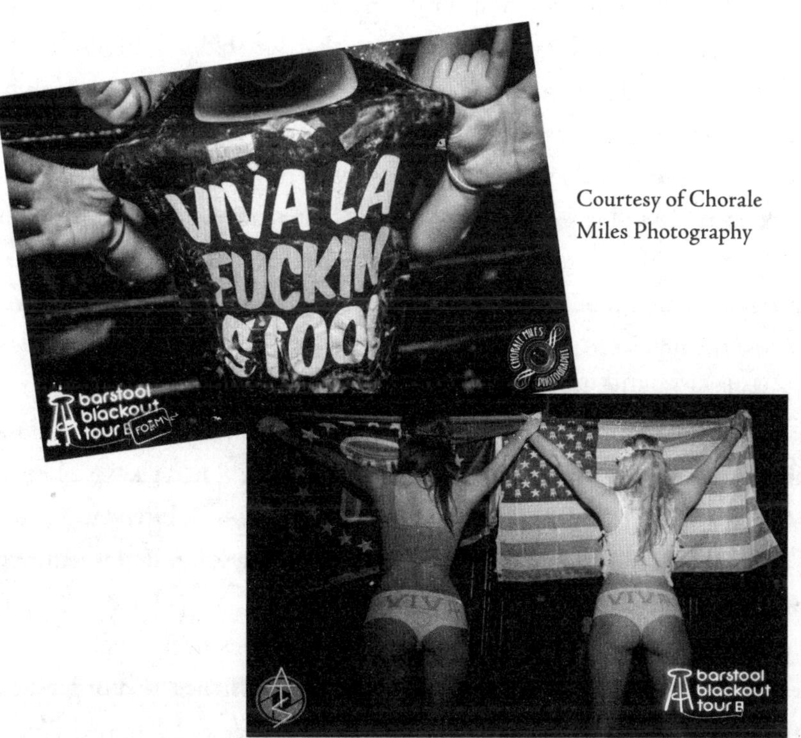

Courtesy of Chorale Miles Photography

I literally hired a guy from Alaska who built homemade foam cannons that could fill Madison Square Garden with foam if need be. Whatever we could do to keep the phenomenon growing we did. I just kept pouring money back into it, feeding the beast, and every day the tour got bigger.

I'll never forget when I got the call from Live Nation, the largest touring organizer in the world. They begged me to close out the Bamboozle festival in New Jersey. They wanted us to close the show. They wanted us to go on after Jon Bon Jovi, for God's sake, as the last act of the night. They offered us $250,000 as a flat guarantee, and the guy was apologetic about it!

"I know it's low, we should be paying you guys more. But all these people will get to hear your music, and it should bring new fans to you guys who might be outside your current demographic," he said sheepishly.

Our music? What do you mean? We don't have our own music. We have a DJ who plays other people's music and is so blacked out onstage that half the time, he doesn't even remember what song he's playing.

The Live Nation rep was utterly confused. He had access to our ticket sale numbers across the country. He saw that we sold out House of Blues in Boston five nights in a row in less than a minute. He saw we sold out the DCU Center in Worcester in thirty seconds. He saw that we were selling out shows from Florida to the Midwest. Scalpers started showing up outside our concerts to sell jacked-up tickets to the poor kids who hadn't been quick enough to get them online. There was a considerable secondary market for the Barstool Blackout Tour. Live Nation couldn't wrap their brains around it. How the hell were we outselling his entire talent roster with nothing? We accepted the $250K and closed out Bamboozle.

At the height of the Blackout Tour I would say we were clearing close to $200K a night. Just profit into the company account. I had visions of retiring in a couple years, a multimillionaire before my thirty-fifth birthday. Little did I know a storm was brewing. And of all places, it made landfall in our hometown, good ol' Boston.

As I mentioned, we sold out the House of Blues five straight nights in Boston. How did we do it? Well, each show was assigned to a different college. So Monday was Barstool Blackout BC, Tuesday was Barstool Blackout

BU, Wednesday was Suffolk, Thursday was Northeastern, etc. Pretty clever marketing on our part because each school wanted to brag that they had the best party. Well, the Northeastern concert would trigger a set of events that I would argue are the most consequential to how Barstool Sports has been perceived and portrayed by the liberal media over the decades. Even when pitching this book to publishers, the more liberal-leaning publishing houses declined to even make an offer, and it all stems from what happened that week at the House of Blues.

7

KO Barstool

Courtesy of Bill Brett

About a week or so before the Northeastern Blackout show, a small group of college girls decided that they were going to put an end not only to the Barstool Blackout Tour, but to Barstool in general. They called themselves KO Barstool, as in they planned to "knock out Barstool."

I think there were four original members, but what they lacked in size they made up for in tenacity. And to their credit, they were far more savvy than I realized at the time. They launched an all-out media blitz against Barstool. They contacted every newspaper, TV station, and radio station that would give them the time of day to alert the world that evil Barstool was throwing a concert for the express purpose of getting women blackout drunk so guys could assault them. As if that's why we called it the Blackout Tour. Who cares that it clearly started as a blacklight party during the DraftStreet days? Who cares that the logo was literally a plug and an outlet, symbolizing the lights going out and the blacklights coming on? According to KO Barstool, we were overtly saying we wanted girls to black out and get assaulted. And worse yet, all these gullible, attractive girls were somehow falling into our trap and needed to be protected from us.

What was their proof? How did KO Barstool get the media's attention? Unbeknownst to me, KO Barstool had gone through every single word I'd ever said, every blog I'd ever written, every piece of trash I'd ever thrown out bearing some scribble of handwriting they could trace back to me—all part of an ammunition-gathering mission to amass evidence that I, El Presidente, was some existential threat to women. And in their quest to ruin me they found exactly one blog that would fit their narrative that was written two years prior. Remember, Barstool had been around for ten years by this point. I had blogged nonstop for six years, a new blog every thirty minutes, trying to entertain people and give my opinions on quite literally everything. Basically every second of my life was public record, and among this gigantic mountain of words, KO Barstool found *one* blog to support their case; a smoking gun that even to this day, as I sit and write this book, is the most commonly cited example of why Dave Portnoy is the antichrist: the size six skinny jean blog.

This 2010 blog post centered on a court ruling in Australia, where a jury determined that a man could not be guilty of the rape he was accused of because—and this is real—he couldn't have removed his victim's skinny jeans without her help. In other words, her pants were so tight that if they were to have come off, it had to be because they took them off together. The case garnered international attention because of the seemingly absurd nature of the ruling. One juror actually wrote a note saying, "I doubt those kind of jeans can be removed without any sort of collaboration."

This court case was viral enough that I decided to blog about it and, in what I thought was plain and obvious sarcasm, put my own spin on it. I went on a rant about how I didn't like skinny jeans, especially on bigger women. I wrote, "I never condone rape. But if you're a size six and you're wearing skinny jeans, you kind of deserve to be raped." If you're cringing reading that line, I don't blame you. In hindsight, it's a terrible joke. Especially since it doesn't really even make sense, as I've come to learn that a size six isn't even a big person. I had thought it was like Lizzo-big, which was how the idea for the blog popped into my head. Still immature and stupid, but it was about skinny jeans and nothing else.

By the way, to me this is the very definition of cancel culture. When a group of people don't like somebody or something and will go back in time searching for something that confirms their preexisting bias. This is what KO Barstool did. It was nothing we said or did in real time. They had already made up their minds that we were bad and they hated us, and then they started sifting through thousands and thousands of older blogs to confirm their opinion. It's total bullshit and they would quickly learn I wasn't going to go quietly into the night.

If they thought I was just gonna roll over and play dead, they had the wrong guy. Oh no. I had literally been working my fingers to the bone for over a decade to get Barstool Sports to where it was at that point. For these self-proclaimed feminist students, who had probably never worked a day in their lives, to try to destroy what I had built was an act of war. I nicknamed them the "Fun Police." We were having a good time, and they took it upon themselves to interject themselves into something that had nothing to do with them. The Fun Police tend to be people unhappy with their own lives. Maybe they were picked on in high school. Maybe they don't like their own reflection in the mirror. Whatever the case may be, they are self-loathing individuals.

Not only did I not back down from the Fun Police, I decided to face them head-on. They had a massive protest planned at Northeastern the night of the concert. I decided I would meet them on their own turf and show them that the guy they had decided to vilify was not the guy they thought he was at all. I thought that by offering my side of the story, I could deescalate the tension and clarify the point of the Blackout Tour.

Walking up to a throng of chanting protesters, all of whom were theoretically protesting *me*, was a surreal experience. There they were, fifty strong, repeating the chants of the chant leader:

If you've been raped . . .

IF YOU'VE BEEN RAPED!

If you've been assaulted . . .

IF YOU'VE BEEN ASSAULTED!

If you feel shitty about this whole thing . . .

IF YOU FEEL SHITTY ABOUT THIS WHOLE THING!

You can go to University Health and Counseling Services . . .

YOU CAN GO TO UNIVERSITY HEALTH AND COUNSELING SERVICES!

I want you to know that, I want you to trust them . . .

I WANT YOU TO KNOW THAT, I WANT YOU TO TRUST THEM!

I wasn't there to mock them. I wasn't there to make light of rape. I was there to explain myself since they previously hadn't let me. For the first few minutes, I stood on the periphery and people didn't notice me. But then someone yelled, "THAT'S HIM! THAT'S DAVE PORTNOY!" And all of a sudden, all their bloodshot, rage-filled eyes turned to me. The auctioneer/chant leader with the bullhorn said, "Dave, is that you?" which I took to be an invitation to come up front. But as I reached her, she simply kept on going with her diatribe with me standing only a couple feet from her. Eventually she was just screaming incoherently into a megaphone into my face. Stool Sales Guy, who was with me, tried to record all the mayhem, only to have angry protesters slap his camera out of his hands.

The crowd continued trying to repeat every sentence she said. Except it wasn't really stuff that was meant to be repeated anymore, so they got pretty clunky and lost. The whole thing spiraled into a confusing scene, and I kept trying to yell, "We don't condone rape!" But nobody gave a fuck and nobody wanted to hear a word I had to say. As I tried to get off the front line, I was confronted by one particularly vehement protester who started shouting in my face and jabbing her finger about what a menace I was to women like her. Exasperated, I simply said, "Who are you?"

None of it made sense. Their minds were made up, their thoughts cast in stone. I was trying to move an unmovable mob, and the groupthink poison had been sipped by all. *Dave Portnoy Bad Man . . . Dave Portnoy Bad Man . . .* There was nothing I could ever say or do that would change their opinion. Worse yet, they had no interest in dialogue or debate. Anything that could disrupt their preconceived notion of me was rejected with prejudice.

I've noticed this trend time and time again over the years with people who pretend to be morally superior to Barstool. They shout and yell and stomp their feet to get their way. But they rarely will defend their positions with logic or engage in dialogue with me. And why would they? It's tough to argue with somebody when you know the facts are against you.

Another observation I had from the KO Barstool protest was that I noticed a lot of familiar faces from another protest I had just been to recently, albeit in a much different capacity. In 2011, Occupy Wall Street had spread throughout the country, including to Occupy Boston. There was a full-blown encampment outside South Station. This was essentially a movement against capitalism and the 1 percent. At this time, I was far from rich. But I was an entrepreneur. I believed, and still believe, in hard work and accountability. I firmly believe in the American Dream and that there is no better country on earth than America in which to create a living. Occupy Wall Street was, to me, essentially a bunch of socialists and communists who just didn't want to work hard for a living. In other words, they were losers.

Anyway, I went to Occupy Boston to make a mockumentary about how ridiculous these people were. And it was every bit as preposterous as I imagined.

Eventually, the Occupy encampments became a huge source of controversy throughout the country. In Boston, there were reports of multiple rapes and sexual assaults within the encampment. The leaders of Occupy Wall Street didn't want the police looking into the supposed crimes. They said they'd handle it internally. And at the KO Barstool rally, many of those same people who may have been actively protecting *actual rapists* were chanting that I was pro-rape because of a joke from years ago ripped out of context. The irony was not lost on me. It would be something I'd notice time and time again. This country is plagued by serial protesters; people who don't actually give a shit about the cause. They just hate their lives, hate this country, and want somebody to blame for their misery.

There was one person in this throng of angry KO Barstool protesters who did have my back though. One bright soul. Through the chorus of boos and chants, one voice pierced through—a young man yelling, "LET HIM SPEAK!" This noble hero would become known as the Angel of Barstool in Barstool lore. After the protest was over, this guy walked up to me and was like, "It's bullshit they didn't let you speak." I thanked him for his support, and he asked, "You don't recognize me, do you?" Nope, sure didn't. Well, as it turned out, this wasn't the first time he'd saved my ass.

A few years prior, I had been in Cape Cod with Renee, planning to propose at dinner at the Wequassett, a fancy hotel in Harwich where we were staying for the weekend. But as I walked in, I was quickly stopped by some stiff in the front.

"Sir, our restaurant requires gentlemen to wear pants."

I mean, it was a beach hotel. Why in the fuck would I be wearing pants? But hey, far be it from me to make a scene. I retreated to my room and went through my bag only to realize that I hadn't packed a single pair of pants. It was fucking July in Cape Cod and I had packed accordingly.

It looked like the proposal I had planned for months would have to wait for another day. Then I heard a knock at the door. You may not fucking believe it, but it was the same guy from the protest—the Angel of Barstool, holding up a pair of black trousers.

"Hey Pres, heard you needed a pair of pants."

Against all odds, this kid *worked* at the hotel and had heard a rumor that El Pres from Barstool had been turned away at the restaurant because he didn't have pants. He quickly found out where my room was, rustled up a spare pair of employee-issue pants, and brought them to me. When he reminded me of this later at the KO protest, I couldn't believe it was the same dude. It was like he just magically appeared whenever I needed him most. And if there was any doubt that he was truly my guardian angel, it happened one more time.

Not long after that KO Barstool protest night, I was stumbling out of a Blackout Tour show in Boston. I was pretty drunk, which was becoming a rare occurrence for me—I'm not a big drinker, and by now I was in my mid-thirties and the hangovers were devastating. But maybe on this night we were wrapping up a long homestand of successful shows in Boston, so I felt the urge to celebrate a bit. Either way, as I walked dazedly along the streets, I quickly realized I was completely lost. My phone was dead and there were no cabs anywhere in sight. All hope was lost, and I had resolved to walk the six miles home to Dorchester.

Out of nowhere, a car pulled up alongside me and the window rolled down.

"Hey Pres, need a ride?"

I peered in through the darkness and, sure as shit, it was the same kid from the protest, the same kid who found me the pants at the hotel. I hopped in and he drove me all the way home. He didn't badger me, he wasn't overzealous or imposing, and he didn't ask for anything in return. Just my guardian angel, offering me a ride as he flew me to the comfort of my apartment on his gossamer wings. The Angel of Barstool indeed.

In May 2012, *Inside Edition* reached out to interview me about the Blackout Tour. I was young, naïve, and unprepared for the gotchaism of crusading journalists who care less for truth and more for engagement. And if you think that's hypocritical because we at Barstool don't exactly fact-check a lot of our blogs, I'll remind you that we are not and have never been journalists. It is not our job to get the story right; it is our job to make the story funny.

Journalists *pretend* to hold themselves to a different standard. Remember, this was a long time before the term "fake news" had come into fashion, and (for the most part) people still believed what the news told us. Conspiracy theories were scoffed at by the majority of people; hidden agendas and deep states dismissed as the coping mechanisms of fringe lunatics.

(By the way, if you're wondering where the Barstool starfish pinnies came from, it's a very Barstool story. One day some dude asked me to sponsor his pickup basketball team. They needed uniforms and said if I bought them, I could design them any way I wanted. Say less. So I bought like thirty of these pinnies. As I was getting ready to send them to the team, the guy emailed me and said the league folded, so they didn't need them anymore. So I was basically stuck with thirty of these ridiculous jerseys.

I blogged the entire story and then decided to put each one on eBay, one at a time. Well, I was the most shocked guy in the room when Stoolies started getting in bidding wars for them. Like they were literally selling for thousands each. Crazy.)

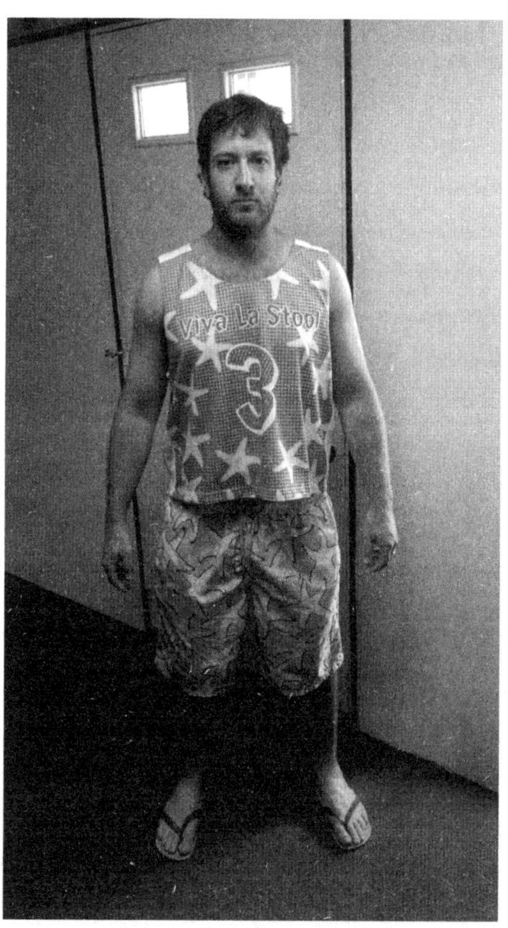

I walked into my interview with Lisa Guerrero, wearing my patented purple starfish pinney, thinking this would be a fair interview. I thought it was about our Blackout Tour and how popular it had become. I had no idea I was walking into a no-holds-barred cage match with a saw-scaled viper. Two hours of intense back-and-forth. Like from the second I sat down till the second I got up, it was war.

"You posted the following on your site: 'I never condone rape, but if you're a size six and you're wearing skinny jeans, you kind of deserve to be raped'?"

"Correct. I stand by that. I think it's a funny joke," I replied.

"Do you think rape is funny?"

"No, I didn't say that. I think it's a funny joke."

"Do you know how offensive that is?" she asked rhetorically.

"No. I obviously don't. [If I had, I would never have written the joke.]"

I put that last sentence in brackets because, even though I did say it in the interview, the world never got to hear it. Why? Because the editors of the interview cut it out. They realized that having me finish the exchange with a stone-cold, remorseless, defiant response fit their narrative far better than me showing any humanity whatsoever. A two-hour interview, in which frankly I bodied Lisa Guerrero and made her look like a fool, was cut down to one minute of edited clips. They knew what they wanted to get from me, and once they had it, I was dismissed.

This clip has been referenced and linked to in hundreds of anti-Dave, anti-Barstool blogs and videos since. It has become the shining example of my purported hatred of women. It still goes viral once every few months on social media with zero context so my haters can gather and declare me the devil. It is the reason why I now insist, whenever I'm interviewed, on having my own ability to record the entire interview myself. That's my only defense against a news outlet selectively editing my words to present me in a way that suits their narrative.

Looking back over two decades later, was the size six skinny jean blog a bad blog? Yup. It didn't hit. It wasn't funny. I wish I never wrote it. But did anybody with a brain in real time think I was actually pro-rape? No shot. This was cancel culture in its truest form. These self-proclaimed feminists did not like Barstool Sports. They didn't like Smokeshow of the Day. They didn't like how we talked. They certainly didn't like the Blackout Tour. They thought they had to protect people, and especially women, from themselves. So they went back in time to find anything they could hang their hats on to get us shut down.

While the KO Barstool protesters did nothing to stop the momentum of either Barstool or the Blackout Tour, they did succeed in another way. Somehow, their outrageous accusations against us created a stench that would cling to the company going forward. From that day, the "size six skinny jeans joke" would forever be brought forward as an example of our misogynistic ideals. From that day on, any time a media outlet or blog wrote an attack piece against us, they would cite that reference as their Exhibit A of evidence that we were a women-hating outfit of thugs. I truly don't know how different the public perception of Barstool would be had KO Barstool never happened. But they set a misperception that I've been trying to combat for the last fifteen years. I certainly haven't done myself any favors by refusing to apologize or blink in the face of adversity. I just firmly believe that you don't negotiate with terrorists. If you give these people an inch, they will take a mile. So I've held my ground and returned fire every step of the way.

By the second run of the Blackout Tour, we were putting out dumpster fires on a nightly basis. We had kids showing up too drunk to get into shows, a girl was bitten on the leg by some rabid maniac, the foam cannon was blasting people in the face and blinding them . . . The problems came in all shapes and sizes and started to snowball against us. Granted, I don't think the problems were much different than those faced by any large-scale concert tour. Whenever you have large gatherings of college-aged kids, there will be a few incidents. The difference with us was that the press reported on each incident like it was Watergate because of all the surrounding controversy.

Cops began shutting the concerts down early as a result of complaints from people who lived in the neighborhoods around the venue. Insurance companies stopped wanting to insure the shows, and bouncers began breathalyzing kids in line, denying entrance to hundreds of ticket holders who would then demand refunds the next day because they never got in.

And still, the venues had no idea what they were getting themselves into. They wanted the shows because the tickets kept selling. We tried to warn them; we tried to say, "You need extra security and EMTs on hand because our crowd *really* likes to party." They'd assure us they could handle anything because they had recently hosted some heavy metal event and it went fine. But they simply had no idea.

I'd get phone calls at 3 a.m. from Gaz telling me the firemen had shown up again. This would happen because the venues started pulling the fire alarms on themselves to shut the shows down because they realized it was beyond their control. This would also catalyze a torrent of refund requests that I'd wake up to the next morning.

Mayors spoke out to warn parents against letting their kids come to our shows. Of course, we would clip these moments and create more highlight videos featuring these warnings. All it did was create more intrigue; what sort of concert would be so controversial as to have public figures speaking out against it? Like horror movies advertising that audiences around the country were so terrified that people were throwing up, we used the negative press to our advantage: kids had to come see for themselves. The literal mayor of NYC was asked during a press conference if they were prepared for the Blackout Tour. That's how infamous it had become.

But eventually, the cost of insurance, the cost of renting venues, and the gigantic headaches caused by all manner of problems made me realize it was time to turn the lights back on. The Blackout Tour ran through its third and final leg and that was that. It had served to expand our reach to many more cities and spread our awareness near and far. For better or worse, Barstool was now a national brand that had stoked the flames of controversy and created an entire army of protesters. This only emboldened our die-hard fans, and both sides dug into their trenches for the mudslinging that would ensue. Through it all, my nana gave me the best advice on the situation. She said, "David, don't pay any attention to negativity . . . just keep making the bucks." And that's exactly what we did.

(Quick story time. The Blackout Tour really started my hatred of politicians. They were just swaying in the breeze, reacting to a small group of protesters who were literally making up lies about us. Why were we being treated differently than any other company? I got so fed up with the way the city was treating me and how anti-business and anti-nightlife Boston was that I actually decided to run for mayor. Not as a joke either. Like I was prepared to go through with it. I even hired a campaign manager. Granted, he was the worst campaign manager of all time, but I did hire one. His name was "Weird Haircut Seth." Why did I name him that? Drumroll, please: he had a weird haircut. I actually later named a horse after Weird Haircut way down the road, but I digress. Maybe Weird Haircut Seth's most lasting impact on Barstool lore is that one day he casually said he could throw a football sixty yards into the air. He was so confident about it that we went to the local park and made him try to prove it. It wasn't even close. He barely threw it twenty yards, never mind sixty, and that clip became one of the most famous early Barstool clips of all time. I laughed my dick off when I saw how far short he threw it, and yelled, "You're a bum! What a bum Weird Haircut Seth is.")

Now back to El Pres for El Mayor (yes, that was our campaign slogan). With a guy like Weird Haircut Seth at the helm, how could I have failed?

Well, to get on the ballot, you needed to get like twelve thousand signatures. So I hired a professional signature-gathering firm. That's all they did. I paid them $20K to get me the necessary signatures to get on the ballot. My thought was that once I was officially on the ballot, I would be able to galvanize all the college kids in Boston to vote for me and I would win by a landslide.

The only problem was that I forgot how rigged politics are. Remember how I said I needed twelve thousand signatures? Well, the city could throw out any signature for one of three reasons: First, if the person had already signed for somebody else. Second, if the person wasn't a registered voter in Boston. And third, if they couldn't read the signature.

I turned in twenty thousand signatures. The city told me only 11,500 of them were valid. What a shocker! They had successfully kept me off the ballot using the most rigged, shady bullshit of all time. The signature company said they had never seen that happen before.

I've always said I hate politicians and politics. The truth is, you can't hate them enough. Granted, I'm not sure what would have happened had I won. There is no shot I could have continued to run Barstool while being mayor of Boston.

8

Go Pres Go

We exited the Blackout Tour era more popular and more notorious than ever. The surrounding controversy had put us into a different sphere. We had more fans than ever and more enemies as well. Through it all we continued to operate at a pace that none of our competitors could match. Every blogger I hired was churning out at least twelve blogs a day, seven days a week. That was the expectation, and if you fell short I wasn't afraid to absolutely destroy you. I had spent the last decade coaxing the tiny flame that was my newspaper into a sturdy, self-sustaining fire. At so many points, it had nearly extinguished without a whimper. A combination of luck, stubbornness, and relentless commitment had kept it going. I felt so attached to the company that anyone who would assail the brand was, I felt, attacking me directly. I expected the same loyalty not only from my employees, but from our fans. And on a cold, blustery winter day in Boston I would give the Stoolies a unifying rallying cry to get behind.

GO PRES GO!

Roll Tide! Go Blue! How 'Bout Them Cowboys! Go Pres Go! All ubiquitous chants to support your team, or in this case Barstool Sports.

By the way, I realize I'm pretty far into this book and I haven't explained my nicknames of El Presidente or El Pres. I've been known as El Pres since the beginning of Barstool. The name came about because I initially thought I was the CEO, but my friend said I couldn't say that because the company wasn't incorporated. (I'm pretty sure we are now.) So I just called myself the president of Barstool instead, and then El Presidente.

And here's how "Go Pres Go!" became the war cry. Every day, I would look for things to entertain our audience. One day, I stumbled upon something called the

6-12-18-24 challenge. Essentially, you had four tasks that you had to complete in the span of twenty-four hours: Run/walk miles, eat donuts, jerk off, and drink beers. You assigned each number to one of the aforementioned activities that you thought would give you the best chance to complete all four in the allotted time. I chose six miles of running, twelve beers, eighteen jerkoffs, and twenty-four donuts. I did my best to document the entire marathon as best I could without literally jerking off on camera. The critics and boobirds were instant. "There is no way he'll be able to jerk off eighteen times in one day! What an idiot for choosing eighteen ejaculations! The arrogance on this guy! Who does he think he is!"

Well, let me remind the readers at home that this was my prime "Fat Dave" era. Long before I had become rich and less gross-looking. These were the days of me blogging 24/7, eating Panera every day for lunch, with a full baguette. I'm not talking the little one that came with lunch. I was ordering a full baguette on the side and eating it while I worked, chained to my desk all day before going home and having a large pizza to myself, virtually every night.

I could barely walk down the street, never mind run six miles, so I had to choose that for the six. It put me behind the proverbial eight-ball from the beginning with this challenge.

As the challenge day wore on and the naysayers continued to doubt me, I finally had enough of the negativity. I made a video where I essentially said the following: "I'm laying it all on the line out here for you guys. I'm doing everything I can to win this 6-12-18-24 challenge. I'm trying to do the impossible. So rather than telling me I have no shot at this, instead of chirping me from the cheap seats, I'd rather you guys just shut up and chant Go Pres Go next time I'm jerking off. Help me win this thing." I ultimately fell short in the challenge because I'm not a huge drinker and I couldn't jerk off enough. But from that day forward, Go Pres Go would be the war cry of my fans. The blog continued to chug along and pick up steam every day. Word of Barstool had traveled far beyond just the Northeast. I picture it like that scene in the movie *Braveheart* where William Wallace is running through the hills of Scotland with dramatic music playing behind him as they narrate that his legend was growing. I'm not sure it was quite like that, but the legend of Barstool was clearly spreading.

Kevin and Big Cat had distinguished themselves as my clear underbosses. We decided to start meeting up around the country for various challenges—from hot dog eating to catching punts from an NFL punter to arm-wrestling female arm-wrestling champions to a go-kart race with X Games legend Travis Pastrana.

Let's start with the go-kart race. Travis Pastrana was promoting his Nitro Circus tour—a live show that featured him and all his buddies riding their dirt bikes and doing crazy stunts—and offered to make a video with us. He was one of the biggest names in motorsports at the time, so it was a no-brainer for us to make some content with him. We did it at a rented gymnasium in the middle of nowhere. There was nothing specifically remarkable or memorable about this video. But the exception was that this was the first time that I, or our audience, got to see our newly hired DMV (DC-Maryland-Virginia) blogger, Barstool Nate. Nate was from the Baltimore/Maryland area and sent us some writing samples that I liked and I hired him on the spot. I didn't fly out to meet with him. I had no idea what he looked like. I just knew that I liked his writing.

And then this guy showed up:

(GASP!)

Get a load of this fucking guy! Little did I know at the time that Nate, aka the Spider Monkey, would not only be the future editor of Barstool Sports, but would also become one of the most cantankerous and reviled characters we've ever had. He has accused me throughout the years of harboring a personal vendetta against him designed to keep him off camera and from becoming a superstar. He calls it "stealing his glitter." I call it him being the most annoying human who ever lived. Throughout the years he's tried to have everybody fired for what he deems unacceptable work. He's been accused of playing favorites on the blog by just about everybody. He's been pied in the face by a fan walking down the street. He lost a $20K heads-up poker match to me after folding pocket kings, and poker is like his big hobby. Hand to God, I don't think I could spend more than twenty minutes in a room with him. But I can't imagine this place without him.

Another time, we did a Nathan's hot dog eating contest when that was all the rage, mostly because we had an American hero dominating the event named Joey Chestnut. I thought that between four of us, we might be able to match or beat his record (sixty-six hot dogs in twelve minutes). I had myself,

Kevin, Big Cat, and Feitelberg assemble behind a basic folding table on which we stacked a ton of hot dogs, as well as cups of water for dipping the buns in like the professional practice.

Only problem was, as we were setting everything up, the moron Intern Handsome Hank caused the entire table to collapse, dropping every single hot dog into the dirt. Which meant that all the hot dogs were crunchy and dusty and containing pebbles and shit. I don't know exactly how that affects how fast you can eat a hot dog, but I know it ain't good.

When our camera guy told us to begin, I immediately submerged my entire first bun in a cup of water and tried to shove the whole soaked mess into my mouth. Turns out, this technique is actually far harder than the pros make it look. That wet bun doesn't just slide down your throat like soup; it's like trying to swallow a sponge.

I made it a couple hot dogs in and realized we weren't even in the realm of Joey Chestnut. My guys managed a couple hot dogs each and I became disgusted with the hot dogs before me. Hot dogs, in general, are pretty disgusting. Nobody eats more than two hot dogs. And to be forced to eat them as fast as humanly possible? I'm out.

"I'm sick of eating. Why am I doing this? I own this company," I declared.

Some people have since accused me of quitting on this sacred July Fourth ritual. They say I'm un-American. The truth is, my neck hurt and I didn't care about trying to win the contest, so my heart wasn't in it. If I had cared, I would have been able to eat at least three or four times as many hot dogs as I did. I only rise up to challenges that I care to win. I don't need to be the king of hot dogs.

We did an NFL combine where we tested our guys on all the stuff NFL players do. I had Todd McShay come to put us through the forty-yard dash, three-cone drill, quarterback throws, and the broad jump. Something about watching three completely unimpressive white bloggers run the same drills as the greatest athletes on the planet hit home for a lot of our fans.

We got Andy Roddick to serve to us to see if we could return any of his 140 mph serves. There was a burger taste test where I had to determine the McDonald's vs. Wendy's vs. Burger King burgers while wearing a blindfold. Big Cat and I played two-on-one basketball against Lions tight end Tony

Scheffler. We did a *Bar Rescue* with Jon Taffer, worked out on muscle beach with the juice heads, and had MLB umpire Gerry Davis rank our best strike-three calls.

It was all over the map. Sports and food seemed to do pretty well with our audience, but I was up to try anything. We went to King Richard's Faire—a medieval village where we cosplayed as knights and jesters and tried to cut people's heads off with fake swords. Ultimately, Big Cat went too far and tried to cut off too many heads and was threatened with assault-and-battery charges.

By the way, I'm not joking about Big Cat getting threatened with actual criminal charges. I'm still not exactly sure how this was possible, but in this land of make-believe, Big Cat was being charged by imaginary cops for killing too many people in the fake world, and that could have repercussions in the real world. Yes, it was as confusing as it sounds. But hey, who were we to challenge the rules of King Richard's Faire? Regardless, it seemed like a preposterous way to treat the honorary judge of the Hot Wench contest, didn't it?

These early videos have aged into hallmark classics for longtime Stoolies. I sometimes watch them back and laugh at how poor the quality is, how simply edited they are, and how young we all look. We were just idiots following our instincts and trying to make entertaining content from nothing. Somehow, it worked.

In addition to the guest appearances and field pieces, we added *The Rundown*. This would just be a repeatable synopsis of the internet's most viral stories of that day. We filmed it on Skype so that Kevin, Dan, and I could cover it every day without having to fly to some place together. Over the ensuing years, *The Rundown* would become must-watch stuff for our fans; an easy way to catch up on the most viral videos of the day, as well as the tastiest Barstool gossip. Naturally, our discussions tended to escalate from friendly debate to personal attacks pretty quickly. People couldn't get enough. *The Rundown* became ingrained in our fans' everyday routines as much as eating breakfast, lunch, or dinner: an unfiltered, off-the-cuff comedy show that covered the entire internet. There was nothing else like it.

9

Boston Marathon Bombing

As a blog, we never really covered the Boston Marathon or running in too much detail. And when we did it was to make fun of marathoners. Marathons in general seem dumb to me. Sure, the people who run them under a certain amount of time are impressive, I guess. But after that, you have this gigantic horde of people trying to simply finish the distance. They can walk for a while if they want. And then at the end they're handed those aluminum foil space blankets to help them retain body heat, like they're standing outside their house as it burns down and we should feel bad for everything they've lost. Uh, you people signed up for this thing. I'm neither impressed nor do I feel bad for you. Stop shivering like the coast guard just fished you out of the Bering Sea.

Anyway, we had an intern at the time named DLo who actually was at the marathon that day. I'm not sure why he wasn't at the office, as I know I didn't assign him to cover the marathon, but he was there and he heard the first bomb go off and tweeted:

"Uhh explosions in Boston." That was the very first tweet that went up about the entire thing. Ironically, we would not just be the first word covering the bombing; we would become the most important source of the entire tragedy by the time it was over.

The bombings happened on April 15, 2013. Three days passed without much information on the suspects. Boston was paralyzed with fear. We didn't know who these people were, why they did what they did, how many of them there were, or what they planned next. All we knew was that there were terrorists on the loose.

To this day I don't exactly know what happened that caused me to turn on a police scanner a few days after the bombing, on the evening of April 18. Somebody must have sent an email that tipped me off to a commotion happening in Cambridge at MIT and told me that I could listen to it all unfold online. To that point I didn't even know listening to police scanners was a thing. But here I was, eavesdropping on breaking news, starting with the murder of MIT police officer Sean Collier. From that moment on until the next evening I was glued to the scanners and relaying all the information via Twitter. I was tweeting the entire time, telling people where they could go to find shelter or loved ones, retweeting different views of the explosion that people were sending me, and sharing updates on the developing manhunt. Obviously, it was a horrific situation that couldn't have hit closer to home for me or our company. While I tried to give out the facts, I also tried to mix in a degree of humor once in a while to keep people sane as best I could; to maybe get a smile from people as the tragedy was unfolding.

I started the day with maybe thirty thousand Twitter followers. By that evening, I had a hundred thousand and growing. When a gunfight broke out between the cops and the terrorists in Watertown, I had Stoolies who lived there taking videos from their bedroom windows of the street as literal bombs were being lobbed around the neighborhood and gunfire was exchanged.

This was the absolute height of Barstool's powers and popularity in Boston. It's no stretch to estimate that every other house in Watertown had at least one Stoolie living in it. These Stoolies were sending me clips and updates at a furious pace, and I was churning out the updates as fast as I could. Our website became *the* place for breaking news on the case. The Barstool logo was splashed across every major news outlet. Not only did we have better sources with boots on the ground than traditional media, we had no restrictions on posting stuff. We didn't have to vet our information like they did. As a result, the local news was at least thirty minutes behind everything we posted. By the time they caught up to us, we were on to the next part of the chase.

From the moment the bombs went off until they finally found the younger brother hiding under the tarp of the boat in Watertown, I didn't really sleep.

That was a four-day stretch when I sat at my computer and furiously, feverishly tweeted and blogged through the night. There is a famous picture of me with a nosebleed, looking like absolute shit from being up for thirty straight hours.

I remember Renee waking up at 4:30 a.m. with no clue what was happening, complaining that the police scanner woke her up. She took one look at me with blood all over my shirt and an empty carton of lo mein next to me, shook her head, and said, "What are you doing?!"

"I'm manhunting terrorists. What does it look like I'm doing?"

Then she just turned around and went back to sleep.

But nothing could shake me from the duty I had to the people of Boston. I simply ordered more Chinese food and kept sending out the information as it rolled in.

Was it all accurate? No, I definitely had a few pieces of misinformation go out. At one point, I reported that some random kid who had died in the Charles

River was a terrorist and was involved with the bombing. Turns out, he had absolutely nothing to do with it. No harm no foul. He was already dead. But besides that, I'd say we were pretty damn close to getting our facts straight.

The mayor locked down the city, telling us all to shelter in place. Nobody was going to work, public transportation stopped running, and the streets were empty. The people of Boston needed information, and they turned to Barstool Sports for it. It wasn't our usual gig, but as I've always said, we're nothing if not adaptable. Barstool's ability over the years to pivot, adapt, remain fluid, and stay up or ahead of the times is what has kept us relevant and fresh to younger audiences for twenty years.

Big Cat also jumped in and became glued to the scanner. And as we have done so many times through the years, we tag-teamed the content, playing off each other perfectly, knowing when to be serious and when to add a bit of levity. I still remember having a bit of fun with a local wrestler who, it turns out, had pinned the younger terrorist twice in a high school tournament. His name was Gleeson, and he became a Barstool urban legend.

BARSTOOL SPORTS

Home The Store Originals Cities Sports Girls Podcasts Odds Tickets

How is Gleeson Not In the Mix Yet?

El Presidente | Apr. 19, 4:02 pm | 0 Comments

Share on Facebook Tweet on Twitter Email

I know this is a serious subject. I've been manhunting for so long you almost forget it's real. You almost forget that there is a real terrorist on the loose in Boston looking to kill innocent people. It seems like it's a movie or something. But having said that how has Glesson not been brought onto the scene yet? This guy OWNS this terrorist. Faced him twice in one wrestling tournament. Beat him like a drum in the winners bracket and then beat him like drum again in the losers bracket. If anybody has this terrorist's number it's Gleeson. Just throw a singlet on him and have him go door to door looking for this asshole. He'll have him pinned, disarmed and begging for mercy in no time. NEED MORE GLEESON!

When the manhunt finally came to a close, and the cops apprehended the younger brother, I was somehow sent a photo of him on an operating table at Mass General Hospital. He was in a really bad state, bloody, blown up, and I tweeted the picture out. I don't know how on earth someone sent that to me as it was probably a major violation of HIPAA rights, but I guess if you commit terrorism against the United States, you implicitly waive your right to patient confidentiality.

We still like to joke that we at Barstool "caught" the Boston Marathon bombers. It's a stretch, I'll admit. But nobody can deny that we did everything we could to help the good people of Boston, and all the brave police who put their lives on the line, bring the Tsarnaev brothers to justice and restore safety to the city once more.

In the aftermath of the bombing, I knew I had to do something to help those who were affected by the tragedy. We instantly put "Boston Strong" T-shirts on sale with the promise that 100 percent of the profits would go to helping one of the survivors, and we decided on Marc Fucarile.

He was an everyday salt-of-the-earth-type guy. A typical Barstool guy. He just picked the wrong time and wrong place to go to the marathon. It could have been any of us. Marc was standing right near the bomb and had to have his leg amputated above the knee. But somehow, the way that the OneFund—the fund to help the survivors—was set up, they paid you more or less based on how many limbs you lost. He actually debated cutting off his remaining, severely mangled leg just to qualify for more money so he could cover his medical costs. As I said, a real salt-of-the-earth guy.

His story hit home for us. When Red Sox legend David Ortiz famously spoke at Fenway a couple days later, he dropped one of the best quotes of all time: "This is our fucking city." We added that quote to our Boston Strong shirts, and we ended up raising $250,000 for Marc. I presented the check in person to Marc as he told his story. It is a moment I will never forget as he was legit stunned by the generosity of Barstool, and he couldn't put into words how much this money would help his family. Barstool had raised money for charitable causes before, but this was by far the biggest sum and the most galvanizing campaign we'd ever run. It helped Marc buy a new wheelchair-accessible house. I was humbled by the entire experience. That this blog I started a decade prior could make this big of an impact. It wasn't that I felt I did anything special. It was our readers who did all the heavy lifting. I was prouder of them for coming through in the clutch. It showed me how much good Barstool could do and how willing our fans were to donate to things that we, and they, believed in. Over the years, I've called upon the Stoolies to help raise money for all manner of causes, and without fail they open their wallets and chip in. We've raised literally hundreds of millions of dollars for the military, dogs, small businesses, and fallen police officers. Again, I don't say that to brag or act like we are some morally superior organization, because we're not. We're just average slobs who know when people need help.

But as always, it all started with Boston.

10

The Brady Four

I think I said this already, but a lot of people think I love fighting, especially when it generates attention and pageviews. Believe it or not, I don't like confrontation. I don't like going to protests or places where people hate my guts. I'm not looking for a fight for the sake of fighting, and I don't enjoy entering high-pressure environments as a means of creating moments or storylines. But if trouble knocks on my door, I'll answer it.

"Deflategate" started on January 18, 2015, after the New England Patriots humiliated the Indianapolis Colts 45–7 in the AFC Championship Game. As the story goes, when the game ended, the Colts allegedly tattled to the league that the footballs used in the game were underinflated. There were a couple initial tweets and newfangled terms like PSI (pounds per square inch) that were leaked, but I didn't pay much attention to them. I went to bed that night not thinking much of it. So I was shocked when I woke up the next morning to a total shitstorm. Deflategate was all anybody was talking about. It wasn't the lead story just on SportsCenter; it was the lead story on the national news. Deflategate somehow had turned into an international incident. Was Tom Brady a cheater? Did the Patriots cheat? Grown men were crying on TV talking about it. Yes, Mark Brunell, football analyst, was *literally* crying. Sal Paolantonio, another football analyst, said Tom Brady's endorsement career with Uggs was over because women wouldn't buy furry footwear from liars.

For the next two weeks, as the Patriots prepared to play in the Super Bowl, every day added a new twist or turn to the story. Bill Belichick held an impromptu press conference talking about the "ideal gas law" like it was a high school science experiment or something. I've never seen anything like it. We had entered the twilight zone. And every day I put on my hard hat and went to work defending the Patriots and debunking Deflategate. It was the perfect storm for Barstool. We were a Boston blog filled with Patriot fans. Our team was under attack and we didn't have to play by the rules of traditional media. We were already on our way to the Super Bowl, so we'd have boots on the ground.

As more info was leaked, the more it seemed like Deflategate was an inside job from the league office. NFL Commissioner Roger Goodell quickly became my sworn enemy. But it wasn't just him. Anybody who besmirched the Patriots—from Marshall Faulk to Bill Nye the Science Guy—was drawn into this war. (At the time of Deflategate, we had a daily show on Sirius radio and were recording at their studios. Sometimes when celebs were in town, they would do a carwash of programs to get as much publicity as possible. Basically, they would just jump from show to show. Well, Bill Nye happened to be there while we were on air and the powers that be at Sirius had him drop in on our show. Poor Bill Nye never knew what hit him. I saw red the second he walked into the room and launched into a tirade about how he was a fake scientist who didn't know shit about the ideal gas law. Just because he wore a bow tie didn't mean he knew the first thing about Deflategate. Everybody was an enemy.)

At Media Day at the Super Bowl, I asked Bill Belichick if he needed anybody killed. I chased Mike Kensil (an NFL league official) straight out of the auditorium and behind a curtain. Nobody knew how to handle me. The media is not used to being accosted by other members of the media. But I was in game mode—the way an athlete describes becoming a different person when they step between the white lines.

The Patriots went on to win the Super Bowl, beating the Seattle Seahawks in dramatic fashion thanks to the iconic Malcolm Butler interception. Roger Goodell was forced to hand the Lombardi Trophy to team owner Robert Kraft while getting booed out of the stadium. Those two weeks firmly cemented me and Barstool as the face of Patriot Nation.

The Patriots' Super Bowl victory didn't end the controversy though. It extended through the offseason until finally, through the most witch-hunty, bananaland investigation of all time, NFL Commissioner Roger Goodell decided that it had to have been Tom Brady who whispered to some equipment manager kid to let the air out of the balls. According to Goodell, this heinous crime gave the league a black eye and warranted death by firing squad; in other words, a four-game suspension for Brady for the 2015 season.

Every single day, from the initial accusation to the suspension, I ranted about it on *The Rundown*. It was all anyone was talking about, so naturally it was all we talked about. The number one story in sports had been gift-wrapped to me for content. I truly saw it as one giant charade to rein in the New England Patriots, who simply could not be stopped by any legal, real football means. And so, like some children's rec league shenanigans, the authority powers had to step in to make it fair for all the other teams by making up a bunch of bullshit or bending rules to favor the slower kids—real socialist ideology being applied to the National Football League.

It seemed impossible to me that Brady would actually receive a suspension, let alone four games. There was effectively zero hard evidence against him. It was all hearsay, and because I believed in the American justice system, it was inconceivable that the league would come down with any sort of concrete punishment. As the case wore on, I said that if they did suspend Brady, I would do something drastic. I didn't know what, but it would be drastic.

So when the four-game suspension was announced, I had no choice: the war was on. To me, the punishment didn't come close to fitting the crime. Consequently, I had no hang-ups about choosing a demonstration that some might have deemed entirely out of proportion for a couple of Patriot fans. I gathered my loyal troops (Bald Paul, Handsome Hank, and Feitelberg) and explained that we would drive to NFL headquarters in New York to stage a sit-in until Roger Goodell agreed to meet with us personally. Given that they had no agency over their own lives, they agreed.

Before we left, I addressed my enraptured audience in a signature Emergency Press Conference. Standing behind a water cooler podium, I compared Roger Goodell to Hitler, announced our plan, and promised to take down the NFL. Then we piled into my car, drove to New York, and slept in a hotel knowing that the next day we'd be handcuffing ourselves together to protest the greatest sports injustice since the Chicago Black Sox.

I say that now. But in truth, as we went to bed, not one of us had any idea what was about to happen.

The next morning, we grabbed some signs we'd made—"FIRE GOODELL" and "FREE BRADY" and "KENSIL IS A BITCH"—and put on our outfits. We wore Brady jerseys, Patriots hats, eye black, sunglasses . . . We wanted to make sure the world knew the cause for which we were willing to risk our lives. Or at least, sacrifice a day of our time sitting on an uncomfortable marble floor with no back support.

We walked a few circles outside NFL HQ, chanting and hoisting our signs in the air. I'd learned a lot about protesting thanks to the KO Barstool protest: you gotta be loud, you have to have a clear message, and you can't give up on that message. Even when the security guards tried to intimidate us by getting in our way, which they did. There was one particularly gigantic security guard who stepped right into my path. But just as mothers are known to summon herculean strength and lift cars when their children are trapped beneath, the cause for which we were now fighting carried me through the man's chest like a running back bursting through the secondary. I absolutely truck-sticked him and kept going.

We marched for fifteen minutes, then went inside. The lobby was your classic New York office building, with a gigantic ceiling, marble floors, and a receptionist desk behind which sat a rather unsuspecting woman. I approached her with the conviction of a Mormon missionary and asked to see Roger Goodell himself.

"Do you have a meeting?"

" . . . Yes."

Then she asked for my name and ID. Against all odds, somehow my name did not come up in the system as a scheduled visitor for the commissioner of the NFL. The fact that she even did us the honor of checking was pretty generous considering that I was wearing eye black under each eye. Then her supervisor came over and let us know that we were not welcome, at which point we pulled out our trump card: four sets of handcuffs. We quickly locked ourselves to each other and took a seat in the center of the lobby.

As we sat, a few curious corporate stiffs slowed their pace to wonder at our intent before remembering that their papers wouldn't push themselves, and they resumed sprint-walking to an elevator bank that would whisk them back to bureaucratic hell. In their defense, we didn't make a whole lot of sense. Were we an art installation? Some performance troupe hired by the players' union to convey a message that football is a prison? And why were we specific to the Patriots? Whatever the case, it wasn't enough to cause anyone to stop and ask us. Which was just fine, because we were now pot-committed. By taking our seats on the floor, handcuffed to one another in a square of camaraderie, we would see this through to the end.

I called into Mike Felger's 98.5 *The Sports Hub Show* to spread awareness of our protest. His show was the most-listened-to show in Boston, and I calmly explained that I was currently sitting on the floor of NFL HQ in New York City, handcuffed to three of my brothers, waiting for Roger Goodell to invite us up for a meeting. All this time, I didn't have a clue that our "stunt" (as some would dismissively label it) was gaining major media attention. I don't know exactly what I thought would happen, but I sort of thought that at some point, the cops might come and ask us to leave.

Sure enough, security called the cops and they came to let us know that we were trespassing. They explained to us that they were there to arrest us, we'd spend the night in jail, and that if we didn't stand up and let them cuff us, we'd be resisting arrest. Which would add another whole layer to the thing.

I'm a cop guy. I like the cops. Historically, I've done my best to make their jobs as easy as possible (see: Howitzergate). But even when they told us they were arresting us, I stupidly assumed they would walk us outside the building and let us go.

Photo by Dan Waters

Wrong. They had us uncuff ourselves so that they could cuff us individually, with their cuffs. Apparently it aligns better with police protocol to have each perp cuffed with one set of cuffs, as opposed to maneuvering some large blob of arms and bodies like a jellyfish across the street to the paddy wagon. But as we stepped through the swinging doors and out into the Manhattan afternoon, I saw at least a dozen news cameras, reporters, and more than a few Barstool fans waiting for us. They yelled out their support, quoting my taglines of "They hate us 'cuz they ain't us!" and "Go Pres Go!" The light bulbs flashed and the sun was a blinding contrast to the muted interior of the lobby, and I was glad I was wearing eye black.

They stuffed us into the truck and drove us down to the precinct.

There, we were booked, had our headshots taken, did our fingerprints, and were processed.

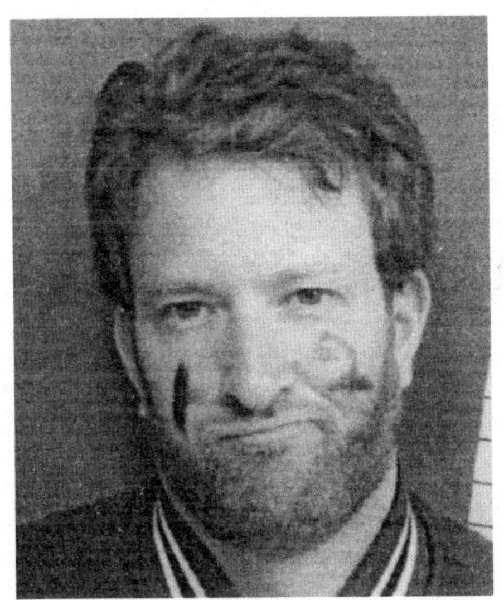

Then they crammed us into a holding cell. I think that's when reality actually set in for all of us. This was real jail. This would go on our criminal records. We would have to sit in this tiny cell for the next twenty-four hours until someone bailed us out.

But as ever, when my back is against the wall and all hope seems lost, my head stays clear and my hands remain steady. They allowed me my one phone call, and I used it to call KFC to make sure that the "FREE BRADY" T-shirts were in stock and ready to go.

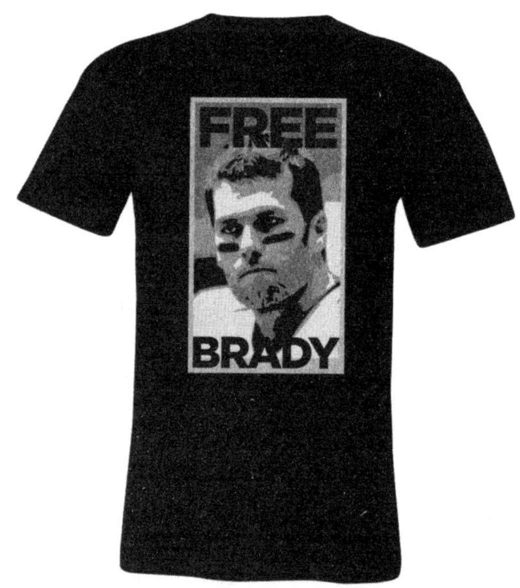

We had a few shirts made in relation to the scandal—"DEFEND THE WALL," "I STAND WITH TOM," etc. It was imperative that we stockpile a bunch with our shirt manufacturer because I knew the publicity from our arrest would galvanize Patriot fans and Stoolies to stand in solidarity—with Tom Brady, but also with us. For now, we were the face of Tom Brady's defense against Deflategate.

Weirdly, the hardest part about jail is the boredom. We went from being the center of a developing national media story to being cut off from the outside world, with no phones, no deck of cards, no books . . . not that we were the biggest reading crowd. We had nothing to do for twenty-four hours as we awaited our hearing before a judge. For someone who had become used to the constant stimulation of the internet, I barely survived that hellhole of a cell.

I should mention that there were other legitimate criminals in the jail. I mean, this was New York City. We were internet bloggers making a half-joking statement about our favorite quarterback, and we're in there with grizzled drug addicts and hardened convicts who basically cycle in and out of the jail on a weekly basis. At one point, Hank calmly stood up and took a shit in the one toilet in the cell. To call it a toilet is misleading; this thing was a tin bucket with no lid, no privacy divider, and no toilet paper in sight. When the guy in the cell to our left heard that one of our guys had actually used the toilet to take a shit, he was in disbelief. Apparently it's an unspoken rule of jail that you don't shit in the toilet.

As the sun set, we settled in for what was shaping up to be a long, miserable, sleepless night. A couple cells down was a guy who called himself "Diaper Boy" and kept yelling at the correctional officers to demand diapers. He complained that he was covered in rashes and yelled all sorts of looney tunes nonsense. I have a hard time sleeping without the AC cranked to sixty-five degrees and an absolutely silent bedroom. As you can imagine, nodding off to the sweet lullaby screams of Diaper Boy with only a metal bench as my "mattress" wasn't in the cards.

Finally, the morning came. I stood up and stretched, my shoulder throbbing in pain as usual. (My shoulder has been injured for twenty-five years, but I play through it as much as I can. Old Pop Warner football injury that I never took the time to let heal properly. Just gritted my teeth and stayed in the fight.) They handcuffed us again and brought us to the court to face the judge and hear our fate. We were still in our full Patriots attire, standing in a line behind a handful of hardened cons, waiting for our number to be called.

Then it was our turn, and I watched the judge's face closely. She looked up from her docket—after issuing a ruling on a serious domestic abuse case—to see four absolute morons in Tom Brady attire. The hint of a smile tugged at her mouth, but only for a moment as she regained her professionalism.

"What are you here for?" she asked as seriously as she could.

"We protested Roger Goodell and his suspension of Tom Brady at NFL Headquarters."

Suppressing a laugh, she told us we were on probation and dismissed us from the court.

I like to think that we brought a small moment of comic relief to her otherwise routine day of sentencing.

We went back to our hotel and opened our computers to immediately join

The Rundown and provide a debrief of our experience. By now, we all smelled pretty bad and were pretty desperate for sleep, but the entire world was waiting to hear from us. I told KFC and Big Cat that jail was no joke, I wouldn't wish it on my worst enemy, provided a colorful character sketch of Diaper Boy, and finished by reiterating that Roger Goodell was Hitler.

The protest of the Brady Four may be the defining moment of Barstool Sports. Not only did it ingratiate us to every Patriot fan in the world, it brought us to the front line of a national media story in a humorous yet harmless way. We had exercised our First Amendment rights to protest what we saw as a deep injustice against our football team. We stood up to the tyranny of upper-office league officials while dressed in tailgating attire. We sat on the floor of a Manhattan skyscraper to voice our displeasure and defend our hero, and we spent a night in jail as a consequence of our dedication. And with that, our small but vital part in the broader theater of Deflategate came to a close. But it was just the beginning of my decade-long war vs. Roger Goodell and the league office.

In Roger Goodell, I finally had an evil enemy I could square off against, and I wasted no time casting him as the heel in my hero's journey. The opening game of the 2015 NFL season was at Gillette to honor the defending Super Bowl champs. Roger Goodell was in attendance, as is tradition for him on opening night. He had to know he was walking into enemy territory, but even he couldn't have imagined what awaited him.

Earlier in the year, I had created a bright blue T-shirt in our store with Goodell's likeness on the front, except with a red clown nose squarely in the middle of his face. The shirt had been an instant hit.

And so, for opening night we printed sixty thousand clown nose towels with the goal of making sure every fan at Gillette had one at their seat. We asked for fans with tickets to the game to meet us at a warehouse a few days prior so they could grab boxes and hand them out for free in the sections around them. Four thousand volunteers showed up. When the Patriots got word of what I was planning, I got an "off the record" call that they never allow promotional items to be handed out in the stadium, but for this particular game they would turn a blind eye. As Goodell walked out onto the field, the stadium was awash in dense pockets of the bright blue towels and T-shirts.

Choruses of boos rained down upon him, and it would have been impossible for him not to know that Patriot Nation, outfitted by Barstool Sports, hated his absolute guts.

Courtesy of Maddie Meyer / Staff / Getty Images

I came to learn that the Patriots appreciated what we did. Though no member of the organization could come out publicly and endorse our behavior, through the years I would learn just how much they loved it. From team owner Robert Kraft to Brady himself, all the way down to the equipment managers and team chefs, the Patriot organization quietly loved us for decrying the farcical campaign against them.

Robert Kraft did eventually tell me outright, on camera, what I meant to his team. As he put it, "It's Brady, Belichick, and Portnoy." It was the highest compliment I've ever received, and one that will forever burn bright in my memory.

Following the 2017 Super Bowl, when the Patriots rallied from being down 28–3 to beat the Falcons and complete the greatest Super Bowl comeback of all time, Patriots then-defensive coordinator Matt Patricia wore the Clown Nose shirt as he walked off the plane in Boston. Saints head coach Sean Payton would also wear the Clown Nose shirt after being suspended by the league. The Goodell Clown Nose shirt became the easiest way to show your discontent with the NFL commish.

Now, it would be easy for a league as big and as powerful as the NFL to just ignore Barstool and carry on with business as usual, but they played the perfect foil. Barstool Sports was banned from all Super Bowl activities after Deflategate. So whenever the Patriots qualified for another Super Bowl, which seemed like every single year at that point, we weren't allowed to partake in any credentialed media activities. They went so far as to print Old West–looking posters with the faces of our employees on them that said "BEWARE OF THESE MEN" and plastered them throughout the city. We looked like the Gang That Couldn't Shoot Straight.

In 2019, the Patriots were set to play the Rams, looking for their sixth Super Bowl title. I had a mole who worked for the NFL, and he sent me his Media Day credential. We counterfeited it, and I snuck into Media

Day for the first time in five years dressed in full disguise as Frannie Lydon. Remember Frannie Lydon, Hank's troll account from the Milton years? Well, he came back to life at Media Day, which is held on the Monday before the Super Bowl, by the way.

After about thirty-five minutes, I was swarmed by a group of NFL employees in black suits and walked out of the stadium. They told me that I was trespassing and was not allowed in Mercedes-Benz Stadium, where the game was being played a few days later. I instantly regretted letting them escort me out of the stadium so easily. I knew that if I had made them drag me out of there, it would have been headline news across the country. I vowed to never make that mistake again. Little did I know I'd have a shot at redemption only a few days later.

On Super Bowl Sunday, I once again donned a mustache and walked into the stadium. I had bought a ticket for $5,000 like everybody else. The mustache was really just to get a chuckle, but I had no plans to do anything other than root home the Pats. Well, at halftime of Super Bowl LIII, in the middle of a Maroon Five performance, I was once again swarmed by security. But I had learned my lesson earlier in the week. This time I refused to budge. With camera phones rolling from all angles, I went dead fish and got dragged out of the Super Bowl.

I'll never forget police officers rushing

over to help NFL security as I was put in handcuffs. They asked what I was being apprehended for. When the NFL security official replied that it was for sneaking into Media Day and protesting Deflategate, the police officers got visibly angry that they were wasting their time with this nonsense. Regardless, I was escorted into a holding cell at the bottom of the stadium for the duration of the game.

As a sidenote, this game was the largest single bet I had ever placed in my life to that point: $300K on the Patriots to win outright. (How was I able to bet this much money on a game, you ask? Just wait until the next chapter.) But as the second half unfolded, I had no clue who was winning or what was going on in the game. The only sense I had of anything was when I heard the crowd roar through the walls, which told me a team had scored. Eventually I was let out and walked a mile outside the stadium in handcuffs. I still had no idea the score of the game. I've never been so nervous turning on my phone and checking a score in my life. To my relief, the Patriots had won. As a cherry on top, I was the number one trend on Twitter—beating anything from the game itself. Old Davey Pageviews had done it again . . .

A few years after being dragged out of the Super Bowl, during COVID, Roger Goodell auctioned off a package for a winning bidder to watch *Monday Night Football* in his man cave with him. All proceeds would go to helping first responders. Naturally, I bid $250K and won the auction. Two days later, I received an email from the NFL saying that after an extensive background check, they had decided that because of my history with the law, they were refunding my winning bid. I always laugh at that. I mean, how much research did they have to do? I've been in handcuffs twice in my life and both were at the hands of the NFL. It didn't take a ton of research to figure that out.

Looking back on my rivalry with the NFL, I honestly don't think I could have scripted it any better from beginning to the end. There is the fact that the creation of Barstool Sports pretty much coincided exactly with the rise of the Patriots. Then the Patriots became not only the best franchise in the history of football, but also one of the most controversial. Or the fact that blogging came around right at the exact moment that allowed us to document it all in real time. Or the fact that the NFL worked so hard to ban us.

When Deflategate began, we were still a relatively small, ragtag group in Milton. By the time I was dragged out of the Super Bowl in handcuffs, we were a multimillion-dollar company based in New York with over four hundred employees. But thanks to Roger Goodell, we were able to maintain that renegade identity even though the true Pirate Ship days had probably ended long ago. It was an incredible journey that ended with Tom Brady himself thanking the Brady Four during his Hall of Fame induction speech at Foxboro. He asked us all to rise and be recognized for our work defending the wall.

We'd come a long, long way from having the state police show up at my door for posting a picture of his son's junk. A long way indeed.

11

Chernin' and Burnin'

A common misconception with the rise of Barstool is that we hadn't already turned the corner before the arrival of the Chernin Group (our first investor, which I'll get into in a minute). Nope, by 2016, when Chernin entered the fold, I was already making more money than I ever dreamed. Remember, I started this thing hoping to just eke out a living doing something I loved; not to become some rich and famous media mogul. But somehow, by 2016, I was making seven figures and had already bought my dream house on Nantucket. I was also able to afford a nice brownstone in Boston from which I could hear the crowd from Fenway Park on my roof deck. As far as I was concerned, I had made it. Life was good.

That's not to say it was all candy canes and gumdrops at Barstool Sports. You know those old VH1 *Behind the Music* documentaries where they interview all the band members and it turns out everybody hates each other? Well, we weren't that bad yet, but we were getting there. I could tell that Dan and Kevin saw me as an unfair boss who was taking the lion's share of income and attention, talking down to them, and who would never let their stars rise to my level. From my perspective, these two had been picked from their shitty desk jobs and plopped into a rocket ship heading for the moon—a rocket ship I had spent ten years breaking my back building before I even knew they existed, and one they continued to mock and doubt even as it paid them a good living.

There was one *Rundown* I remember in particular, when I was telling Kevin and Dan that other media companies were starting to see what we were doing and were going to copy the way we did things. I believed we had cracked the code and we were the future, truly. I had heard a rumor that ESPN literally had a meeting on how to be authentic like Barstool. Umm, buddy, you already lost the second you turned on your projector. I knew that our ability to blend personality, humor, and informed sports takes was setting a tone that the broader media landscape would eventually want to shift toward. But Big Cat and Kevin laughed in my face. They told me I was insane.

We were coming at it from two different worlds. I knew how far Barstool had come, and I felt that the future looked brighter than ever in 2016 because I knew how bleak things had been just a few years earlier. But they weren't with me in the newspaper days. The blog was their starting point, and they were trying to envision what their futures would look like under the thumb of Dave Portnoy. They thought I was an egomaniac who would only allow for there to be one star player at the company. They thought I only cared about myself.

Now, I can certainly understand why Kevin and Dan were getting restless. The job was both easy and hard, if that makes sense. It was easy in that these guys were required to write two paragraphs about some fight at a Waffle House, and they didn't have to change out of their crusty pajamas or take a shower to do so. It was hard because they had to find a story worth blogging twelve times a day, and the world doesn't have off-hours when it comes to generating blog content. On Saturday night, if a star athlete got caught cheating on his wife, someone needed to blog that. And I didn't give a shit if they were at a wedding, on a boat with their buddies, or under anesthesia for wisdom tooth removal—the blog never slept. They were working and grinding every bit as hard as I was. They were every bit as responsible for the modern-day growth and success of Barstool as I was while still being treated as second-rate citizens, in their minds.

Raise your hand if you know who Jared Lorenzen is (RIP, big fella). Aka the Hefty Lefty. Aka the Pillsbury Throw Boy. Aka the Abominable Throwman. He was a quarterback sensation for the University of Kentucky largely because he was the biggest and fattest QB anybody had ever seen in their lives. He was also in the NFL for a cup of coffee as the Giants' backup QB for a few years. His unique build made him a fan favorite and we blogged about him throughout the years. He also became a fan of Barstool and we did a couple collab videos with him. We went to the Breeders' Cup and the Final Four with him. In fact we single-handedly brought back chicken fries on the Burger King menu with him.

Well, one day Jared called me and said his old agent was friends with some big money guy out in California named Mike Kerns. This big shot was potentially interested in investing in Barstool. Jared asked if he could pass my contact info along.

Now, up to this point I'd really had zero intention of looking for investors. Because outside the growing discontent with Dan and Kevin, I was happy with my life and the course of Barstool. The last thing I wanted to do was put together some grand business plan, do a big dog and pony show, dance like a clown, and beg for money. Plus, the entire reason I started Barstool was so I wouldn't have to work for anybody else. Regardless, having said all that, it still would have been stupid not to even take a call—especially when it was a friend asking. So I said sure, what the hell . . . it can't hurt to see what this guy says.

As it turns out, Mike Kerns worked for Peter Chernin at the Chernin Group (even bigger money). Professing his fandom, Kerns said he'd hop onto a plane from California to Boston the next day if I'd meet him for lunch. Right away, I knew this was the most serious inquiry I'd ever had about Barstool. Throughout the years, I had been approached by various types of investors/companies/clowns. It always felt like they were doing me a favor by meeting with me. That I had to explain why they should give me money. That I had to prove myself to them. And in the end it always turned out to be a gigantic waste of time and energy.

(Total sidenote: I get asked for business advice all the time. I never know what to say because I think every business story is sort of different and what worked for me may not work for you. But I do think there are some universal lessons regardless of your company. If you ever have to beg for an investment, if you feel like a used car salesman during the process, if you aren't 100 percent comfortable saying yes to a deal, then don't do it. Investment should never be a last resort or come out of desperation. That won't save your company any faster. Too many companies go looking for money way too soon. Or maybe I don't know what the hell I'm talking about, but I digress.)

Anyway, back to Mike Kerns. Within twenty-four hours of being introduced to him I was sitting across the table from him at Mistral in Boston. Right off the bat, I liked him. I liked that he dropped what he was doing and flew across the country on a moment's notice to meet with me. I liked that he knew us, knew me, knew my story. He was clearly a legitimate fan, not some guy who had read two of my blogs to prepare for our meeting. Kerns got right to the point: Would I be interested in a major investment in Barstool, and what would I do with the money?

For a while, I had been kicking around an idea of how to transform our group of satellite bloggers into one cohesive ecosystem. Maybe cohesive is the wrong word, because I didn't exactly expect us all to get along. More like a consolidated system, with everyone moving from their respective cities into one office, under one roof, with cameras rolling 24/7 to capture the madness of our island of misfit toys. The first-ever blog reality show, if you will.

This idea had sprung from the obvious success that came whenever we did get together on camera. Our fans liked us as personalities, liked our interplay, and always wanted more of our interactions. What held us back was the disparate geography of our star players: I was in Boston, Kevin was in New York, and Dan was in Chicago.

But what if we had one giant fish tank to operate from? One office, equipped with microphones and recording studios and proper camera equipment; real videographers and editors and producers available to shoot whatever dumb ideas we envisioned at the drop of a hat. Maybe a few actual salespeople to sell ads and slap sponsors on content. A tech guy to reboot the system when the website crashed. Someone to track T-shirt orders and make more of the bestsellers before they sold out and fewer of the non-sellers so we didn't end up with boxes of unsold "BALL DON'T LIE" T-shirts to give to Goodwill. The possibilities were endless.

For the most part, though, these were just daydreams. While I was pretty sure this concept would work, I also didn't want to risk everything I had built up to that point to create this new universe. Like, I was thirty-eight years old and had been living check to check most of my adult life with Barstool. Anytime we made money, I poured it back into the company. Did I want to risk it all at this point in my life? Did I want to sell the Nantucket house to fund this and be right back where I started financially? Nah. Even though I loved the idea, it wasn't a risk I was willing to take. But would I do it with somebody else's money? Well, that's a whole different story.

Having the Chernin guys take over 51 percent of the company meant that for the first time, I was not going to be on the hook personally for whatever financial problems we might run into. That was a huge relief and selling point for me. Also, their timing couldn't have been better either in terms of quelling the uprising within Barstool Sports. It instantly solved my issues with Dan and Kevin. I genuinely think they would have quit or given up on me and Barstool if Chernin hadn't come in to show them there was a light at the end of the tunnel. Whereas I'd always been sort of just a "close your eyes and trust me" type of leader, the Chernin Group brought instant credibility. They proved that maybe I wasn't as insane as they had accused me of being on that *Rundown* day. It also allowed us to put some of my "just trust me, bro" vibes onto paper. Kevin and Dan were officially each given 4 percent of the company. Gaz and KMarko were also given equity. And with the 51 percent acquired by the Chernin Group, I went from owning 100 percent of Barstool to less than 40 percent of the company in the blink of an eye. Both KFC and Dan now officially owned a significant stake in Barstool and saw a path to future success.

I guess I should put a little tidbit in here about Feitelberg. He was our early intern who blossomed into a full-time employee. In fact, he has the dubious distinction of being the longest-tenured Barstool employee who did not get equity in this original deal. If I could go back in time and give it to him, I would. But with equity it's kind of hard to put the toothpaste back into the tube. He and I have spoken about it. I've told him directly what I'm about to say here. At the time of the Chernin deal, I didn't think much about him. I wasn't even sure if he would come to NYC with us. If he wanted to come, great. If he didn't, great. He just wasn't really in my orbit. And at that point I was already giving away over 60 percent of my company. It already felt like a lot, so there was zero consideration in my head to giving it to anybody I couldn't live without. I feel like I've been more than fair with him over the years and have made it right, but only he knows deep down whether he agrees with that.

One thing is for sure: without him coming to NYC, there is no "Saturdays Are for the Boys" slogan. This was obviously a huge movement for Barstool and we probably made millions upon millions in selling SAFTB merch. Essentially it all started one day when Feitelberg was recounting a story he heard at the bar where a guy said Fridays are for men and Saturdays are for the boys. Well, the slogan instantly caught fire and became a rallying cry for dudes who just wanted to have a boys' day on Saturday. You literally couldn't turn on the TV or go outside without seeing SAFTB somewhere—from sporting events to celebrity interviews and beyond. Without Feits, this entire movement doesn't exist.

However, after a few weeks, he—along with a few others within Barstool—

wanted to stop promoting it because they thought it became sort of lame and cliché. They were probably right about that. But the cash registers were ringing, so we were like, "Fuck no." We are going to milk this thing for all it's worth. We are going to beat it into the ground.

Either way, it did present a philosophical debate. Should Feits have made life-changing money or gotten a huge bonus for this? Well, I fell on the side of the street that Barstool was mostly responsible for the explosion. Like yes, Feitelberg invented it, but without Barstool it goes nowhere. That's really how I look at our entire merch business and company. That's what we pay our employees to do—to come up with ways to make money, and we need to hit home runs to pay for the entire thing. That's the business model. It's the old McDonald's question: Who owns the McNuggets? The guy who invented them while working at McDonald's or McDonald's?

Either way, all our other original Milton guys have made seven figures, so I don't lose too much sleep over it.

Now as far as the Chernin deal itself, people always seem to be interested in this shit, so here is how it went. As I briefly mentioned before, I wasn't about to put on a dog and pony show for the Chernin Group. If they wanted to invest, then invest . . . if not, good luck to you. So the only thing I really did was give them access to our Google Analytics numbers so they could see what was under the hood. And they quickly discovered what I already knew: there was a Ferrari engine under the hood of this ugly, beat-up-looking pickup truck. Barstool Sports, the website, had become a unicorn on the World Wide Web. The vast majority of the people who visited our website on a daily basis would arrive there by typing in our URL—BarstoolSports.com. They didn't come via some roundabout Google search or a linktree or by clicking on a pop-up on some other website they were reading. They were direct, intentional visitors who knew where they were going and what they wanted to find. I remember some guy from The Chive once reached out and wanted to know if I wanted to join some link share program where our link would be bounced all over the internet. I declined because I didn't see the point of it. I wasn't trying to rack up fake clicks and numbers. Those people didn't buy T-shirts. I was trying to round up real fans.

On top of that, our fans would *stay* on the page. If you compare the internet in 2016 to old-fashioned cable television, where a viewer would flip through the channels, every channel would get one view from that viewer. Except that once our viewer arrived at our channel, they simply stayed on our channel. So our one view was far more valuable than that same view on other websites where the user might read one sentence and then move on to some other site.

We literally had an army of fans who would hit refresh on our website to load new blogs once they finished reading one. They were fans, plain and simple; they weren't site visitors, or strangers, or lost travelers along the highway of the internet. Our people were there intentionally, and they stayed for a while once they got there: Barstool Sports. Take your shoes off, stick around, you're home.

They wanted everything we were able to throw at them, and in turn, they engaged with us—through commenting in the comment section, creating a gigantic Reddit forum, interacting with us on social media, and buying our merchandise.

This stickiness was extremely unique. Kerns, who had worked at Yahoo Sports prior to the Chernin Group, said people interacted with our site like it was a fantasy sports site. Meaning they were on it all day long, refreshing. It was unheard-of.

So naturally, Chernin rolled in with a huge offer, right?

Nope. The opening bid from Peter Chernin and Mike Kerns was $7.5 million for 51 percent of the company, and I would retain all creative control over the content. It wasn't just low; it was embarrassingly low. In hindsight, it was an offensive starting point. I'm not a big negotiator in any space; I'm a sticker price guy. If that's the cost of the car, I'll pay it. If I think an employee of mine deserves a raise, I give it to them often before they ask for it. I pay people what they're worth, and I pay the worth of things I want.

When the Chernin guys said $7.5 million, I knew that was too low and I figured that was that. No deal, sorry, guys, see you down the road somewhere. I really didn't expect them to raise their offer.

But then they came to $12.5 million.

Twelve years earlier, my Astrovan—filled with newspapers handed out by homeless people—had exploded on the highway. Now the company that I had created was worth $12.5 million dollars.

I took the deal. For so many reasons, not the least of which was that it let me put $5 million into my bank account. At that time, that was more money than I thought I would ever need or make, and it allowed me to breathe easy. Whatever pinch I felt about carrying my Nantucket house was gone instantly. My financial future felt safe.

It also solved my issues with Dan and Kevin, making them happy. Since I'd given them each 4 percent of the company, there was now a lane for them to become more successful doing this than they would ever have become in their steady corporate jobs. Whatever shit they had to put up with, whatever frustrations they had with me, it might be worth it given the money they were now seeing was real.

I took the deal because I liked and trusted Peter Chernin and Mike Kerns. I had done my research and Peter Chernin was a highly respected, proven investor in the media space. This deal would legitimize Barstool in ways that I simply couldn't. I trusted that they would stay out of my way as far as running the creative side of the business.

Lastly, I knew that we needed this money to grow Barstool to the next level. We needed it to become a real multimedia company with offerings beyond the blog, to level up our video content, to attract bigger names to drop in and collaborate with us, and to build our own stable of homegrown stars.

The timing was right and the number seemed right. It wasn't even close to what the company was actually worth, but it all worked out in the end.

In an initial meeting with the Chernin Group they said they wanted to 4- or 5× the value of Barstool in five years. The dream scenario would be to sell it for $50 million in five years. (We sold it for $650 million in five years. Not bad.)

Barstool Sports had grown up. We were a real company now, a recognizable brand that elicited both respect and disgust, loyalty and hatred.

PS: I've gone back and forth over the years on whether the Chernin Group screwed us with that $12.5 million offer. Do I think they knew it was wildly low? Yes, probably. But at the same time, it's not like any other investment companies were beating down my door. They were the only ones who showed any real interest. So for that, they get a lot of credit. And there is no chance we become who we are without them. But I also wouldn't trust them as far as I could bowl them in terms of any future negotiations.

They also learned a very early lesson on how to deal with me during the final stages of closing this deal. As long as you always do what you say and say what you do, I will always get along with you. I can take bad news. I don't always need to get my way. But when you say something to me, it's in stone. Somewhere in the early negotiations, Chernin Group agreed to pay for my legal fee to get this deal done. It was around $50K. But when we reached the goal line and there was literally nothing left to discuss, they said I was on the hook for it. I absolutely refused to move forward. I told them the deal was off if they didn't honor their word. There would be no negotiations. I wouldn't pay 50 percent or five dollars of it. They agreed to pay it and that was that. In the scheme of things, it wasn't that big of a number; it was the principle of it that mattered to me. I doubt they've ever had somebody seriously threaten to walk away over something so minor, but I was 100 percent ready to torpedo the entire thing over it. Do what you say. Say what you do. Always.

Once we got past that last little snafu, we were off and racing. Somewhere along the way we all agreed that the new HQ would be in New York City, for three reasons. First, Kevin had a family and couldn't move. His kids were in school and he had a legitimate reason for why he couldn't come to Boston. Second, NYC made sense as a place where big stars from all walks of life could come through the office and do content with us. It was, and is, the center of the promotional circuit for anyone trying to get out the word that their new album is dropping, or raise their profile to sell more jerseys, or drum up interest in a new movie they've made. I figured we might as well plop ourselves directly into the center of it all to make our office as accessible as possible. Third, we were already as big as we could get in Boston. New York, meanwhile, presented a huge growth opportunity.

So in January 2016, Kevin, Dan, Keith, and I met in Times Square to film a video announcing the Chernin deal and the future of Barstool. I revealed the big move, explained why this would be good for the future of Barstool, and pushed back accusations that I had sold out.

"When you're a young comedian in the eighties, and you graduate, you had to send your résumé to SNL. In five years, all these little kids, all these beautiful people, there's only going to be one place they'll be sending their résumé to—Barstool Sports. We're the best, brightest, funniest . . . but only Stoolies know that. We want to take it to the world."

It was a lofty promise, and I meant every word. I had moved us out of our comfort zones in our home cities to take a shot at greatness. Like aspiring actors moving to Hollywood or wannabe models heading to Milan, we needed to thrive under the bright lights of the Big Apple.

There was definitely some backlash from our Boston faithful that we were all moving to New York. People said I had sold out, or that I was leaving the city that helped build us. Umm, the last place I wanted to move was New York City. I didn't want to leave Boston at all; I just knew we had to all be together in order to keep growing this thing. It definitely took some time for people to realize I wasn't forgetting where we came from.

To try to smooth over the move with the fans, I promised I would review every single pizza place in New York City. I didn't exactly count how many that would be, but I figured I'd start nearby and expand my radius around the office and into Brooklyn and the other boroughs as needed. I was just talking to talk at that point; I don't think I was really planning on doing it. But just like with most organic things at Barstool, I would quickly learn that these simple, daily reviews would become essential to my personal brand and growth.

Within two weeks of signing the deal with Chernin, Renee and I uprooted our lives and moved into the Meatpacking District in NYC. We moved in, sight unseen. A realtor did a walk-through and sent us a video and we took it. I was sad as I taped up the last of our boxes in Boston. Renee and I had loved our house there. We had friends and family all around us, as well as the love of the entire city behind us. Now we were heading for enemy territory.

Looking back on it now, if there was one singular event that I could point to that ended Renee's and my marriage, I would say it was the Chernin deal and this move to NYC. Of course, nothing is that simple in retrospect, but it definitely played a major factor. I had been working on Barstool relentlessly for thirteen years—literally since the day I met her. I had finally gotten to the point where I could take my foot off the gas a bit. I could enjoy a weekend off without freaking out. We could take a normal vacation. But once the Chernin deal happened, in many ways it was like starting over. I had made a promise to do whatever I could to make this investment work. That meant I was back to a never-ending work cycle right when it seemed like maybe I had been going to take it back a bit. And for Renee's part, she had left her job and was now stuck in the middle of Manhattan with me working nonstop. We just started to grow distant.

Going our separate ways was the hardest thing I've had to do in my life. There was no big fight. We still loved each other and honestly wanted the best for each other. But it just wasn't working anymore. Renee had been a true day one for me and Barstool. There is a video out there in which she tears up talking about me long after we had separated. It's hard for me not to get emotional when I watch it or even as I write this. There are very few "drop everything" people in my life. Like hey, this person needs something so drop everything you are doing and come help. But she is one of them. And if you're wondering if we stay in touch, the answer is that we do. She's always been there for me and vice versa even after all these years. She's still my best friend.

On a little less emotional note, through all the hit pieces and all the attacks on my character, do you know how many times the media has contacted Renee to ask about me? The woman who I was married to for five years and spent over ten years of my life living with? The answer is a big fat ZERO. Not once. Because the media doesn't ever want to hear from somebody who will contradict the story and narrative they've already written about me in their head. They'd rather get a quote from some girl I've met once or regurgitate a quote from twenty years ago from one of my blogs. It's insanity.

Once I got settled in NYC and found office space, the next order of business was hiring a CEO. Now, I want to clear something up right here. We didn't hire a CEO because I'm a dummy who couldn't run the company. I don't want to toot my own horn, but I have a gigantic brain. I worked in corporate America for five years before starting Barstool and did pretty good. I took us from a startup newspaper to getting sold for $12.5 million without anybody's help. It wasn't overnight and I got lucky a ton along the way, but I still managed to do it.

The bigger issue was that I had too many balls in the air between my blogs, my exploding social media platforms, and my video content. Running a legitimate business meant hiring HR people, retaining legal counsel, building out a benefits plan, expense reports, taxes, vacation days, blah blah blah. All shit that I had absolutely no interest in doing. Also, I guess it should be mentioned that I was largely perceived as a crazy person across the internet. Oh, you don't want to take a meeting with the guy who went to jail over Deflategate and tried to jerk off eighteen times in the 6-12-18-24 challenge? There had to be some separation of Church and State. So with the help of the Chernin guys, we began the hunt for our new leader.

To initiate the search, we hired a high-powered recruiting firm. Their job was to find qualified candidates. I'd interview them and then if I liked them, they'd make it to Dan, KFC, and Keith for the next round. I want to say I interviewed about thirty guys. All men. I didn't like any of them. I'm not even sure if any of them made it to the second round. They were all know-it-alls to me. "Hey Dave, this is what you got to do. You gotta change this . . . do that blah blah blah." Well, you guys actually don't know the first thing about us, so how do you know what we should do or shouldn't do?

The search was exhausting and frustrating. Like I knew within five minutes these weren't the right people, but then you gotta be cordial and pretend you're still interested. It sucked. We were getting nowhere.

Then at some point during the search, I got a call from a woman named Betsy Morgan. Betsy was actually the old CEO of the *Huffington Post* and, like me, enjoyed spending her summers on Nantucket. The Nantucket connection, plus running a huge website in her past, were the reasons the Chernin Group thought it made sense to introduce us. We became friends and Chernin made Betsy the first and only advisor in Barstool history. (At least I think she was an advisor. I honestly don't even know what that means exactly. I assume she got stock and made some money down the road when we sold again to Penn?) Anyway, Betsy was going to be in NYC and asked if I wanted to meet for coffee and discuss how the CEO search was going. She also asked if it was okay if a friend of hers came along. I was like sure, whatever. I'll meet you in an hour. Her friend who was tagging along was Erika Nardini.

Erika and I hit it off instantly. Right away, it was obvious Erika was very familiar with the brand. She was a Patriots fan. She had bought all our Pats merch. She knew everything about us. And then she just started asking a million questions. What are you gonna do next? Have you thought about this? What about that? It would be cool to do this. It would be cool to do that . . . and I vividly remember her saying, "The hardest thing you guys have to figure out is what you want to do because you guys can do anything."

And there it was. That's exactly how I felt about Barstool. We didn't need to change. We didn't need fixing. We just needed to be let out of the garage and let our Ferrari engine roar.

(In my head as I write this, I'm picturing our little jalopy car rolling to the starting line next to all the fancy cars like ESPN and Bleacher Report and Deadspin, and we rev our engine and those drivers look at us stunned like, *What the fuck was that?*)

Anyway, after meeting Erika, I called Mike Kerns and asked him if he knew who she was because I had met her that day and she was the one. That was our future CEO. Turns out they knew exactly who she was. They had just met with her a few weeks prior for something else. The only problem was, Erika had just left her job at AOL to run a different company called Bckstg—a Scooter Braun company (more on Scooter later). So it would take some convincing to get her to accept the job.

As it turns out, it didn't take nearly as much as I thought. Erika was sold as much as I was from that first coffee meeting. The more we talked, the more excited she became. She talked to each of our guys individually and we kept moving the ball forward. It seemed like we had our CEO.

The last step was to get everybody together before she took the leap of faith. At some point that winter, I told Erika to meet the team in New York. I got us a reservation at Buddakan—a chic, club-like restaurant with ridiculously overpriced Chinese food. Buddakan is the type of place you might go for dinner in Vegas on a bachelor party. It was not the ideal venue for introducing a group of schlubby bloggers to their potential new boss. But it was across the street from my apartment and I could get a reservation, so that's where we went.

I'm not one to patronize my employees. But that night, I should have told everyone to be on their best fucking behavior. The goal was to impress Erika, to put any doubts she may have had about accepting the job to rest. After all, it was only the most important decision of her professional life.

Well, how did our guys act? Umm, if I had to describe it in two words I'd say . . . not great. Or maybe a better way to describe it is that we were just us. From the first round of appetizers, my guys were doing everything they could to dissuade Erika from taking the job. Dan and Kevin skewered the company, shared all our worst moments, and opened up the inner blueprints to point out every mold spore and broken pipe we had in our house. *Hey Erika, wait till you get a load of Nate and Smitty! You'll never regret a decision more in your life. And we haven't even mentioned our sales guy Lightswitch Lou . . . total psychopath. Oh, and our website? Total piece of shit.* On and on it went. In hindsight, it was probably better that everybody was just their usual, miserable selves than put on some fake act. At least Erika got to see firsthand what she was getting herself into.

I held my breath waiting to talk to her the next day. I was waiting for her to be like, "You know what, Dave . . . this may not be for me." Thankfully, that dinner didn't scare her off. The next day, she signed the contract to be our CEO. And as I'd find out over the years, almost nothing could scare Erika.

A month or so later, it was time to announce Erika's hiring to the Stoolies. We'd kept it somewhat secret even though she'd started weeks earlier. We went back to Times Square, our unofficial tableau for any and all major Barstool announcements. Standing behind me, hidden from view by Big Cat's gigantic torso, was Erika.

"We have found our man after a search long and hard," I said. "We need someone who can control the city. Finally, the day has come to announce our new CEO. My boss, big old balls"—pausing here for dramatic effect—"Erika Nardini."

We stepped apart and Erika stepped forward, introduced herself, dropped the mic, and walked off.

The New York era of Barstool Sports had begun.

* * *

There are a lot of decisions that I can look back on over the history of Barstool and say that was the most important decision I made. If this didn't happen the exact way it happened, I don't think Barstool turns out the way it does. The hiring of Erika Nardini is certainly at the top of that list. It wasn't just the growth that she oversaw during her tenure at Barstool; it wasn't just the constant juggling of egos, the constant babysitting. It wasn't just the fact that she and I got along perfectly. I've often said we respected each other so much that we would defer to each other if we ever had a disagreement, but we almost never did. Instead, to me, the most important quality she brought to the table was that she was ride-or-die Barstool. Once she did her homework on me and Barstool and decided she was all in, she never wavered. She was *all in*. There were probably hundreds of times when she could have apologized or taken a step back, but she never did. The more heat we got, the more she dug in to defend us. I've seen so many people who think they know what it's like to be in the eye of the storm, but it's hard to truly prepare for it until you're in it. And Barstool was in it a lot, and I personally was in it a lot. From sex tapes to sex allegations to sexist allegations to racism allegations to any type of allegation you could be accused of, I was accused of it. And she never blinked. She fought for us like how I fight for us. Even though she wasn't there handing out newspapers back in the day, it felt like she was there with me. That's how much she fought for and believed in the brand. And I knew she'd always do her best to protect me from the storm as best she could.

One of my favorite stories with Erika is when she wore a sweater one day that said "Feminist" on it. Naturally, the losers at our mortal enemy Deadspin got on their high horse and made fun of her for it. They called her a "Token Female CEO." They implied that I only hired her to divert sexism allegations, to put a woman at the front of the company to prove that we couldn't possibly be sexist because, hey, we were led by a woman. *So how dare she wear a feminist sweatshirt?* they screamed from their ivory tower.

How did Erika respond? She quote-tweeted their story and said, "It's cashmere, bitch." That was all I needed to know about Erika Nardini.

By the way, I always find it comical when self-proclaimed feminists try to dictate how other women should act. Or determine what jokes they can laugh at. Or what companies they can lead. As if poor little Erika was so incapable of thinking on her own and just not smart enough to realize that she was a pawn in my giant game. Like isn't true feminism empowering women to think and decide for themselves? Not treating them like helpless babies who need every decision made for them by the self-proclaimed moral police? I've always found that so ironic. It's the same as in the KO Barstool days when these women who hated us were screaming at other women who enjoyed coming to our parties. KO Barstool felt they had to protect these women from themselves because they weren't smart enough to make good decisions on their own. Frankly, it's patronizing. And it's the exact opposite of feminism.

The facts are that me hiring Erika had absolutely nothing to do with her being a woman. She was better than all the men I interviewed, period. Erika became one of the most powerful CEOs in sports media while she was here.

She led us to incredible highs. At one point, three out of the four top business positions at our company were held by women because she hired other women. Yet our detractors still called us a boys' club. They still said we were sexist. They still said she was a token hire. Then you'd look at their executive board and they literally had all middle-aged white dudes. It's surreal how hypocritical it was looking back on it. But just like always, we let our actions speak louder than our words. While others took shots at her and us, we continued to grow at warp speed while our competitors continued to fall by the wayside.

12
Mudgills

So now we had our new office in NYC. We had our new CEO. We had money to hire people. And it was time to test my theory: that if we poured a little gas onto this fire that I started over a decade ago in my parents' house in Swampscott, we'd have an explosion. And boy did we ever.

I don't want to say the NYC experiment was an overnight success, but it pretty much was. We outgrew our first office space—which we thought would last us five years—in a few months. I was constantly adding new talent to the mix. PFT Commenter, Caleb, Rone, Ria, Fran, Glenny Balls, Pat McAfee, Alex Cooper, Biz, and others were all hired during the NYC office 1.0 generation (I'll get more into some of those people later on). The content was riveting. How could it not have been with that many big personalities all crammed under one roof? If I had to describe the early NYC years, I'd call them a constant state of war. And it was war within, as well as war against the outside. Because one thing that has been true with Barstool since the days of KO Barstool is that the more success we had, the more people would try to tear us down.

I am not a perfect person. There are probably a lot of things I could be way better at. But one talent I have, if you want to call it that, is that I thrive in the mud. I am a naturally sarcastic, combative person. I don't go looking for fights, but I certainly don't run from them either. You want to go low? I'll go lower. If you hit me with a feather, I'll hit you with a wrench. I've been this way my entire life. Maybe it's the East Coast Boston personality in me. But I'll tell you this much: the last thing I'd ever do is sit back and let people who don't know me and have never bothered to talk to me attack a brand I spent fifteen years building. I've always viewed an attack on Barstool as an attack on my family, and I've responded in kind. You know that quote from *The Godfather,* "It's not personal, it's business"? Well, I don't subscribe to that theory. For me, all business is personal.

As we continued to settle into New York, the attacks against Barstool were seemingly growing by the day. The same interchangeable group of social justice warrior "reporters" came out of the woodwork to blame all society's woes on us. I put reporters in quotes because these weren't even real reporters to me. They were rich, spoiled kids who just graduated from their elite, small, East Coast liberal college fifteen minutes ago and had never worked a day in their life. While they sat around in some classroom sucking each other's dicks about how smart they were and how they were gonna save the world, I was doing a seventy-two-hour paper route and handing out newspapers outside South Station at 4 a.m. The last thing I was going to do was sit back and be lectured by these hypocritical, entitled douchebags about how awful Barstool Sports was. I was going to attack back, make fun of them, humiliate them. I would make them regret getting into the ring with me.

I swear we literally launched a cottage industry of lunatics whose entire career was just to follow what I said and then attack me for clicks. Deadspin, the Daily Beast, Business Insider, the *New York Times,* and the *WaPos* of the world, aka the No Fun Squad. It was just the same exact people writing the same exact stories year after year after year. Their recurring complaints about us came to be known as the Big J (Big Journalist) News Cycle in Barstool lore.

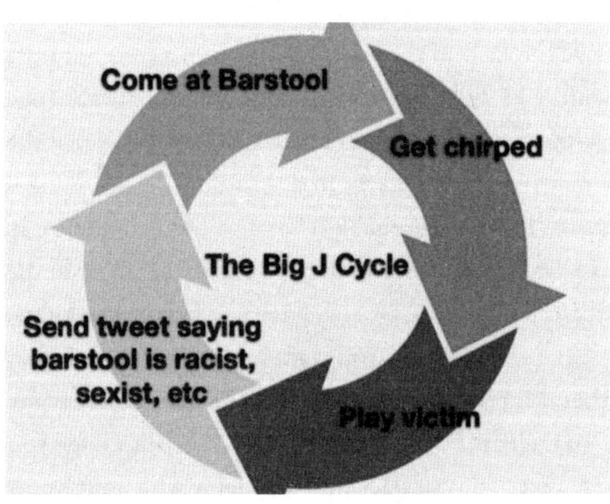

Here's how the Big J News Cycle goes: The media attacks Barstool with either out-of-context or made-up stories. Barstool then responds, defending ourselves from the unprovoked attack. Then the journalist who launched the original attack complains they are being attacked by Barstool and our fans. And around and around we go.

I've been thinking about how to write this chapter for a while now to accurately capture how crazy the entire Barstool hate cycle is. I don't think there is any way I can do it justice without actually showing you some of these hit pieces and how they unfolded in real time.

Let's start with Robert Silverman. That original KO Barstool movement walked so Robert Silverman could run. He has essentially dedicated his life to trying to cancel Barstool Sports. I'm not sure how many times this guy has written about me over the years, but it's a lot and borders on obsessive. And to his credit, he is still going. He was on a podcast as recently as 2025 still mumbling incoherently about how I'm the bogeyman and how he sees Dave Portnoy ghosts everywhere.

Now, Silverman wrote what I would call the original Barstool Hater's Bible. While KO Barstool just called the media to complain about us, this guy was actually *part* of the media. He worked for a publication I had never heard of called the Daily Beast. It's essentially a low-paying liberal website filled with people who think they are far more important than they are and who hate seeing fun in the world.

Anyway, Silverman wrote the first true hit piece on Barstool Sports. This article would be quoted by virtually every single Barstool hater from the moment it was published until the end of time. Here's his title: "Inside Barstool Sports' Culture of Online Hate: They Treat Sexual Harassment and Cyberbullying as a Game."

Here is what has always infuriated me about the "journalists" who cover Barstool (and I've probably already said it thirty times during this book). They all are already Barstool haters before they pick up their pen. They all already have their preconceived notions about us. Anything that could possibly contradict their narrative is ignored.

This is from my reaction to the hit piece.

All I know is when I first heard about this hit piece I had no idea who he was. I literally didn't. But then I was told this was the same guy who tried to insinuate we were selling drugs out of our Superbowl House in Houston. Yes he really tried to craft a story around that narrative. In fact he reached out to twitter and asked for help from anybody who had dirt on us. Of course this was wildly untrue and Stoolies mocked him and made fun of him and he deleted all the tweets from it. However that isn't all he's done apparently. It turns out he's been stalking me for literally years. He comments on virtually every single thing I do. It's amazing. I don't know whether I should be flattered or scared. He's called me anti Semitic. (For the record I'm Jewish).

He's inferred that I'm Hitler and all the Stoolies are Nazis. That's quite a hot take given that the *Jewish Journal* declared me one of the biggest and brightest Jewish stars in media. I still hate them for the photo they used though.

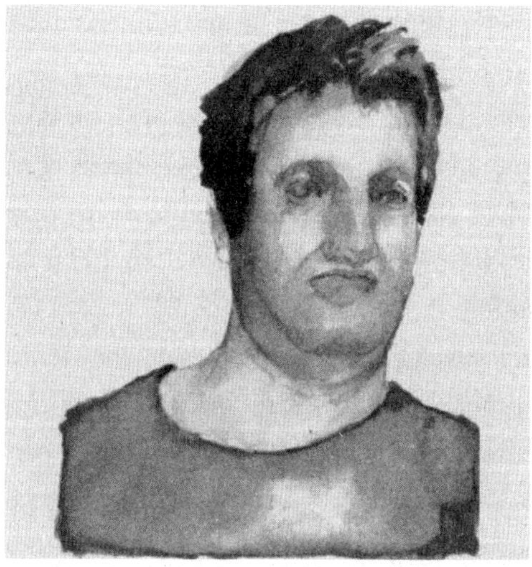

Courtesy of Jay Ehrlich, Illustration by Michael Berson, the *Forward*

He's called us homophobic. Ask Gay Pat about that.

He's made fun of my marriage, saying Renee left me. That's incorrect but still pretty mean-spirited from somebody who always claims to have the moral high ground.

He basically responds to every tweet I write, regardless of what I tweet about. I could tweet about the Red Sox and he'd have a problem with it. If somebody compliments us, he has a problem with it. If somebody compliments Erika, he gets mad. If somebody says PFT is funny, he gets mad. Hell, if anyone anywhere talks about Trump, he gets mad at *us*.

Like I said, he's totally and completely obsessed with me and the success of Barstool Sports. If you showed him twenty straight ink blot photos and asked him what he saw, I guarantee he'd say Dave Portnoy twenty times in a row. And he'd talk about how he is writing what he calls a fair and balanced hit piece on us.

Listen, I don't care about the negative press. I'm the straw that stirs the drink. I understand that. To quote Reggie Jackson, "Fans don't boo nobodies." When you need pageviews, you write about me. I move the needle. I'm the guy all the other guys worry about. I love that. But all I'm asking is that the Daily Beast include this standard header on all his articles before they press publish:

> Robert Silverman has been obsessed with Barstool Sports for five-plus years. He slanders them at every turn. He is jealous that David Portnoy has made millions and millions of dollars and Barstool Sports is now worth hundreds of millions of dollars while he languishes as a freelance writer. He can't accept the fact that Dave Portnoy outhustled, outworked, and outwrote every other blogger on the planet and that his success did not come overnight. That Dave grew Barstool Sports brick by brick. That he poured every cent he made back into the company. That he assembled the most talented crew of bloggers in the country. Robert Silverman hates the American Dream. He wants Barstool so bad, it's like acid in his mouth. Nothing he says can be taken seriously.

I stand by everything I wrote in this blog, especially the last sentence. This man actually went to clown college. For real, he went to CLOWN COLLEGE. Like to become a performing clown. That's who our haters love to quote: a literal clown. Of course I offered to sit down with him and go through every accusation. Of course he refused. That's a commonality with almost every person who has ever attacked me: they never want to sit down one-on-one.

Now I don't want to make this chapter too long, but it really is important to our story. And even after all these years and all the success we've had, it still infuriates me. Let's talk about my other major nemesis: Deadspin. How do I describe Deadspin? Well, they were actually one of the few blogs that predated Barstool. They were a sports blog when nobody knew what the hell that meant. They became famous (or notorious, depending on how you look at it) for breaking a few huge sports stories. They broke the Manti Te'o fake girlfriend story. They broke the Brett Favre sexting to Jenn Sterger story (without asking Sterger if they could publish it, going against her will and ruining her life). They posted a story about an Indiana coed having sex in a bathroom, which ruined her life. Their former owner published Hulk Hogan's sex tape without his consent and eventually got sued and put out of business because of it. Now, if it seems like Deadspin had no moral compass, it's because they didn't under the leadership of A.J. Daulerio. We looked like the *SS Goody Two-Shoes* compared to Deadspin. Like they were literally and openly willing to ruin people's lives for clicks. They made no bones about it.

Then one day, they switched. After the whole Hogan thing, A.J. was out at Deadspin and a new editor came in. It would be the first of like twenty new editors Deadspin and their previous parent company, Gawker, would employ as they floundered to stay relevant. Overnight, Deadspin went from one of the most vile, crass websites on the internet to a holier-than-thou, left-wing moral authority website. All they did was critique and complain about anything and everybody they deemed not up to their journalistic standard. And we were target number one.

For a number of years, it seemed like every other day Deadspin wrote a hit piece on us. The switch-up was actually amazing, but how could anybody take them seriously with their past? Well, they deleted their entire social footprint so nobody could look up all the things they had said and written before this magical transformation. They wrote an apology blog saying everything they had done in the past was a mistake, and that was that. Their entire sordid history was supposed to be forgotten.

One of the new young gun reporters Deadspin hired straight out of college was a gal named Laura Wagner. And boy, she hated my guts. Laura was definitely the type of girl to put pronouns in her bio before that was even a thing. If you were having fun, she wanted to stamp it out. She was a true nod back to the KO Barstool days and the No Fun Squad. Laura literally once blogged that Drew Brees should be ashamed of himself when, after breaking the all-time career passing yards record in the NFL, he said, "See, boys, anything is possible" to his two young sons on the field but didn't say it to his young daughter who was being held in his wife's arms, so that made him sexist in her eyes. That's a real article she wrote. That's who she was at her core and that's who I was dealing with.

From the second Laura arrived at Deadspin, she attacked me. Not just for what I wrote but personally too. I didn't respond for a year. Just one attack after another that I ignored. Then finally, I took inspiration from *Seinfeld*. There is an episode where George falls in love with a woman because she hates him so much that he finds her irresistible. So here was my response:

> Another day and another hit piece by the indominable Laura Wager. I honestly think I love this fucking woman. She's just so potty mouthed and so vile and so vindictive. She's just so obsessed with hating Barstool I can't get enough. I legit think her enitre day is just listening to Power 85 and reading our blog waiting for us to say something remotely controversial or stupid so she can sprint to her computer and blog about it. It's the type of dedication, hatred and pure jealousy you just don't see every day.

This would be what the Robert Silvermans and the Deadspins of the world would then qualify as sexually harassing female reporters. It would be linked in countless future hit pieces with no context, no backstory—just that I was sexually harassing women. A woman who had been launching grenades at my feet for months nonstop. If that's sexual harassment, then lock me up.

It wasn't just that they took things wildly out of context, or removed all context entirely either. These "reporters" would seemingly just make things up out of thin air. In 2019, the Boston Bruins were making a playoff run. They had rally towels that they handed out and needed a sponsor to pay for them. In exchange, we'd get our logo printed on the back. We agreed to do it. Then all hell broke loose. The reporters who hated our guts descended like vultures.

It started with the *Boston Herald* and a reporter named Marisa Ingemi. She contacted the Bruins, armed with all the articles Laura Wagner, Robert Silverman, and the rest of the No Fun Squad had written about us, and said, "How dare you partner with these people?"

(I'm not sure if I can legally put Marisa Ingemi's picture in here, so I'm begging you to put down this book and google her. You'll spit out your coffee and you're not even drinking any. Legit she looks like she came from central casting. These are the types of people I was dealing with. Yeah, it's mean, but it's truthful and it's my book, so I don't give a fuck.)

Anyway, this was a full-blown controversy started by Ingemi in our backyard. Naturally, the Stoolies were pissed and I'm sure were sending her all sorts of nasty comments on Twitter and leaving mean comments under the article. So the Big J victim cycle that I described earlier began: a reporter who hates our guts writes a hit piece on us, we respond that it's bullshit, our fans go after the reporter on social media, the reporter cries that life is so unfair and that Barstool is a bunch of bullies. From A to B to C to D, as reliable as the sun coming up each day.

Remember, this was after Ingemi attacked us, unprovoked. Now, I obviously never condone any Stoolies who go over the line with threats. That's idiotic. But I also never saw it as my job to protect these Barstool haters from themselves. You attack me in a public forum and try to interfere with my business that I've been building for two decades, you better believe I have the right to respond. Yes, I have a large audience. Yes, I have lots of fans who have been with me for years. They view an attack on me as an attack on a family member. So maybe you should have gotten your facts straight or attempted to do legit research before coming after me. Because like I said, if you hit me with a feather, be ready for the wrench.

The next shoe to drop in this controversy came when Jessica Heslam from the *Boston Herald* wrote a pair of articles slamming Barstool. One was for attacking Marisa Ingemi, who apparently is allowed to attack people but not vice versa. And the second article was a plea to the Bruins to not do business with us. The article was titled:

THE NFL BROOMED BARSTOOL'S DAVE PORTNOY, SO SHOULD THE BRUINS

Here are the opening paragraphs:

> BostonHerald.com - Not too long ago, Sasha Goodfriend was a college student trying to stop men from carrying unconscious young women out of Barstool Sports Blackout parties in Boston.
>
> Goodfriend, a Boston University student at the time, was among the students protesting Barstool baron David Portnoy's lucrative club parties in the city's Fenway neighborhood that were popular in 2011 and 2012.
>
> "I remember seeing girls being unconscious and thrown on the backs of guys and taken into cabs and literally, me and my fellow group of activists would intervene to protect those girls," recalled Goodfriend, now the president of the Massachusetts chapter of the National Organization for Women. "It was really upsetting."

I don't know who Sasha Goodfriend is, but she should be in prison—as should Jessica Heslam for printing this outrageous lie. To think that our party at House of Blues was so out of control that guys were carrying women over their shoulders like cavemen and throwing them into cabs? What are you even talking about? We had police and security lined up and down the street. There was not one complaint from any one of our parties about sexual assault or anything even remotely similar to this crazy lie. Now, almost ten years later, this girl was just blatantly making stuff up that was so obviously untrue, and this reporter prints it? What are we even doing here? But as I've learned over the decades, people can legit lie and say whatever they want and get away with it.

Also, how about the headline of the article? The NFL banned us because of Deflategate and for protesting for Tom Brady, not because of any sexual harassment or misogyny. Talk about a false equivalency. It drove me nuts.

Years later we would find ourselves embroiled in another hockey controversy. Erika had started playing hockey in her free time and developed a love for the sport. She had a few players from the NWHL (National Women's Hockey League) on her podcast promoting the league. Well, once again, the gatekeepers of morality came knocking. *How dare the women's pro hockey league associate with evil Barstool! Vice* magazine wrote a hit piece filled with all the usual links from the same rehashed articles about how bad we were. But one part of their article, in particular, caught my attention:

vice.com

On Tuesday night, Barstool Sports founder Dave Portnoy tweeted a video riddled with inaccuracies and mocking the devastating, career-ending injury suffered by Denna Laing in the league's first season of the league in 2015. (The NWHL honors Laing every year with an award, and her number is retired by the Boston Pride.) Portnoy also expressed a

Now not only was this just a complete mischaracterization of my video, but Barstool actually had a deep history with Denna Laing. We were the first media outlet to cover her devastating hockey injury, where she went into the boards headfirst and became paralyzed from the waist down. We put Denna Laing T-shirts up for sale in our store and raised a ton of money for her. We made a documentary with her about the entire thing. She said those shirts were some of her proudest moments after the accident and helped her get through it. It was mind-boggling to me that a reporter could openly and maliciously lie like this.

Oh, by the way . . . do you want to know who the author of that article was? Marisa Ingemi. Ding, ding, ding. The same one who started the Bruins controversy from the clouds. Years later, she was using the same exact playbook. It was the same exact circle of reporters citing their own fake journalism to support their narrative about Barstool Sports.

After I posted the documentary of us with Denna, which directly contradicted Ingemi's reporting, *Vice* quietly deleted that portion of the article and removed her name from it. The rest of the bullshit stayed. No apology. No nothing. Ho hum, just a reporter of ours totally making shit up, but we'll let it go because she was probably picked on in high school.

I could go on and on with stuff like this. It could literally be the entire book. I'm not sure anybody would care. But it has clearly shaped how I perceive the media. I know they lie. I know you need to do your own research. I don't trust shit because I've seen it firsthand.

People say I hate unions and am a union buster. Why? Because when Gawker laid off a ton of my archenemies (after going bankrupt), I celebrated and said their unions couldn't help them now. This somehow caught the attention of AOC (yes, that one), who tweeted this:

> If you're a boss tweeting firing threats to employees trying to unionize, you are likely breaking the law & can be sued, in your words, "on the spot." ALL workers in the US have the protected freedom to organize for better conditions.

Then she followed up by asking for donations so she could help stop companies like ours.

Naturally, Barstool employees created a fake union to pretend like I was suffocating them. It's what we always do: make fun of the people making fun of us. But the haters ran with it, fell for it hook, line, and sinker. The National Labor Relations Board, whatever that is, got involved. I actually had to send an email saying I wasn't going to fire anybody for making a union, per the orders of the government. Everybody at Barstool got a huge laugh out of it. And my anti-union stance is now mentioned in every hit piece against us.

Or how about when people say I'm racist? When Black Lives Matter happened, the same people who hated us went back and dug up a clip from five years prior of me singing the N-word. Out of context, it sounds bad. But with context, you learn that I was announcing our Super Bowl party, for which I hired Ja Rule and Ashanti to perform. I sang the first minute of five of their most popular songs to reveal who we booked. One of the lyrics contained the N-word and I sang it, and to be honest I didn't give it much thought in real time. Five years passed. Nobody said a word. Then when BLM happened, suddenly this video came out and I was being labeled a racist. All for singing a lyric to a song to announce a Super Bowl party. None of the articles that called me a racist mentioned the context, either. They just said I had a habit of saying the N-word. Okaaay . . . I had never said that word before and I'll never say it again. Even if I'm rapping along to a song that contains it.

By the way, you want to hear an interesting story regarding this controversy that I've never told publicly before? A couple months before BLM started, I formed a partnership with High Noon. They had just launched as a company, and our partnership was a smashing success right off the bat. But they were getting inundated with complaints about me after my Ja Rule video surfaced. *Dave is racist blah, blah, blah.* It was bad enough that they were really feeling the pressure. It was the very beginning of our relationship and everybody was saying I was the devil. So we had a conference call where they wanted me to publicly apologize to anybody I offended for singing the lyric. It would help them lessen the pressure they were getting to disassociate with me.

I flat-out refused. In my mind, it wasn't just about apologizing for this one instance (even if I had thought I had done something wrong, which I didn't). This was cancel culture and all my haters had been trying to get me to apologize for over a decade. It didn't matter if it was rape culture, #MeToo, BLM, or whatever the latest cause du jour was. Some people hated my guts and just wanted to end Barstool at all costs. They would complain about everything I did. If you give these people an inch they will take a mile. I would not apologize for something that clearly wasn't done out of hate and happened five years ago. I stopped repping High Noon for a couple years after that. Barstool still worked with them but not me personally.

Fast-forward a few years and Alex Cooper and I were getting ready to launch a competitor to High Noon called "Not Water." It was basically a similar drink to High Noon. I hadn't spoken to High Noon in years. I reached out and told them what I was about to do and essentially gave them an ultimatum: pay me this much and I will go back to being the face of High Noon or I'm launching a competitor. It was one of the best decisions both High Noon and I made to let bygones be bygones and start fresh. It's been one of the best partnerships I've had in twenty years of doing this. High Noon is the number-one-selling canned vodka drink in the United States. And I've gotten a few nice beach houses out of the deal too.

For all the shit Barstool has dealt with over the years—all the bullshit, all the accusations, all the hit pieces—as crazy as it may sound, our ability to stand our ground against our haters may be the most important ingredient of our success. Yes, I know that sounds nuts. But the people who hate us are just a loud vocal minority. They're the same group of haters, left-wing publications, fake journalists, and woke losers crying about the same spilt milk over and over and over again. And the more they cry, the more our fans have defended us and become loyal to us. The more I fought back, the more our fans rallied around me. Every hit piece against us created an army of new fans who were not only ready to defend Barstool but eager to buy our merch, support our advertisers, and fight for everything we did. Our fans treated us like a sports team they rooted for rather than a media empire. It certainly isn't how they'd teach it in business school, I don't think—make sure your founder is a sarcastic East Coast asshole who takes everything very personally—but it worked, and every time we dragged an enemy into the mud, our power grew.

13
Pardon My Take

In 2013, long before the Chernin investment in Barstool, KFC started a podcast. It was called *KFC Radio,* and Kevin, Big Cat, and Feitelberg would just sit around and shoot the shit about ridiculous questions.

Things like "If you could only eat one food the rest of your life, what would it be?" Or "How much would somebody have to pay you to put your baby in the microwave for a minute?" Or "How many seven-year-olds would it take to beat you up?" etc. Just dumb shit.

Now, Barstool lore claims that I thought podcasting was stupid and told KFC this endeavor was a waste of time. Well, I don't know if I thought it was stupid, but I definitely thought it was a waste of time. It didn't seem like something we could monetize, so I just didn't see the point. Okay, so maybe I thought it was stupid. But one of the beauties of Barstool is that anybody can do whatever they want here. If podcasting gets your dick hard, so be it.

So off Kevin went, building truly one of the first podcasts on the internet. *KFC Radio* would go on to have a long, illustrious run at Barstool. The show recently ended after a thirteen-year run. There is no doubt that it brought legions of new fans to Barstool and was very profitable during its heyday. But maybe its most indelible mark is that it paved the way for *Pardon My Take*.

I don't think *PMT* ever comes to fruition if Big Cat wasn't inspired by being part of the early *KFC Radio* days. And I don't mean that to knock *KFC Radio* because *KFC Radio* was hugely successful in its own right; it's just that *PMT* is arguably one of the top five most important podcasts of all time.

So how did *PMT* come together? Well, once Chernin invested in us, two things happened instantly: we had more money to hire people, and we got instant credibility. The first hiring target was Eric Sollenberger (aka PFT Commenter). PFT was a satirical internet personality who basically made fun of NFL comment sections on sites like Pro Football Talk by cosplaying as these people in their most exaggerated form, hence the nickname "PFT Commenter." He wrote frequently for SB Nation and was a great writer, although his style of calculated irony and intentional typos was very different from our typical Barstool voice. In fact, when Dan introduced me to PFT, I was legit concerned that he would be too intelligent for our audience. That they wouldn't pick up on his sarcasm or be able to differentiate his intentionally sloppy style from our traditional blogs, which were unintentionally littered with typos and misspellings.

But Big Cat really wanted him. They had struck up a friendship over the years and the two of them believed they'd be the perfect combination to launch a podcast together. *Okay, Dan,* I thought, *if you want him, I'm on board. Let's hire him.*

The only problem was that PFT had a problem with me.

Now I didn't realize it at the time, but Eric Sollenberger was not a fan of Dave Portnoy or Barstool Sports; he was a fan of Dan. He wanted to work with Dan. But prior to us hiring him, I think that if Barstool and Deadspin were walking down the street and a brawl broke out, like in the movie *Anchorman*, PFT would have hit me over the head with a baseball bat.

So how did I come to realize all this? Well, it became painfully obvious the first time we met.

In February 2016, Barstool went out to San Francisco for the Super Bowl.

This was right after we finalized the Chernin deal. Mike Kerns was based in SF and held a little get-together during the week to celebrate at his house. PFT was also out there for the Super Bowl and we were in the process of trying to hire him, so we invited him to the event to meet everybody.

At some point during the cocktail party, PFT came up to me. I'm not even sure we had spoken yet, and he said the following:

"That size six skinny jean joke. Why'd you make that?"

"I thought it was funny."

"It wasn't funny enough to make it."

"I thought it was funny at the time."

"It wasn't funny enough to get away with that type of joke."

Ironically, PFT was making the same point I always make to our own employees: don't put the ball on a tee for our enemies. If you're going to make a joke on a sensitive subject, it better be hilarious or else it's not worth it. Regardless, I felt like I was back on *Inside Edition*. I was totally caught off guard by it.

I assume he remembers it, but after this book comes out, I'll have to ask him. Either way, I'm not sure what he wanted from me, but I wasn't about to suddenly reverse course and apologize to him. I walked over to Gaz and said, "How about this fucking guy grilling me about the size six skinny jean joke?" I mean we're at a fucking party, for Christ's sake. I had no idea whether PFT was going to accept the job at that point, but I really didn't care. If that was how our newest employee felt about me, I saw no reason to fight for his approval. He was Dan's hire, not mine. If he wanted to be here, great. If he didn't, great. I wasn't going to lose sleep over it either way.

Now, I don't know what type of internal mental gymnastics PFT performed to convince himself that it was morally okay to work for Barstool. But whatever it was, he eventually signed. It could have been Dan whispering in his ear that I wasn't as bad as people said I was. It could have been the fact that I no longer was the majority owner or the CEO. He could tell himself that he was coming to work for Erika Nardini or the Chernin Group, but certainly not Dave Portnoy. In any event, whatever he told himself, it worked. Despite clearly not liking me, PFT joined the Pirate Ship, and both our futures would forever be changed as a result.

A few months after our tense introduction, PFT Commenter and Big Cat launched their new podcast—*Pardon My Take*. One week after that, ESPN sent us a cease-and-desist letter, claiming the name of their podcast was a blatant ripoff of the ESPN shows *Pardon the Interruption* and *First Take*. Can you be any dumber, ESPN? Thank you for the free publicity, you morons. We threw the cease and desist into the trash and off we went.

Pardon My Take took off like a rocket ship. It was the fastest-growing piece of content we had ever put out, and it instantly changed my mind about podcasts. I guess KFC and his brother, super producer Brendan Clancy, were right about podcasting after all.

(Sidenote: Kevin's brother Brendan has worked for us for as long as Kevin has and is still on payroll. I haven't seen him in a decade. I have no clue where he lives or what he does. I've probably asked KFC about him two or three times over the decade. Like "Hey Kev, is your brother still alive?" Kevin swears that not only is he alive and well, but he works hard for us. That the whole company would grind to a halt without him. Okay, if you say so. For all I know, Kevin is just collecting two paychecks at this point. But those are the perks of being an early guy. I'm not going to dig too deep into what Brendan Clancy does anymore. He's grandfathered in for as long as I own the company, even if I count it in my mind toward KFC's salary.)

Anyway, back to *PMT*. They went to number one on the iTunes podcast charts and stayed there week after week, beating out major names like Bill Simmons and ESPN radio hosts who had leaned into podcasting as well. The show allowed Big Cat to hone and utilize one of his biggest strengths: networking. He started to reach out to the people behind major athletes to lay the groundwork to get them on as guests. His ability to play the long game was incredible, and he started to strategize on how to get major guests to come on the podcast months in advance.

For years, professional athletes had been coached on how to deliver postgame interviews: say as little as possible, defer praise to your teammates, thank God if you want, and get out as quickly as you can. To sit down at a microphone and participate in an extemporaneous conversation with two goofballs went against what these athletes had been coached to do by their teams' PR specialists. What if they were asked a personal question? What if they laughed at an inappropriate joke? Barstool was a controversial brand; would appearing on a Barstool podcast limit marketing opportunities for that athlete down the road?

Somehow, Dan and PFT threaded the needle on all these issues. They made the athletes feel comfortable and drew responses out of them that went beyond the canned responses offered in press conferences and TV interviews. Through humor, they got their guests to drop their guard a bit and show more of themselves. Before long, *Pardon My Take* became a must-do appearance for athletes wanting to promote themselves or a new book they'd written. It truly was a phenomenon.

Now, this isn't to say it was all smooth sailing with *PMT*. Far from it, in fact. Because the more successful *PMT* became, the more their relationship with Barstool (and me) began to strain. Now keep in mind, this book is written from my perspective. *PMT* has their own book coming out where they may tell this story differently, but I think we can all agree my recollection is the recollection of record for Barstool.

The bigger *PMT* got, the more uncomfortable I started getting with their success. Not because I was jealous. Despite what people say about me, my goal has always been to build megastars. If people become bigger than I am, that is good for my wallet and the company's bottom line. That was the entire point of uprooting my life and moving to NYC. Instead, I couldn't help but notice that *PMT* was creating an entirely new universe outside the Barstool world, that was eerily similar to Barstool in my eyes. It almost felt like *PMT* was competing against us.

Pardon My Take created a new name for their fans: Award-Winning Listeners, or AWLs. They built social media channels that would post viral stories before the Barstool main accounts could get to them, and they used our employees to do it. Whereas Dan and I had driven around in an RV doing interviews on a tiny couch at the Super Bowl, *PMT* now had "Vanny Woodhead," their own van from which they would also do cramped interviews. They were spinning off a new universe, and I was paying their salaries. The math did not add up. It would be one thing if we were working in lockstep with them, but we weren't. Tons of the AWLs openly professed to hate Barstool. If I had a nickel for every time I heard "I love *PMT* but hate Barstool," or their fans begging *PMT* to leave, I might be richer than I am today. And Dan and PFT didn't exactly quell those rumors. They seemed to distance themselves from Barstool every single day.

Now, you've got to remember that while *PMT*'s growth and mainstream appeal were exploding, I was at war with the No Fun Squad on a daily basis. To make matters worse, I was fighting with lots of PFT's old colleagues and friends. He had preexisting relationships with the employees of the Deadspins and the Daily Beasts of the world. So from PFT's perspective, he had a guy (me), who he didn't really like to begin with, fighting with his former friends and constantly making headlines for all the wrong reasons and seemingly jeopardizing the growth of *PMT*.

Both PFT and Dan were on the record saying they'd prefer that I just turn the other cheek when somebody picked a fight with Barstool. They didn't want me to engage, and they didn't want our fans to get into the mud and make things worse. Well, I'd rather stick a pitchfork in my eye than turn the other cheek. I'd never taken the high road and I wasn't about to start then just to appease *PMT*. When you go low, I'll go lower. Needless to say, it was two very different strategies. So while *PMT* continued to explode, I'm sure for them it seemed like for every step forward they took, it was two steps back. They'd make headlines for a great interview, and the next day they'd see headlines about toxic masculinity and how Barstool CEO Dave Portnoy told a young employee that she would be too ugly to be on camera in five years.

Yes, I told Ria—from the wildly successful franchise "Chicks in the Office"—when she was twenty years old that she would be too ugly to be on camera in five years. On live radio. And yes, she ran out of the studio in tears. Yes, it became headline news everywhere, from the *New York Times* to the *Washington Post* to Deadspin.

DEADSPIN BASEBALL FOOTBALL BASKETBALL

Barstool Sports Founder Tells Employee She'll Be Too Ugly To Be On Camera In Five Years

TOM LEY | Published: Thu 28th June, 16:02 2018

Barstool Sports Chief Tells 20-Year-Old Female Staffer She Will Look Too 'Gross' for On-Camera Work in 5 Years

"There is no apology coming for that," Dave Portnoy adds on Barstool Radio

Jon Levine June 29, 2018 @ 5:36 AM

Okay, it looks bad on the surface. But just like with everything at Barstool, there was context. At the time of this fiasco, Hank was dating Ria (Ria is now married to Marty Mush, which is a whole different saga for a different book). Anyway, Ria's sister got engaged. Hank and Ria had been dating longer than her sister's relationship. So we asked Hank if that put pressure on him to pop the question. Hank said no because they were both still so young. To which I countered that working at Barstool ages you in dog years. Hank had already been working for us for like seven years, so he was like fifty in Barstool years and already looked like a beaten dog. I continued that since Ria was also working for us, she'd also age so quickly that she'd be too ugly to be on camera in five years.

Now keep in mind, Ria is universally attractive.

She was twenty at the time. It was an absolutely preposterous statement I made. Ria heard the end of the conversation and ran into the radio room and demanded an apology live on air. I refused. She burst into tears and ran out of the room. Now, till the day I die, I will say I didn't do anything wrong. The entire tenor of the conversation was a joke. There wasn't an ounce of seriousness to it. She ran into the studio during live radio. What did she expect to happen? However, the second the radio show was over, I walked over to Ria and asked if she was okay. She had stopped crying and said she had only heard the end of the conversation. She actually apologized to me for running into the radio studio.

I didn't care. It was great content. We were a reality show. If that happened on MTV's *The Real World*, nobody would have blinked. But with us, it sparked an international incident. Reporter after reporter reached out to Ria. I told her she could say literally whatever she wanted about the situation and it wouldn't change our relationship at all. Ria defended me at every turn, but the people who hated me and Barstool didn't care. It was just another example of how bad of a guy I was for the haters to feast on. Also, I'd put Ria on the short list of people who would defend me and Barstool with her dying breath.

Back to *PMT* again. I get how frustrating this entire ecosystem must have been for them. They were sitting on a rocket ship and the only thing that could seemingly slow them down was the company and the man they worked for. But from my perspective, there was no shot *PMT* would have even achieved liftoff if it hadn't been for all the years I spent building the rocket ship in the first place. My combative personality and refusal to back down are what made headlines and got us all here. All the while, you had people whispering in *PMT*'s ear how much better they could be doing their show out from under the thumb of Barstool.

Enter Michael Klein. This guy was probably the loudest of these voices in their ear. Michael Klein was PFT Commenter's agent. As far as I know, PFT was Klein's only client. Maybe he had others but nobody of significance. Meanwhile, PFT was the first person I ever hired at Barstool who brought an agent with him to negotiate a contract. To be honest, prior to the Chernin Group, I didn't even have contracts. You worked here until you left or got fired. And I didn't fire anybody . . . so nobody left. If people wanted more money, they asked for it or I gave it to them because I knew they deserved it. If there was such a thing as the honor code for paying people, that's how I operated. But times, they were a-changing. Barstool was growing up, and contracts and dealings with agents were a natural progression of events.

Now, I obviously still had a bitter taste in my mouth from dealing with agents from the Back to Stool days. But it's not like I instantly hated Michael Klein. The original contract negotiation with PFT was easy and painless. Money was a nonfactor. He was also pretty much a nobody at that point. It wasn't like he was some huge star I had to woo; he was just a friend of Dan's. It was only after *PMT* started taking off when the problems began. Somewhere along the way, Michael Klein had talked his way into repping Big Cat as well, and he called for a sit-down with me and Erika. We met across the street from the old office at The Smith. Now, I'm paraphrasing what was said here, but it was something to the effect that Dan was violently underpaid and needed a raise ASAP. He also wanted to put PFT and Dan on the same contract term so that their contracts would expire together.

The whole thing infuriated me. I had known Dan for six or so years at that point. I'd just given him 4 percent of the company. Like me, Dan had just signed a contract with Chernin Group. Dan and I had always worked out pay fairly between ourselves. But now this dude who had been in the picture all of five seconds was telling me what Dan deserved? Umm, fuck you, buddy. I didn't deliver all those newspapers to have some four-eyed, condescending dork deliver his list of demands to me (yes, Michael Klein looks like an Ivy League dork know-it-all).

All the hate I had for agents came flooding back in a heartbeat. I was so mad that I couldn't even talk to him anymore. I just got up and walked out. Erika handled all the negotiations with Klein from that point forward, until I eventually got the company back. I couldn't even look at him without becoming irate.

We would have to deal with Michael Klein a lot during the coming years. Because like a true leech, Michael Klein proceeded to build his entire career repping Barstool talent. He went from PFT to Dan to McAfee to *Bussin' With the Boys*. I found the talent and then he'd swoop in and make life impossible for us. I've described him as a world destroyer. He doesn't give a shit about how Barstool Sports is doing as a whole. He just wants the most money he can get for his clients and if that bankrupts Barstool, so be it; he'll just move on to the next planet to destroy.

Despite my personal feelings for him, I can't deny his success. He parlayed his success with our talent to lure in lots of big clients in the digital space. The dude has never even thanked me. Without Barstool, he's probably shining shoes. Instead, he's become one of the biggest agents in the game and even started his own content company that competes directly with Barstool while actually still repping talent. That's where *Bussin' With the Boys* went, I think. It seems like the biggest conflict of interest of all time, but what do I know?

I'd say the entrance of Michael Klein into the Barstool world began a mini–Cold War between Barstool and *PMT*. There wasn't much communication between me and those guys after that. You could cut the tension with a knife. And it all came to a head during Super Bowl week 2017 in Houston.

We had booked a weeklong special on Comedy Central. The plan was to have *The Rundown* air live on their network. For us, it was a huge deal and another sign of our growth. In fact, four years prior, Dan and I had gone to Hollywood to pitch *The Rundown* to TV networks. We met with everybody—from HBO to Showtime to Comedy Central. Every meeting went the same way: Dan and I would think we had killed it, and we'd leave each meeting weighing the pros and cons of accepting each offer that surely was coming our way.

Needless to say, we didn't get one nibble. Nobody seemed to get what we were doing, or they didn't believe in us, I don't know.

We did get a funny story out of the trip though. As we were driving from one of the many meetings we thought had gone well (but hadn't), we passed a big group of crunchy, hipstery musical people tuning their instruments on the side of the road. Ever vigilant for a content moment, Dan told me to film him as he rolled down his window. "Hey hippies, get a job!" he yelled.

We later found out it was the Lumineers.

Fast-forward four years and we had successfully made it to the boob tube. The only problem was, Dan and I were barely talking at this point. It was me and Kevin vs. Dan. All Dan's time, focus, and energy were on *PMT*. It sucked that we had put in all this time and energy to get to this place, and when we finally arrived, we were borderline dysfunctional. It got so bad that I actually asked Hank if a civil war broke out between Barstool and *PMT*, which side would he fight for? At the time he said, "Barstool, of course," which I believed. I'm sure it would be a different answer now, but luckily we don't have to worry about it.

Meanwhile, the Chernin guys found themselves in the middle of it all, trying to play peacemakers. They had the guy who started the company (who was notoriously vindictive) feuding with the most valuable entity at the company. There is no doubt the Chernin guys thought throwing all their weight behind *PMT* was the right bet, but they couldn't figure out how to navigate it. I remember one phone call between me, Erika, and the Chernin guys when they were basically asking me to acquiesce to whatever requests or issues *PMT* had. I told them I was not changing anything I was doing. If they wanted Dan to lead this company into the new age, I had no problem with it; I'd go on my merry way. But I had built this company my way and I wasn't changing for anybody.

Erika then followed up and I think painted a much clearer picture to the Chernin guys of the inner workings of Barstool Sports. In no uncertain terms she told them if Dave left, she'd be gone too, and that they should not underestimate the loyalty I had within our walls. I think she was right about this. For all my shitty leadership skills, the one thing I tend to engender in my employees is fierce loyalty. They know that when the chips are down, I will have their back, and the feeling is mutual. I don't think anybody thought that *PMT* had the larger goals in mind like I did; they were just out to grow *PMT* as big as possible.

So after that conference call, I think Chernin realized they were right back to square one. They needed me, and they certainly needed *PMT*. Word of the tension bubbled all the way up to the big guy, Peter Chernin, and he flew Dan and me out to LA to try to broker peace between us. I'm not sure we really accomplished much. We both just yes'd him to death about how important the other of us was to the overall success of the company. But it didn't really settle anything.

Ironically, the only thing that could repair the rift between us would not come from within Barstool. It would come from an enemy who would unintentionally bestow the greatest gift possible to us: unity. Thank you, ESPN.

One of the things that has pissed me off about Michael Klein is that throughout my dealings with him, he has pitched his clients to other networks and actively pursues outside opportunities. Now, if you are his client, that all sounds good and dandy. But the way Barstool works is that when you sign with us, we have the right to sell all the stuff you do. So we can't have Michael Klein or any agent running around pitching deals when we have our own sales force doing that; it creates confusion in the marketplace. Not to mention that lots of clients will try to undercut us by going around our sales team and trying to pick off our talent individually. So as *PMT* continued to explode, Michael Klein was doing his best to monetize them and it seemed to me he didn't really care what rules he broke. I'm sure somewhere along the way he reached out to ESPN and said, "Hey, would you look at these guys who are all the rage in the sports industry? Let's do something."

And that's how the initial conversations around ESPN's *Barstool Van Talk* began.

Now for those unfamiliar with *Barstool Van Talk,* it was a TV version of *PMT* that was made to air on ESPN. The deal felt like it took a year or two to finalize, and the actual show lasted one episode. (Still a record, I think, for modern TV. Who has a show canceled after one episode? Only us. I'll get to that in a second.)

Now I hated this idea from the jump. It was painfully obvious what ESPN was doing: they wanted to test-drive *PMT* and see how it did. If *Barstool Van Talk* performed well, they would make a gigantic offer to our two biggest stars that Barstool wouldn't be able to match, and Dan and PFT would be off to the World Wide Leader. You didn't need to be a rocket scientist to figure this out. It was also obvious that ESPN hated me and Barstool. They were very much in the camp of "we love *PMT* but hate evil Barstool." I wasn't included in virtually any of the contract negotiations. The guy who ran point for ESPN was Burke Magnus, who would later bring over McAfee and *Bussin' With the Boys* to their network. I think I've said five words to him in my life. I've heard he's a nice guy, but he's never really spoken to me. He just tries to poach our talent. Anyway, like I said, I wasn't involved in any of the negotiations.

So I know what you're thinking: *Hey Dave, weren't you in charge of all content? Why didn't you just kill this deal instantly?* Well, great question. The answer is because I was the only one against it. I don't think Erika loved it, but Chernin certainly did. And Dan and PFT were dying to do it. I think they saw it as a huge opportunity in their careers. There was so much momentum for it I was kinda damned if I did and damned if I didn't. Like if I used my content veto power on this, I'm pretty sure I would have lost *PMT* forever. But if I let them do it and it was successful, we would also probably have lost *PMT* forever.

To this day, I'm not sure what the endgame for Chernin was. Like why were they so gung ho about it? Did they think they'd make more money from how much ESPN would pay us to own *PMT*? Because the actual licensing deal ended up being peanuts. My thought was that ESPN would just wait until PFT and Dan's contracts were up and then take them, and we'd get nothing. I still can't figure out what Chernin was thinking with this. Regardless, the only point that I held firm on was that if *PMT* was going to do a show on ESPN, it had to say Barstool in the title. This was something that nobody at ESPN wanted to do. It looked like they smelled a dead fish every time I mentioned Barstool Sports. Erika and Chernin wanted me to just let it go. I refused. Like I already thought we were getting fucked. At least lube me up a little bit. But rather than let the entire deal fall apart, the name was changed from *PMT Van Talk* to *Barstool Van Talk*, and off we went with me grinding my teeth.

Little did I know I wouldn't have to grind them long. On October 17, 2017, *Barstool Van Talk* launched on ESPN. Six days later, and before the airing of the second episode, it was canceled.

Everybody on our side found out the same way: after working on the show for nearly a year, we all found out from a press release from the president of ESPN—John Skipper. To this day, it is one of the most ridiculous statements ever made in the history of mankind. He said, "I erred in assuming we could distance our efforts from the Barstool site and its content."

Umm, you didn't realize that *Barstool Van Talk* would be associated with Barstool Sports? THE NAME OF THE SHOW HAD BARSTOOL IN IT!

Now, was John Skipper the driving force behind getting the show canceled? No, he wasn't. He was just the spineless jellyfish who didn't have the nerve to defend his decision to partner with us. Instead, the honor of executioner would go to Sam Ponder, an analyst and sideline reporter who was making a name for herself at ESPN.

The day before *Van Talk* was scheduled to air, Ponder dropped a tweet from the clouds, and it exploded like an atomic bomb.

Ponder tweeted: "Welcome to the ESPN family @barstoolbigcat (&

welcome to all ur minions who will respond to this so kindly)." Then she embedded screenshots from a blog Feitelberg and I had written about her in 2014 (three years prior to this deal). The blog was in response to a tweet Ponder had posted regarding the Ray Rice case. As you may remember, Ravens running back Ray Rice was caught on tape beating the shit out of his fiancée in a hotel elevator. It was absolutely brutal, and I was very outspoken in demanding stronger punishment against Rice. In response, Ponder tweeted this:

Blogs/websites that constantly disrespect women & objectify their bodies, then take a strong stand on the Ray Rice issue really confuse me.

9:33 PM · Jul 24, 2014

Well, this tweet really confused me. Clearly, Ponder was taking a shot at us. So I took a shot back and told her to shut the fuck up.

"So give it a rest with your righteous indignation. Your entire career and livelihood is based on appealing to guys like me and blogs like ours. Bottomline is guys thinking chicks are hot is natural. It's Darwinism. It's never going to change. But that doesn't mean we don't respect women and think it's ok to hit a woman. I have no idea what's so confusing about that. Go fuck yourself."

Then Sam Ponder responded with audio of an old podcast that Dan and I had made years earlier, when we talked about her on *College GameDay*. In this podcast, Dan and I were going through the slate of games and we started riffing on Ponder, who was the female lead on that show. She had just had a baby and the baby was now becoming part of the show; kind of like how Kirk Herbstreit has now made his dog a member of the cast.

Well, I didn't like it and said something to the effect of: "Nobody cares about your baby. We want to see you sex it up and be slutty and not be some prude."

Now, was the language rough in this? Sure it was. We were a blog that was always meant to be just a couple guys shooting the shit. But I will actually defend the point behind the language for the rest of my life. Sam Ponder is a beautiful, blond reporter who followed in the footsteps of another beautiful blond reporter, Erin Andrews. I'm not saying they weren't talented. There are lots of beautiful blondes in the world who would love that job. But to deny that their sex appeal is part of why they got the job is just denying reality. There is no shot that when ESPN hired her for the *GameDay* gig, they thought she'd be toting around her newborn on set.

Anyway, it was sort of a throwaway line that I had forgotten I'd ever said. Clearly, Sam Ponder had kept the receipts. She had been waiting years for the perfect moment to deliver a knockout punch as retribution for what I'd said about her three years prior.

To refresh the timeline here: Ponder dropped this tweet the day before *Barstool Van Talk* was scheduled to premiere. What we learned long after the fact was that there was already a rebellion underway within the walls of ESPN to make sure this show never saw the light of day. Sarah Spain, Katie Nolan, Sam Ponder, and others were all loudly complaining about this relationship, and in some cases crying that the *PMT* boys got a show before they did. The Ponder tweet was their last-gasp effort to force the hand of John Skipper in the court of public opinion.

For one week, I basically remained silent as Barstool's name was dragged through the mud yet again. I wasn't gonna start firing back and jeopardizing this relationship because that would have been the end of my relationship with *PMT*. So I just sat quietly and took enemy fire. I sat and listened as Sam Ponder said that I "wished her newborn child had been aborted," which was a flat-out lie. She was never able to produce any evidence of that ever being said.

But John Skipper just couldn't take the heat. It's my experience that people make rash decisions in the heat of battle. Everything seems worse when you are in the middle of a controversy. So he caved to the pressure and canceled *Barstool Van Talk* the day before episode two was due to air.

And with the show officially canceled, I finally took the gloves off.

Believe it or not, I was not mad at Sam Ponder for holding a grudge for three years. To this day, I respect the move. Anyone who can keep that level of a grudge close to their chest for that long, waiting patiently for the exact perfect moment to release your ammo when it will cause the most damage, is someone to whom I tip my cap. I always say I never throw the first punch in a war, but in this case, I did. Granted, I didn't realize I had as I hadn't talked about her in three years and to me, it wasn't that serious. But it's not for me to tell her how to take what I said.

Regardless, she made one critical error when dealing with me: she lied. She just blatantly made up the part where she said I wished her newborn had been aborted, and that's what I latched onto. The rest I could deal with. Sure, it's cringey reading it back and I'd phrase it differently today, but my logic is sound. But wishing her newborn was aborted? That's what people were reporting I said? I demanded she show proof of it. After all, she provided links and proof of everything else. Where was this quote from? Why didn't she have it? It's obvious: because it didn't happen.

And so I pounced. I launched a Sam Ponder Lies campaign. Everywhere she went on ESPN, "Ponder Lies" shirts started appearing. She, along with people who hate me, would call this harassment. I call it "welcome to the mud." You wanna get a show canceled and make stuff up about me? Well, ding, ding, ding. I'm sure PFT fucking hated it. I didn't care. I knew this ESPN deal was idiotic to begin with and this just proved my instincts right.

(A quick sidenote regarding this story: it was later mentioned in an article that the Wizard of Oz who pulled the strings behind the whole Ponder incident was rumored to be her superagent, Nick Khan. He was the one who dug up the screenshots of the blog and sent them over to ESPN to get the ball rolling against us. I was shocked to hear this because only a few months prior, Erika and I had met with him, and he was effusive in his praise of Barstool and how much he respected and loved us. But now I had come to find he was the guy behind the scenes who started this entire shit show? Strange way to show you like us, no?

What was even crazier is that a few months after this incident, I got an email from his secretary inviting me to sit with Nick at a boxing match at

Madison Square Garden. I emailed the lady back asking if he was serious. Like does he think I'm a moron or something? Why the fuck would I want to sit with the guy who blew up *Barstool Van Talk?* Typical slimy agents. I asked Erika if she cared if I posted the exchange because I knew she had a relationship with him. She asked me to sit on it, which I did. I kind of regret that move but hey, it wasn't my company anymore. It was the least I could do to try to calm tensions after this entire disaster.

Oh, by the way, Nick Khan is now the CEO of WWE. I wouldn't trust him as far as I can bowl him.)

What I didn't realize at the time was that this entire ESPN fiasco was the absolute best thing that could have ever happened to Barstool Sports. I've mentioned a few defining moments already thus far: the advent of the blog, Chernin, Boston sports success, hiring Erika, etc. The failure of *Barstool Van Talk* is as critical as any of them. Because what it did was realign the Barstool Universe. Dan came to the painful realization that for as much as he may have wanted to distance *PMT* from the perceived stink of Barstool, it was impossible. Every success he would ever have would be followed by critics screaming bloody murder. On top of that, as the weeks and months went by, I think both Dan and PFT came to realize that the show wasn't just canceled because Dave Portnoy was a meanie pants; there was internal politicking happening at ESPN that had nothing to do with morality issues. Jealousy, backstabbing, and egos were also very much in play. Maybe the devil you know is better than the one you don't.

From that point on Dan and I were back on the same team. It was Barstool vs. the World again. I knew we were fully healed when, not long after the show was canceled, John Skipper left ESPN because he was being extorted by his coke dealer. Seriously—he said he met a random coke dealer from whom he bought coke once, and now this coke dealer was extorting him. This was like weeks after he canceled the show. I'm crying laughing even writing this sentence. Like seriously how lucky am I? The engraving wasn't even fresh on his champagne bottle and he had to quit ESPN because of a coke problem. I popped open the bottle during *The Rundown* and toasted my vanquished foe as Dan laughed, and we clinked glasses and took a few sips together. I growled, "You don't cancel me. I cancel you!"

The Pirate Ship was back.

Funnily enough, about six years after this all went down, I was on a date in NYC at a popular restaurant in the Meatpacking District called Catch. As I was leaving, a blond woman wearing a hat at the bar came straight up to me.

"You don't recognize me, do you?"

I actually didn't. I assumed it was a girl I had hooked up with in the past. But nope, not even close—it was Sam Ponder. And boy, was she ready to read me the fucking riot act. Over the next hour, we went jaw to jaw, reliving and rehashing the entire saga. I'm pretty sure she was there for some professional business dinner because Colt McCoy was there too, nervously checking in on us every so often, not sure if he should deescalate the situation. But each time he tried, Sam shooed him off. It seemed like she'd been waiting for this moment, and she didn't want to leave out a single word of what she had always wanted to tell me.

For my part, the girl I was on a date with left and went home without me. I don't blame her because we were going at it for an hour. She was relieved when I told her it wasn't an ex; just some old ESPN reporter I told to start slutting it up on camera that led to *Barstool Van Talk* being canceled that led to World War III . . .

Anyway, our talk was like two heavyweight prizefighters, both with iron chins, swinging from their hips in a phone booth bout with no round limits. Enough time had passed that both of us had slightly inaccurate memories of every tweet and word that was said, so we spent a lot of the argument defending misquoted words whose meanings had been twisted through the years. But somehow, in the end, we squashed it. We're not enemies anymore. At least not from my perspective we're not.

That encounter made me respect the hell out of Sam Ponder, even if I didn't agree with a lot of what happened. It takes a ton of courage to come up to me in public like she did and have a face-to-face conversation. Most people would let others fight that battle for them or hide behind a keyboard and slug it out on Twitter. Not Ponder. She gained my full respect that day by ambushing me at the bar. That's something I could see myself doing, and I can't say that about too many other people on earth.

(Quick funny story: the Sam Ponder controversy pales in comparison to the headaches that the *Pick Em Podcast* would cause down the road for Dan and me. Not only did the *Pick Em Podcast* get *Barstool Van Talk* canceled, it would also introduce us to one of the most infamous and nefarious characters in the history of Barstool Sports. A man whose reign of terror has lasted nearly four presidencies. I'm talking about Rico Bosco.

For those who don't know who Rico Bosco is, he was a frequent caller to the early *Barstool Pick Em* show. He would always fly off the handle at the blink of an eye and he truly was the best part of the show. He was an absolute electric factory of madness and mayhem. We thought it was an act. It was not. He would eventually elevate his role from caller into part-time contributor, then to full-time host on the *Pick Em* show. And now he is a full-time employee at Barstool Sports.

Now, when I say Barstool Sports attracts weird brains, Rico does not have a weird brain. His brain is a *demented* brain. By all accounts, he is a truly awful human. A bad guy. A literal terrorist. Ayatollah Boscolla has launched more terrorist attacks than Iran over the years. He has forced multiple employees to quit or resign due to his nonstop attacks. He threw a full High Noon can as hard as he could at another employee from close range that barely missed his face, all because that employee called Rico by his government name: Terrence Mayrose. He commands a lunatic army of Twitter trolls who he sends to attack his enemies and their family members for perceived slights against him, such as not saying hello for long enough in public. Like I said he is just the absolute worst guy on the planet.

Unfortunately, he is also Dan's and my Kryptonite because we both love him. He's one of the few people who consistently can make me laugh out loud with his insane mental breakdowns. He may be a psychopath but he is our psychopath. He should have been fired at least twenty times, but I guess if you can consistently make me laugh, you have a job for life at Barstool. It's not right, it's not fair, but I never said I wasn't a flawed individual.

Now, before you judge me too hard, just know we have made Rico go to anger management therapy in the past. And he is on meds now. I also once told him that as a friend, I didn't think he should work at Barstool anymore because it was bad for his mental health. But the problem with a sedated Bosco is that he is very boring. Like would Picasso or any great artist have been as productive if they were on sedatives? Probably not. True madness, like Bosco's, needs to flourish in the wild until it combusts. And when it finally does, I'll have nobody to blame but myself for keeping him employed.)

One last thing on *PMT*: if this was the only chapter you read in this book, you'd probably walk away and be like man, Dave hates PFT and PFT hates Dave. And maybe we were close to hating each other during this saga. And I'm sure it was a hard transition for him coming to Barstool from a world where lots of his former colleagues turned their noses up at us. Yes, our politics and personalities don't always align. When he first got here I definitely think he looked at me as a necessary evil he had to deal with. And I definitely looked at him as a bit ungrateful for the platform we provided. He had sixty thousand followers and made less than $100K before he arrived at our doors. However, over the course of the decade that he has been with us, I've grown not only to appreciate him but truly to like him and trust him. We'll never be best friends, but I'm not best friends with anybody at our company. I think he's come to see that I'm not the guy so many of my haters portray me to be, and he knows Barstool certainly isn't the cesspool people make it out to be. You don't have to agree with everything everybody says all the time. And I know he appreciates that at Barstool, people can voice their opinions about virtually anything so long as they're not trashing advertisers. There is no doubt that PFT has been critical to the growth and success of Barstool Sports. We are not where we are without him and despite all my complaining about his agent, PFT has wanted to stay here the entire time, even when he could have easily left for more money. My currency is loyalty and he's earned it from me

100 percent. Not only that; I think I've earned it from him. I honestly believe if PFT was with a group of people—including even his brother, who openly hates me—and they were bashing me, he would defend me even if I was never going to find out about it. That's about as much respect as I can have for a person and I truly believe he feels the same way.

14

Grudgement Day

If you are a Barstool Sports fan and somebody mentions Grudgement Day, you know exactly where you were when it happened. It's a day that is as much a part of Barstool lore as, say, the JFK assassination or the moon landing is to American history.

We'll once again jump back to 2016. I was thirty-nine years old, single for the first time in about a decade, and I had money in my pocket for the first time maybe ever. I was also starting to become F-list famous. Granted, it was the very bottom rung of fame, but it was still something. I was trying to balance running Barstool Sports as well as being single and ready to mingle in the biggest city in the world. It honestly wasn't the worst situation to be in.

To keep up with the demands of my life, I started taking Adderall basically every day. I'm talking thirty milligrams or whatever they measure Adderall in. Like the more wired I was, the better I felt. Now, contrary to popular belief, I'm not a coke guy. People love to say I did coke all the time but that's a lie. Later, when I moved to Miami, ecstasy would become my drug of choice; never coke. I've never been a huge drinker either. During the Blackout era, I'd go to the parties, show face, hype up the crowd a bit, and then leave through a back entrance as fast as I could.

Anyway, to wake up early to run the company, I took Adderall. To stay up late to go out, I took Adderall. My day became an Adderall sandwich, which made it a lot easier to turn down actual sandwiches. Adderall is an appetite suppressant, and I went from eating my Panera chicken caesar salads and an entire baguette for lunch to just a few bites of pizza and roughly a hundred gallons of coffee. I literally had people at the office who would replace my coffee the second it became less than half-full.

The other major lifestyle change was that unlike in Boston, where I drove to work, I now walked everywhere. Our office was a forty-minute walk from my apartment, which I did twice a day. I even started a video series called "Dave Walks to Work" where I'd livestream myself just walking through the streets of NYC, remarking on the assorted smells of homeless encampments and saying hi to dogs that seemed friendly. It actually became a pretty popular series. I guess you could say I was a forerunner of all these livestreamers and vloggers who document every second of their lives now.

Granted, the only reason I did it was to prove how useless one of my employees was. Nate had started a poker podcast and it was awful. He refused to accept the fact that he sucks at making content and nobody likes him. So out of spite, I told him that a content series of just me walking to work would draw bigger numbers than his poker podcast. I was obviously right and ended up creating an entire series around my morning commute. You can probably see how another title I considered for this book was *Barstool Sports: The House That Spite Built.*

As my diet and lifestyle changed, so did my body and my wardrobe. The weight poured off me, and the Fat Dave Era came to a close.

I threw out my shitty sneakers and bought a couple pairs of white Common Projects (aka fancy sneakers). My jeans became skinny to the point that I would skin my knuckles pulling my phone out of my pocket. My entire wardrobe was overhauled: out went the purple starfish lacrosse pinnies, replaced by gray hoodies layered beneath black bomber jackets or peacoats in the winter. Lots of people look back on certain eras and think, *How the fuck did I ever dress like that?* Well, not me. I loved my skinny jeans. I thought I looked fucking great. I will die on my skinny jeans sword. They looked good on me. You know what they say . . . if you can rock size six skinny jeans, more power to you. No pun intended, but intended.

Photo by Tom Briglia

For the most part, I kept my new dating life private. I knew this girl named Jordyn Hamilton from back in Boston. She had been a Smokeshow of the Day, and we reconnected in New York. "JHammy" was young, hot, and enchanted by the thought of living rent free in NYC. And I was enchanted by her.

She basically didn't have a job, or a home. I had an apartment that was too big for me and more than enough money to share. It was a match made in heaven. It didn't take long before she had effectively moved in.

I gave her a credit card for her essentials. I'd go off to work in the morning and she'd go about her day. I didn't have much of an idea of what she did, honestly. I knew she was obsessed with SoulCycle—the stationary bike fitness class that was all the rage back then. Jordyn often went to two classes a day. It was nuts, but we all have different ways of staying trim, I guess. I prefer the "don't eat or sleep much thanks to pharmaceutical speed" approach.

I liked her a lot. She was the first girl post-marriage I was totally and completely obsessed with. I sound stupid even writing that sentence because it was pretty evident to anybody with a brain that she was just into the lifestyle I was providing. I was lost in the sauce, dazed by my new world, swept up in the attention and adoration of a twenty-three-year-old. I started making some pretty dumb decisions. At the office, we were doing "Electric Chair" viewings of major sports games, where we'd put a camera on ourselves and stream as we watched playoff games live. After a long day of bopping around the city with JHammy, I brought her into the office to watch a playoff game. Live, on camera, in front of our entire audience. Oh, and I should mention that this was the first time they learned that I was no longer with Renee.

This was probably one of the top three dumbest things I've done in the history of Barstool, and I can't think of the other two. I guess I should throw a bone to *PMT* as well. This is when I was fully at war with them, and I'm sure they looked at this like I'd lost my mind. Like this is who we need to be loyal to? Dude has fucking lost it. Michael Klein probably had this footage playing on loop for them.

Look, JHammy and I were a little drunk. As I said, I wasn't the most reasonable person during this period of my life. People had started calling me "Club Dave." My judgment was severely impaired by lust. I like to think I was smarter than that, but I wasn't. I'm human. Cut me and I bleed blood. I was infatuated with JHammy.

The Stoolies were up in arms. They absolutely hated JHammy off the rip, hated that I brought her on the stream, and hated that Renee was no longer First Lady. I had to write a blog the next day to do damage control, where I explained that we'd been broken up for a while and I'd met someone new. Normal adult stuff; life happens, grow up, deal with it. I called

JHammy a "cool-ass chick." She had that in her bio on Instagram for a long time.

What I love most about Stoolies—their loyalty and stickiness—can also be the hardest thing to deal with at times. They can be obsessed with the private lives of Barstool personalities, starting with me at the top of the list. And they have every right to pry and want answers and me to be an open book. That's the world I created. That's the world I have profited from. You can't just take your ball and go home when you don't like it. There are no real boundaries for them to respect, so why wouldn't they dig for any and every tasty rumor about my private life? I get it, and I accept it.

Yes, the Stoolies hated JHammy. Whatever. I didn't care what they thought. I was a consenting adult dating another consenting adult who just happened to burn five thousand calories per day on a stationary bicycle. Sure, her daily exercise budget rivaled the per diem afforded most professional athletes during road swings, but if that's what she felt she needed to keep herself in top form, who was I to complain? Plus, she had an undeniably great ass as a result, and it's a well-known fact I'm an ass man. A hundred bucks a day was no skin off my back.

I took JHammy to the Super Bowl in Atlanta. This was the same Super Bowl at which I was feuding with *PMT* during the week of the Comedy Central *Rundown* special. I'm sure they could argue that part of the reason they were trying to forge their own path was because their leader was seemingly distracted chasing JHammy around. But I wouldn't be the first man to be undone by a pretty woman.

(As a sidenote, the Houston Super Bowl was also the first Super Bowl where we threw a Barstool party. We thought all the traditional Super Bowl parties like the legendary *Maxim* party had become dated and corporate. A few years prior, I had paid $20K for a table at the *Maxim* party. I had to put it on my credit card and pay it off over time. I thought I was gonna be a big-swinging dick at this party. It was the most I had ever paid for anything. It was more than Renee's wedding ring. Well, when we walked in, the hostess actually seated us in a satellite room. Meaning the DJ and the party were going on in one room and we had a table in a different room where we could watch the party on closed-circuit TV. I was so mad I made the VIP host cry. They tried to claim that they told me I wouldn't be in the main room when I bought the table. There was just no way that was true. I would never have paid $20,000 to sit in a closet and watch the real party on TVs like I was at some old offtrack site, betting on horses.)

Photo by John Parra

Anyway, just a few short years later we were hosting our own Super Bowl party and it was undeniably the party of the year. It was the hottest ticket in town. You couldn't buy your way into it. It was an open bar for the entire event. We bussed in all our local smokeshows from all the local colleges. This was the Ja Rule–Ashanti party in 2017 that would come back to bite me on the ass five years later thanks to a lyric I apparently wasn't supposed to rap.

Whereas all the other Super Bowl parties were corporate, ours was like a giant house party. Except it was a house party filled with superstar athletes and celebrities. Bald Paul, my sales guy turned head of social media, was working the door, chewing his gum loudly, telling people like Cowboys running back Ezekiel Elliott that we were at max capacity. And we were. We had owners of NFL teams getting shut out at the door.

After the party was over, our crew plus a few friends of Barstool moved back to our Airbnb that we rented for the week. Now, there's a phrase that became popular a few years ago that people would say to describe something that was awesome. People would say, "Last night was a movie." Personally, I never liked the phrase and the *Bussin'* guys drove it into the ground, but there is an outside shot that our afterparty to our Super Bowl party is where this saying started. It was like *Project X* meets *The Hangover.*

Friend of the program (and NFL quarterback) Blake Bortles actually watched JHammy give me a blowjob. I thought the shades were shut on our bedroom but they were see-through. After we finished hooking up, I walked into the kitchen and he goes, "Just saw you getting head . . . nice." Another quarterback, Jared Goff, almost burned down the house by cooking Totino's Pizza Rolls (they were a big sponsor of ours at the time) and forgetting to take them out of the toaster oven. A mini-fire broke out in the kitchen. While all this was going on, Loud Sean (our production manager at the time) was trying to put coke into his eyes and had to be fished out of the pool by PFT Commenter so he didn't drown. Loud Sean would then spend the rest of the night challenging people to $10,000 one-on-one basketball games even though he was too blacked out to even stand.

I guess I should mention who Loud Sean is or was. He was one of those shooting stars who streaked across the Barstool galaxy, shining so brightly until he faded out of our universe. As I've already mentioned many times in this book, I think that's been part of the charm of Barstool over the decades—we've always had that unique ability to attract weird brains. I interviewed Loud Sean in a small coffee shop in NYC right when I moved to the city. It was before we had an office, so I had nowhere to meet people. The coffee shop was packed and in strolled Loud Sean. Even though we were sitting like two inches from each other, he was talking so loudly you would have thought we were in the middle of a club with techno music blasting. It was stunning. It took five minutes before another customer in the coffee shop walked over and politely asked Sean if he could speak a little more quietly. Sean quickly apologized and said of course. But his quieter voice lasted seven seconds. The man just couldn't talk without screaming. He cleared out the entire coffee shop within fifteen minutes. An entirely new group of customers eventually came in before they, too, quickly cleared out from his booming voice. It was insane. I knew I had to have him.

The name Loud Sean stuck. And while this chapter is about Grudgement Day, many could argue Loud Sean was responsible for the most famous day in Barstool Radio history. Loud Sean was not just a loud talker; he was a belligerent drunk too. He didn't get tipsy. He got blackout, out-on-your-feet, white girl wasted. To the point I eventually gave him a two-year suspension from drinking at Barstool events. But before that, he got into a verbal fight with a coworker at a karaoke bar one night. Apparently, things got really nasty when discussing basketball. Loud Sean told another employee (who won't be named) that in a game to 21, he would back him down in the paint seventeen times and shoot four jumpers in his face and beat him 21–4. To which the other employee responded that Loud Sean was a bad father and a drunk, and he was going to steal Loud Sean's wife. They retold this story on Barstool Radio the next day and there wasn't an ounce of humor in it. Like they told this story with a stone-cold face and it was clear they despised each other. You could cut the tension with a knife in the studio.

Well, naturally we had to set up this basketball grudge match at a local park and livestream it. It was the most physical, ugly, awesome basketball game I've ever witnessed. Loud Sean gassed himself in warm-ups and could barely stand by the end of the game. The winner (an employee whose name we shall not mention) then celebrated by hoisting a picture of Loud Sean's wife and parading it around the court. And that, my friends, is the Barstool Difference. I'd argue it was the second-biggest day ever on Barstool Radio.

Of course, the biggest Barstool Radio day ever was Grudgement Day.

As I continued to date JHammy, I couldn't help but notice her Uber charges piling up on my credit card. That didn't make any sense, because the SoulCycle studio was three blocks from my apartment.

One day, I waited for her to come back from class for a couple hours. When she finally came home, I asked her where she'd been. She casually mentioned that her instructor had brought her into the back, to the employee area, to hang out for a bit.

Huh? Must be that VIP treatment you get when you pay for two classes a day.

You know that queasy feeling you get in the pit of your stomach when your twenty-three-year-old girlfriend is cheating on you with her SoulCycle instructor, and you've been funding the entire sweaty affair for weeks?

I didn't have that feeling. Because I liked her. And I only saw what I wanted to see. But at some point, where there's smoke (and firetrucks, billowing flames, and people screaming that their grandfather is still inside), there's fire.

I finally confronted her about all the troubling signs one day, and she immediately came clean. By that point, she liked the other guy anyway and didn't want me anymore, so she admitted that she'd been sleeping with him for a while now. I was bummed, angry, and humiliated. And like any person going through a healthy breakup, I went on Twitter to announce that I would be going scorched-earth the next day on our Sirius XM show:

"Remember when I wrote the blog defending @jhammmmmy when nobody else would. I take it all back. Tune in to @barstoolradio tomorrow."

I then promised that Grudge Dave was back.

Consider me the Don King of promoting internet fights.

When I walked into the office the next day, every single employee at Barstool was pulling out their popcorn. You could almost smell the excitement in the air. Sitting down for the radio show at noon, I didn't know exactly what I wanted to say. But I knew I wasn't going to hold anything back.

We went live at noon and I told the whole story to tens of thousands of listeners: from the early warning signs to Jordyn's eventual admission and all the sultry details of their affair. I told the world I'd been cucked by a SoulCycle instructor. By 12:30, #CuckCycle was trending. By 1 p.m., I had "CuckCycle" T-shirts on sale.

By 1:30, SoulCycle had disabled comments on their social media channels. *Does every SoulCycle class come with getting to fuck your instructor?* It was all stuff to that effect. They sent mass texts to all their studio managers advising them to be on guard for any Stoolies who might come in to ask about the scandal, and to call 911 if they "don't know how to handle the situation."

Of course, as soon as I saw that, I quote-tweeted the text warning with my own thoughts:

"Best way to avoid calling 911? Don't have your instructors fuck the girlfriend of [the head of a] major media company. #DailySoul @soulcycle."

This, folks, is guerrilla warfare. This is how you fight on the internet. I turned a *Hindenburg*-level detonation of my relationship into a trending story and an all-time moment in Barstool history. And we made money off it through merch sales.

March 10, 2017, would forever be known as Grudgement Day. Stoolies who had expressed their disgust with me for becoming rich, for "selling out," for splitting up with Renee—anyone who felt that I had traded away my principles for fast cash and hot girls—flooded back to my camp in droves, reaffirming their loyalty because Dave clearly had his fastball back.

I didn't care about that. I've never really cared about whether the audience loves me or hates me. I don't play to their desires or try to stay in favor. Because I've done this long enough to know that some days they'll love you and some days they'll hate you. But they'll always come back.

When we moved to New York, my vision was a 24/7 reality show. The good, the bad, the ugly—we'd lay it all bare for the world to see. There were times when I had to swallow shit for the sake of the company, particularly in regard to the *Pardon My Take* tension. My calculus for determining what should be kept hidden from the public came down to a few things: Will revealing this hurt the company? If I put it out there, will I lose that person forever? But when it came to my life, I was willing to share anything and everything. And as embarrassing as it may have been, that policy included sharing the sordid details of being cucked by a nipple-pierced SoulCycle instructor.

Great leaders lead from the front.

One question I get asked a ton is if I have any regrets with Barstool, or if I would have done anything differently. I always answer the same way: I feel like Barstool is a one-in-a-billion story. Like everything had to break the exact right way for us to get where we did. So how could I ever have any regrets or want to do anything differently?

Grudgement Day, though, is one situation I do wish I handled differently. I wish I hadn't gone bananas on JHammy. It was pretty obvious she didn't like me the way I liked her the entire time. I was a moron. Renee was like, "What the fuck are you doing?" Even my parents called me after it was over and asked if my brain was okay. I acted like JHammy killed somebody when all she did was cheat on a boyfriend who should have seen it coming a mile away. She definitely didn't deserve the hate she got, but that's my personality. I will burn a million bridges and sink my own ship just to make sure you sink with me. We have talked since then and are cordial and both can kind of laugh about the situation. And no, I'm not above reminding her of a quote I said during Grudgement Day: "JHammy is going to look back at this and rue the day she picked a guy riding a bicycle over a guy building a 100-million-dollar empire."

The only thing I got wrong was how much I underestimated how vast my empire would become.

15
Building Superstars

By now, you're all familiar with the intergalactic talent of Pat McAfee. The ESPN titan has built himself into the most multifaceted asset maybe in all sports media. From ringside announcing in the WWE to *College GameDay* to his daily three-hour show, the man is relentless and seemingly everywhere.

But it wasn't too long ago that I was hiring him for peanuts because nobody else would take a shot on him.

I first met Pat in 2016 in San Francisco when Big Cat and I were doing interviews in our RV for Super Bowl week—an RV so old it actually couldn't drive up hills. If you're at all familiar with the streets of San Francisco, you know that's a major problem. The entire city is basically built on a hillside. So we'd have meetings or interviews that were ten minutes away but it would take Bald Paul two hours to get there because we had to navigate a path that avoided anything larger than a moderate incline.

Anyway, Pat was a guest on the RV. I can't remember how that booking originated. I'm pretty sure he was a fan of Barstool and wanted to meet us. For our part, we would take any interview we could get with a pro athlete. We hit it off with him immediately, and right from the jump it was clear that his personality would fit right in with us. I think he felt the same way because he was asking lots of questions about Barstool and hinting that he might retire from the NFL soon and wanted to get into media. I told him we'd certainly be interested in hiring him if he actually made the jump, but it seemed like a long shot at the time because he was still making millions to punt a football.

Well, I was wrong. In 2017, Pat decided to retire from the Indianapolis Colts. Following his third knee surgery in four years, he was ready to trade in his cleats for a microphone. Now, I'm pretty sure Pat tested the waters with a few traditional media entities like ESPN and didn't get much interest from them. But I was very interested.

We worked out a deal and announced Pat's signing with Barstool during the Super Bowl week in February 2017. We had longtime friend of the program and NFL insider Ian Rapoport as part of a skit where we held an NFL-style press conference announcing the move. It was probably the biggest announcement of a talent acquisition ever for us, even though I was able to sign him for relatively modest terms.

The move made a lot of sense to me: Pat had a following in Indiana and the Midwest, and he had proven himself to be funny both on camera and on social media. He also performed stand-up comedy to enormous crowds here and there. I'm not a stand-up guy, as it goes against everything I know and am—speaking off the cuff, honestly, no polish, no rehearsals. But I could still appreciate Pat's ability to captivate a crowd and tell stories about his time with the Colts.

The first thing we did when we hired Pat was try to build a universe around him, much like what we had going on in New York. He wanted a cast of characters he could interplay and work with in Indianapolis. So we held an open casting call for him, and a ton of Stoolies—whose dream it was to work for Barstool—showed up, and he picked the people he liked. They were all put on our payroll, and slowly "Barstool Heartland" was built.

In the beginning, it was all hunky-dory; all gumdrops and rainbows. Pat fit like a glove and his star began to rise. *The Pat McAfee Show* was born. He and I were both on the first iteration of *Barstool College Football Show*—a live show we produced ourselves at Barstool on Saturdays before big college football games. It's kind of funny to look back on it now. Pat currently stars on ESPN's *College GameDay*, their premiere college football Saturday show; and I'm over on Fox's *Big Noon Kickoff*. It was hard to predict we'd both end up on major networks, being paid insane money, competing against each other a decade down the road. It's a long way from an early Iowa show we did with no sound. Yeah, that's right—we did an entire game day show where nobody could hear a word we said. I remember walking offstage thinking we had absolutely killed it. Then I opened my phone and tweets were pouring in about how it was like a Charlie Chaplin silent movie. The Barstool Difference . . . Good Ol' All Business Pete (our head of live programming and technical stuff) had done it again.

It was also during this season that I taught Pat how to gamble. He had never placed a bet in his life prior to coming to Barstool. Me, on the other hand? I was a degenerate. I had action on almost every game every weekend. Well, one Saturday, Pat started asking me about it. He wanted in on the action and just told me to double every bet I had. I was like, "Are you sure, man?" He was adamant. "Okay, if you say so." So I doubled my bets from $5K a game to $10K a game with Pat splitting it. The only problem? Pat thought I was betting like $100 a game, not $5K. This is something I clearly should have clarified before placing the bets. Now, the games hadn't started yet, so I had the chance to cancel them if I wanted to. But anybody who has ever gambled knows the dilemma I was faced with. If I canceled them, I was positive I'd go undefeated and cost myself a ton of money. Nope—I'm a firm believer that once you place a bet, you have to just let it ride, and that's exactly what I did.

Needless to say . . . I got absolutely smoked. It wasn't my best gambling day, but for Pat, it was a game-changer. He started to learn how to gamble, how to talk like a gambler, how to appeal to gamblers. This skill would be something that would bring him a fortune in the future with FanDuel.

(Sidenote: the *Barstool College Football Show* was also where I introduced him to A.J. Hawk, who joined us at Ohio State for one of our tour stops. A.J. is now a mainstay on his ESPN show. The influence of Barstool is undeniable.)

Now, Pat's deal with us was not a traditional Barstool deal, in the sense that we didn't just pay him a flat salary and that was it. Instead, we were more like partners. We agreed not only to pay him a salary but also to finance his Indiana operation. We paid all his expenses and then we would split all the ad sales once we broke even. Our sales structure was such that our sales team could sell ads to any of our shows, but of course they'd receive the largest commissions when selling ads for our biggest show (*Pardon My Take*).

When a deal for Pat's show fell through (because the advertiser switched their buy to *Pardon My Take* last minute), Pat was upset. He thought we were fucking him over, intentionally pushing advertisers to our show because Pat would get 50 percent of the revenue sold for his show (and thus we'd get 50 percent less than an ad for *PMT*). This wasn't exactly true: our sales team received the same commission regardless of whether they sold ads for *PMT*, *Chiclets*, or *The Pat McAfee Show*. They didn't give a fuck. But it was simply easier to sell *PMT* because it was tried and proven. Pat's show was new, and advertisers like what they know works. But when that ad went from Pat to *PMT*, he was pissed off and lost trust in our entire sales operation for him.

Pat wasn't exactly low-maintenance when it came to dealing with him on the business side. I had constant complaints from our salespeople that he was impossible to work with, and Pat would complain that our business side was equally impossible to work with. I remember we had our sales upfronts one year (basically an event where you try to wine and dine all future advertisers and pitch them on all the content you have coming up for the next year. You try to close as much business as you can there.) Well, we had a hype video featuring all our talent, and whoever made the reel forgot to include Pat in it. Pat went ballistic. He stormed off and left the upfront. I totally understood his point of view, but at the same time it was an honest mistake made by a low-level editor employee. It made absolutely no sense for us not to include one of our rising stars in this video. But these types of mistakes would fester like an open wound for him, and he began to see them as a sign of disrespect. Now, whenever I spoke to Pat directly, we were always able to hash things out pretty efficiently and quickly. We just cut out all the bullshit and figured things out. But as time wore on, we weren't always able to talk directly and clear the air.

I should mention he wasn't the only one during these years who was complaining about the lack of transparency with our sales force. I remember getting on the phone with Biz (Paul Bissonnette, former NHL enforcer and one host of our hockey podcast, *Spittin' Chiclets*) one time and just screaming at him about some ad deal and every other word was "fuck." At the end of the call Biz was like, "That's how I need to have conversations. Talk to me like I'm in a hockey locker room. I can take bad news. Just give it to me straight." I think that's a valuable lesson for anybody in life and has actually been one of the keys to Barstool's success. I am brutally direct and straightforward with people. I don't sugarcoat things or promise things I can't deliver. Some may call it blunt. But people know where they stand at all times with me and I think they appreciate that. I also come from a shitty sales background, so I know how hard the sales team's job is. I think sometimes the ex-athletes just don't initially understand the concept of a sales cycle or why things that seem obvious and simple aren't always obvious and simple.

Anyway, back to Pat and his developing mistrust of our sales and business organization. I knew I had to do something so that these issues wouldn't keep coming up. Enter my old pal Lightswitch Lou. I'm pretty sure I already mentioned Louis earlier in the book, but I've been writing this thing for so long I'm beginning to forget what I wrote in the early chapters. For years, Lightswitch Lou was our only sales guy. We called him that due to his tendency to explode at the flip of a switch. Louis had been with me since Milton, and I considered him a close friend. Like we hung out away from work all the time. He's also a complete psychopath and someone you can yell at, swear at, call names, and he'll give it right back. In short, Louis was someone I let into my inner circle because I felt sure he'd never fuck me or get sensitive.

As the complaints from Pat continued to escalate, I assigned Louis to him directly. I sort of thought of Louis as an extension of myself. For all Louis's faults, he just got shit done. He also knew our company inside and out. The mandate was simple: keep Pat fucking happy at all costs. This was the beginning of the end of the Pat McAfee era at Barstool.

Here is the thing you gotta know about Lightswitch Lou: if Louis made a hundred bucks, he wanted to make a thousand. If he made a thousand, he wanted to make a million. If he made a million, he wanted to make a billion. He was just never satisfied. I guess it's not the worst trait to have as a salesperson, but it also can be toxic, and in this case it was.

Now, for the majority of Louis's career at Barstool he was never more than a stone's throw from where I sat. His was the closest desk to mine in the old Milton office. We'd yell and scream at each other. He'd come up with cockamamie ideas that he'd pitch to me. He literally signed contracts under my name without telling me. I mean, that would be a big problem for most bosses, but Louis was grandfathered in as an early employee, so I gave him a lot more rope than others would get. And for all the liberties he took, I could always reel him back whenever he went too far.

But when we moved to NYC, Louis's desk was a little farther away, but he was still close to my office. We also hired a head of sales and other salespeople. Louis never played nice with any of them. He'd come into my office ranting and raving about how everybody sucked and was out to get him. I kind of thought it was funny, to be honest. Louis always entertained me. We'd yell and scream and hash it out like always. All the while, Barstool Sports kept growing and getting bigger. We went from the entire company being on one floor to expanding to a second floor. It was content on the third floor and businesspeople on the second. And that's where it all went haywire.

Louis is a crazy person with a crazy brain and crazy ideas. Once he left my sight and went down to the second floor, I could no longer reel him in. He became a rogue agent. Not only that, but a hostile rogue agent. He hated Erika Nardini. Absolutely despised her. He didn't trust her at all. I didn't realize how much he hated her at the time and I'm still not exactly sure what his problem with her was. I think it was just that she was trying to implement some rules and procedures in our growing company and Louis wanted to go back to the old Barstool days of the Wild Wild West.

The chaos started with a drink called Anyday Rosé. While Louis was supposed to be selling Barstool ads and managing McAfee, he was secretly launching a sparkling, canned rosé cider company.

Maybe "secretly" isn't exactly fair. Louis did come to Erika and me, asking if we wanted to start this company together. We looked at all the financials and everything around it and decided it wasn't something we wanted to be involved in. Well, if we weren't going to do it, Louis was still convinced this was a billion-dollar idea and wanted to do it himself. I sat him down and told him I was fine with him starting a company but he had to do it on his own time, away from Barstool, without utilizing our resources or anything to do with us. And to be abundantly clear, I added that if he was so confident in Anyday Rosé, he should quit his sales job and focus all his energy on the drink; if it didn't work out, he always had a job with me, no questions asked. Like if anybody understood the urge to try your own thing, it was me.

As far as I understood, that put it to bed, because Louis said he'd shut it down.

He didn't; he just moved it underground. Or more accurately, to the second floor.

The fact that he kept it secret clearly showed that he knew he wasn't supposed to do it. Barstool is a content company, not a startup incubator. But Louis quietly offered investment opportunities to people close to him who he knew wouldn't report it back to me. It actually seemed the only four people who had no clue this was happening were me, Gaz (one of his best friends and his *roommate*), Big Cat, and Erika—all people who would have shut it down immediately.

Anyday Rosé launched one morning out of the blue. I was actually at the Belmont Stakes the morning it launched when I got a call from Chernin's lieutenant Mike Kerns asking about the rosé company we had started. It was news to me. Nothing like being called by your investor to be asked about a liquor company that was started under your nose against your express orders. The thing was everywhere. There was a press release about it. Lots of our employees were tweeting about it. Pat McAfee was tweeting about it. Instantly I called Pat. He claimed to have no knowledge that I wasn't on board with Anyday Rosé; he couldn't believe I didn't know about it. I told him he either had to quit Barstool or give up the beverage brand. He said his hands were tied because he already had invested significant money into it.

I was furious. Not at Pat but at Louis. I called Louis and went ballistic on him. What the fuck was he doing? He had to either stop Anyday Rosé or he was fired. Well, he said he was in too deep with the drink, so he quit/was fired from Barstool. Louis apologized and promised never to take another job in media doing something similar to what he had done with us. But that turned out to be a blatant lie.

Meanwhile, Pat and I reached an agreement that he just wouldn't promote the drink anymore. But it was already too late to salvage the relationship. It was doomed the second I assigned Louis to Pat. Rather than smoothing over our relationship with Pat and putting Pat's concerns at bay, Louis confirmed and amplified them. Louis planted the idea in Pat's mind that our sales team was intentionally screwing him out of ads, and probably suggested it was intentional and supported by Erika. He was a poison pill. By the time the whole rosé fiasco happened, it was only a matter of time till Pat would leave for good.

A few months down the road, there would be another minor business issue that Pat took umbrage with. It was so minor to me that I don't even remember it exactly. I think a commission check was a few weeks late. He told me he was quitting and he had lost total trust in the business side of our company. I tried to talk him out of it but his mind was made up. He was going to make a go at the media business alone.

Except it wasn't quite alone at all. I'd find out later that Old Lightswitch Lou would be his right-hand man, bringing over a decade's worth of Barstool knowledge and contacts with him. So much for Louis's promise not to take a competitor job.

On top of that, after Pat launched his new company, I got a phone call from an ad agency that told me Louis had reached out about selling ads for Pat and his new operation a month before Pat had publicly quit Barstool. The message was clear: Pat's decision to quit wasn't nearly as spontaneous as it first seemed. This was a plan a few months into the making.

The hits from the rosé controversy (which came to be known as #Bubbly-Gang) kept coming. After Pat left the company, one of our tech employees told me there were suspicious similarities between McAfee's new website and our very own Barstoolsports.com. The page layout was identical, among other striking parallels. I'm no computer programmer, but when a legitimate tech geek pulls me aside to say there is no way our two websites should be this identical, even I can read between the lines of code.

Louis had taken the code with the help of my chief technical officer, a guy named Jeff Hunter who had been with me for ten years. Jeff had built every new version of our website, dealt with the ever-expanding traffic growth, and fixed every bug and glitch along the way. Both Jeff and Louis were listed as admins on the site. Apparently Jeff was also part of #BubblyGang. He was fired instantly as well. I both called and emailed Jeff asking him why he had done that. This guy I had known for a decade never responded. We haven't spoken since.

In the space of just a few months, I learned that one of my best friends (and one of my longest-tenured employees) had orchestrated the launch of two companies that were a galling fuck-you to me: one that was a direct rebuke of my orders, and another that was built to be a direct competitor to us. He did it by secretly enlisting my own employee to copy and paste code from us. And he turned one of our biggest stars against us. And people wonder why I have trust issues. I declared Louis dead to me, which absolutely sucked because I don't have so many friends as to be fine losing one overnight.

Somehow, through all the bullshit, there were enough credible "I had no ideas" between Pat and myself that we didn't totally detonate the bridge between us. When I called Pat and told him that our tech guy had taken our code and used it for his new website, Pat shut it down immediately. He swore up and down that he had no clue Louis and Jeff had done that. And knowing Louis, that was entirely plausible. I offered all the Indiana employees who were suddenly left jobless by Pat's departure jobs in NYC if they wanted them, even if I didn't know what to do with them. I just felt bad that they were suddenly unemployed. A bunch of them took me up on it and are still with us today.

I respected Pat then and I still do to this day. We actually toyed around with doing a show together years after he left, but then FanDuel swept in with a huge offer for him that made it impossible. Nice work by his agent (and my old friend) Michael Klein.

Pat is an interesting cat. Like I really do think he believed he was being treated like shit by our businesspeople here. I also think he's sort of sensitive and borderline diva-ish at times. There was no way he was ever going to be with us forever because eventually we would have pissed him off one way or the other. He's not really motivated by money either; he lives by his own code of respect. He felt disrespected by the Colts and he quit. He felt disrespected by us and he quit. It's hard not to respect that even if you think the reason he feels disrespected is somewhat flimsy.

These days, I'm often asked whether I think Pat would be the same megastar he is today had he never started with Barstool. That's hard to say, but my best guess is probably not as huge as he is today. He'd clearly still be wildly successful, but if he had gotten hired by ESPN right when he first left the NFL—as opposed to starting with us, then going off to do his own thing, developing his brand and voice, signing a huge deal with FanDuel, and *then* going to ESPN—he would have been locked into the type of content they make. Instead, he got a crash course on the internet, podcasting, and everything traditional media sucks at. He got to study at the school of Dave Portnoy and

Barstool. ESPN had been wanting to hire Barstool talent without having to attach the name Barstool long before Pat joined the scene. To this day, they still can't find new talent like we can. They just try to poach ours and then have the audacity to stick their noses up at us. True hypocrites in every sense of the word.

Whenever people leave Barstool and go on to future success, I get ripped by our fans for letting them go. Like *How stupid is Dave for not locking Pat McAfee up to a long-term deal.* As if I didn't realize that he was going to be a huge megastar or something. Of course I knew. But it was never going to work out forever with Pat. He was destined to become a planet unto himself. I remember him distinctly telling me he wanted to be a WWE champion when we first hired him. This was before he had done anything with wrestling. His ambition is huge, his talent is huge, and he's a complicated guy.

Pat's story is similar to those of many superstars we've helped launch. Pat, Alex Cooper, Caleb Pressley, *Bussin'*, etc. They use our platform and expertise to build their brands, and then when they don't need us anymore or somebody offers more money, they take what they've learned (and sometimes some of our employees) and go off into the world. I think sometimes people think I'm jealous or upset when guys like McAfee explode. I'm not. That's the *SNL* model I've professed for a long time here. We want to create superstars, and if they leave for more money or better opportunities, that just proves our business model works and helps us find the next star.

For me, how I view ex-employees is all about how people leave. Pat's exit was a bit murky just because of the #BubblyGang aspect to it. I was far more upset with Louis than anybody else. Probably because Louis was in my inner circle and I felt truly backstabbed by him both on a personal and professional level. I've only talked to him a few times since this all went down. He did email me maybe a year ago apologizing and basically saying he was on drugs and shit during this time period. They say time heals all wounds. I still need more time. Because I'm nothing if not a grudge guy.

But when it happened, I didn't have much time to wallow about the loss of McAfee or Louis. Because I had another storm brewing on the horizon.

Let's talk about *Call Her Daddy*.

16

Call Her Daddy's Daddy

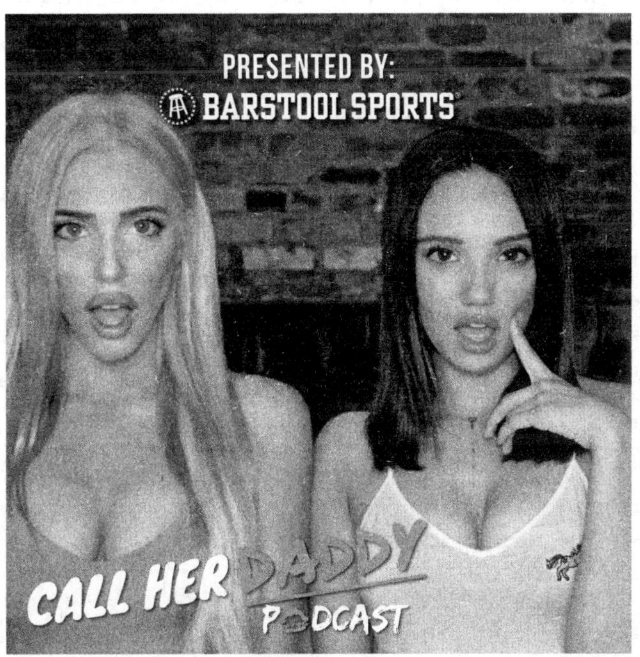

In 2017, I started following Noah Syndergaard's girlfriend on Instagram. Look, when you're the tip of the internet spear, you have to know who's dating who. The people expect me to know these things, so I do my duty. Syndergaard, aka "Thor," was the Mets' star pitcher and was photographed around New York with a hot blonde on his arm—at Knicks games, Rangers games, dinners . . . a classic New York pro athlete showing off his rocket girlfriend, playing to the cameras with plenty of PDA.

I took an interest because she looked vaguely familiar. Once I followed her on Instagram, I came to find that we had featured her as a Smokeshow of the Day years before, when she was playing soccer at Boston University. Of course, Gaz was already following her. Gaz knows every girl in the world and if he's not following them on Instagram, it probably means they're not attractive. Or young anymore.

One day, this girl Alex Cooper posted a teaser for a podcast she was in the process of launching. Gaz brought it in and showed me. The clip was a sizzle reel featuring Alex talking unabashedly about her sex life.

I'd never seen anything like it. I immediately DM'd her and asked her what the hell it was. She said it was a trailer for a new podcast she was starting called *Call Her Daddy*.

I then asked who had made the trailer, and she replied that she had learned to edit herself and she had cut it together. She also planned to edit and produce the podcast entirely herself.

That told me everything I needed to know. To this day, I have people working for me at Barstool who insist they can't put out content because we don't have an editor available for them. They gripe about not having access to the same talented producers we offer our stars, and they believe this is what holds them back. Meanwhile, Alex Cooper is probably the biggest star we've ever had at Barstool, and the first step in her ascendance was learning to edit from a YouTube tutorial on Adobe Premiere.

Alex Cooper was a self-starter, not just a pretty talking head. She was far more than met the eye and had a vision for herself that extended beyond the podcast. She was thinking long term, finding missing pieces of the zeitgeist and filling them in a way no one else had. If she presented ditzy, it was intentional. Behind the facade of lip gloss and platinum blond highlights stood an ambitious, enterprising woman with a fierce belief in herself and a willingness to learn whatever skills necessary to become the absolute titan we now know her to be.

I asked her if she might want to start the podcast with Barstool, explained the launching power we had, and offered her $75,000 per year for three years—with steps up to $85K and $100K in years two and three based on hitting performance thresholds. She agreed to the terms, and thus began the era of *Call Her Daddy.* My initial dealings with Alex set the tone for my entire relationship with the *Call Her Daddy* duo. I had no face-to-face with the woman who became her cohost, Sofia Franklyn. In fact, I didn't even know that she existed yet. Alex told me she was bringing her friend along and needed her, so I said fine and extended the same offer to Sofia. But make no mistake: it was Alex Cooper who caught my attention and impressed me so much that I was willing to accede to any copilot she wanted.

The first episode of *Call Her Daddy* was released on October 3, 2018. At the time, the main Barstool Sports Instagram account had over ten million followers. We posted a couple clips from their episode, and they blew the fuck up. There were all-out wars in the comments: people decrying the duo as the death of the feminist movement, people pronouncing them the coming of a new age of women warriors, and a bunch of horny dudes simply expressing their desire to bang them. I remember KFC marching into my office telling me I needed to fire these two girls before they ruined our reputation with every athlete on the planet. As right as KFC may have been about podcasting being the future, he was more wrong about dumping these two.

The podcast charted number one on the iTunes podcast charts that week. And the next week. And the week after that. It leapt forward at a pace not even *Pardon My Take* had achieved. Wherever I went, whoever I talked to, the questions were *always* about them.

"Are they really like that in person?"

"Who do you like more, Alex or Sofia?"

"Have you slept with either of them yet?"

We had caught lightning in a bottle. The only challenge now was keeping the bottle.

Call Her Daddy was wholly unlike anything we'd ever put out before at Barstool. The only sports content they featured was references to the various athletes they'd dated and the size and strength of their erections. But they were funny and utterly fearless in their vulgarity. Here were two attractive young women who seemed to have New York City by the balls, and they were completely unabashed, transparent, and eager to share the steamy details of their dating lives with a swelling audience of thousands.

Plus, they had an incredible knack for branding. The listeners became Daddy Gang. Alex and Sofia became the "fathers." Their signature blowjob technique was introduced to the world as the "Gluck Gluck 3000." That was on episode three, by the way—just three weeks in, they were offering advice on how to create a vacuum seal with your hands to "guzzle the sperm from your man like it was the only bottle of water in an endless desert."

Their words.

Remarkably, Alex and Sofia didn't seem to care much about the polarizing reaction they created. They just barreled forward, harnessing an army of young women grateful to finally have a female counterpart to what men had been doing for years—speaking openly, candidly, and sometimes even a bit demeaningly about their sexual adventures. I might have been a decade too early with Jenna Marbles and Stoolala, but the world was ready for these two. Meanwhile, I stayed out of their way. I'm not a micromanager in any sense; I like to let my people do their thing and if it doesn't work, we'll talk at your next contract negotiation. But it didn't take long for Alex to come barking to me that our social media accounts weren't featuring enough posts of their podcast. (Personally, I like it when my employees issue this complaint because it means they care and want to grow. Everyone should be fighting for more publicity, which is our equivalent to playing time on a team.) I had no problem telling our social team to post them more. Hell, the engagement was insane—from furious incels demanding we muzzle these insidious broads to tens of thousands of young women sharing the clips with their group chats. It grew, and grew, and grew.

In December, Alex came to me to ask for a raise. She explained that due to her greater work deliverables for the podcast—she still cut and edited the show herself and ran the *Call Her Daddy* social accounts—she deserved a raise. It made sense to me, so I quickly agreed and bumped her up to $150,000. That was a 100 percent raise just three months into her contract. Pretty good if you ask me. We also proactively decided to bump Sofia from $75K to $90K without her asking. This was a 20 percent raise three months into *her* contract. Again, more than fair in my book. Now, this $60K difference between their salaries would become a major source of contention down the road, but I really didn't think much about it at the time. From where I sat, Alex was the breadwinner on the podcast. It was her show. Her idea. She was who I negotiated the original deal with. Her entire pitch, when she asked for the raise, was that she was doing the lion's share of the work, and it all checked out. I mean I hadn't even met Sofia before she signed with us. And we have plenty of podcasts where the hosts aren't making the same amount. It's like a band or a baseball team. Not everybody is paid the same amount of money. The lead singer doesn't get the same paycheck as the backup vocals.

With that settled, we ended the year on good terms. There was no indication that Alex and Sofia were unhappy with their situation.

Until they met Logan Paul.

In April 2019, Alex and Sofia flew to Los Angeles to appear on Logan Paul's podcast. If you don't know who Logan Paul is, you probably haven't understood about half the references in this book so far. Logan Paul is one of the biggest media personalities alive. He's one of the founding fathers of the vlogging game, and he has reinvented himself so many times that it's impossible to summarize him with just one title. These days, I guess you could call him a wrestler-boxer-entrepreneur-podcaster-sports drink titan, but I still prefer YouTuber. I've always respected him for his hustle and ability to stay one step ahead of what the people want, getting to the game before they take their seats. In fact, I think Jake and Logan Paul will go down as two of the greatest marketers of all time.

Except when my two star female podcasters jumped on Logan's show, he planted some rather poisonous seeds in their minds. They got into a discussion about their current contracts and pay, and Logan was unimpressed. In learning that they were salaried employees, the king of YouTube let out a snort of disapproval that reverberated through the minds of Alex and Sofia, shaking loose their faith in the fairness of our partnership.

Keep in mind, this is six and a half months since they *started* the show. They're barely halfway through their first year of their three-year contract. They're on a rookie contract, and I'm fully aware that they're outperforming what I'm paying them. I think Logan had forgotten that he had built his brand for well over a decade. How much was he making six months into his journey?

On the other side of their Logan Paul appearance, Alex and Sofia slowly began to show their growing dissatisfaction with being tied to Barstool. First, they stopped coming into the office. They were nowhere to be found except on the one day of the week when they recorded their episode. I guess I allowed it, because their show was now paying the salaries of all the daily office attendees, who, of course, quickly voiced their resentment that the girls were being granted special treatment. In particular, Nate had a major issue with it. Nate. Whose work has never paid a cent of his *own* salary, let alone subsidized half the content team the way *CHD* did.

The first demand that *Call Her Daddy* made after the Logan Paul trip was a fairly innocuous one. Apparently, there was a third member of the *CHD* team I was totally unaware of. His name was Muj Fricke. He was known by the Daddy Gang as "The Milfhunter," and he wore a ski mask on the podcast to protect his identity. I was told that he had grown up with Alex and was critical to the show. I also learned he had been there from day one, which was news to me. Both Alex and Sofia said I needed to hire him full-time. The pod was crushing it, so if they said he was integral to it, then so be it. We paid him $75K a year—less than Sofia by the way, but she didn't seem to have a problem with that.

I got bad vibes from this guy right from the jump. He would privately tell me that he was the brains for the entire operation and that he did all the work. That *Call Her Daddy* would be nothing without him. It was just an odd dynamic considering I was under the impression Alex and Muj were lifelong friends and that the only reason Muj had a job with us was because Alex demanded we hire him. Yet here he was, bashing her every chance he got. I didn't trust him at all.

Near the end of 2019 was really when the major trouble started brewing. *CHD* had hired a lawyer and wanted to have a meeting with us. The lawyer brought a list of demands so preposterous that I couldn't even make it through the meeting. Both girls wanted a million dollars a year, the right to sell their own ads, ownership over the intellectual property of *Call Her Daddy*, and 90 percent of their merch sales. Oh, and they no longer wanted to be qualified as employees of Barstool Sports.

It was the dumbest thing I've ever seen. They weren't even a full year into their contracts and they wanted to basically blow up their deal with us. At least, that's what their new demands felt like. *Hey thanks, Barstool, for giving us millions and millions of dollars worth of free promotion, and thanks for taking a chance on us, but we don't need you anymore. Smell ya later . . .*

The contract demands were so ridiculous that we didn't even counteroffer. What was the point in negotiating? I looked at it as I often do—like an athlete signing a contract. If a baseball player signs a new three-year deal and then hits thirty home runs before the All-Star Break in their first season, they don't get to rip up the contract and start over. That's what the team paid you to do. And this isn't just lip service. I signed a five-year contract with the Chernin Group when they bought Barstool Sports. My salary was $400K a year. I hadn't been given a raise in four years despite Barstool absolutely crushing it and my personal brand exploding. I was being paid peanuts on the dollar for my worth on the open market, but that was the contract I had signed. And now the *CHD* girls wanted to make more than double what I was making, and they'd only been here for a cup of coffee. It was insanity.

Alex and Sofia had spent eleven months putting out one podcast episode, once a week. They would come in, sit down, and run through a list of ways in which guys had given them the "ick." I had spent a decade delivering newspapers in my Astrovan, literally shoveling shit out of my newsracks before I saw a nickel of profit. Work that paved the way for these two to have this opportunity. You don't need to be a sports fan to understand why I laughed their lawyer out of the room.

What I didn't know at the time, but I would come to learn, was that behind all this ungrateful, entitled behavior apparently was a puppetmaster pulling the strings; an insidious conductor who stayed in the shadows, seeking to turn the girls against me. A guy by the name of "Suitman."

Now, this Lord Farquaad-looking, factory-reject Ken doll was Sofia's boyfriend. He was also Peter Nelson—an executive at HBO, a Harvard graduate, and in my eyes quite possibly a human incarnation of Satan. This dude was in Sofia's ear, expressing his disbelief at their deal with Barstool and how far off it was from the "industry standard." I'm fairly sure he's the one who connected the girls with their lawyer, and I have strong reason to believe he helped them come up with their list of demands. Fucking Suitman did everything he could to convince them that they were not being paid what any other podcaster with their success was being paid. Specifically the girls were directly comparing their numbers and salaries to *PMT*'s numbers and salaries. They ignored the fact that *PMT* had been around for four years already. It was almost like *Call Her Daddy* and Suitman had access to Dan's and PFT's contracts. But how would that be possible? It was as though Suitman and Michael Klein (our favorite agent) were exchanging notes.

And then I found out that Suitman and our favorite agent Michael Klein were actually very good friends. Fucking agents, man . . .

Now, I'm not saying that the girls weren't underpaid at this time. But how do you quantify the value that Barstool had given to *Call Her Daddy*'s success? They had used our model, our tools, our gigantic social media springboard. We built them their own studio and posted their clips on a ten-million-follower Instagram account, tagging their podcast and directing people to download the latest episode. They had healthcare and a fully built merchandise infrastructure ready to print their hoodies with whatever catchphrases they came up with that week, shipping them to the masses without the girls having to lift a finger or walk to the goddamn Kinko's to print shipping labels. As I had done. For so many years.

What's the "industry standard" value for promotion on that level, Suitman? Riddle me that, you Winklevoss wannabe.

I took the risk when they were absolutely nothing. Now they were something. And they wanted everything.

Fuck off, Suitman. Go Gluck Gluck 3000 yourself.

In the early months of 2020, Suitman started shopping *Call Her Daddy* around to other podcast networks. Quietly, unethically, he reached out to major distributors like Wondery, letting them know that superstars Alex Cooper and Sofia Franklyn were not happy with their current deal at Barstool and wanted a new home.

Suitman must have had some sort of deal worked out for himself. I have to believe he stood to make a percentage of any new deal they might have made with a rival network, because why the fuck else would he have done all this work? He was already dating Sofia; he didn't need to land her a humongous raise in order to bang her. Plus, guys like that don't do anything out of the goodness of their hearts. He was hunting for himself, in shark-infested shallows with swiftly rising water that would soon be over his head.

In March, the COVID pandemic began. I'll get into that plenty in a bit, but it didn't really mean much in terms of the *Call Her Daddy* saga. As the timeline goes, it was toward the end of March that New York City went into quarantine. And it was April 8, 2020, when Alex and Sofia released what would be their final episode of *Call Her Daddy* together—just a year and a half after they'd started.

I didn't know it at the time. Out of nowhere, they simply stopped putting out their podcast. The only job they had, they stopped doing. The next week, when no new episode of *Call Her Daddy* came out, I didn't even think too much of it. By now, I was entirely accustomed to what I thought was the lack of professionalism from Alex and Sofia—who had stopped contributing to any sort of broader company effort or event long ago. I figured they would release the episode late and maybe I'd send them an angry text.

Nope. Radio silence.

When they skipped the next week, I knew something was seriously amiss. We hadn't spoken about any contract stuff since I had shut down their first approach with the lawyer a few months before, but it was obvious that they were basically going on strike to try to improve their deal.

The Daddy Gang started clamoring for answers. My Twitter timeline was littered almost exclusively with demands for updates on the mysterious *Call Her Daddy* holdout. Everyone in my personal circle wanted to know the tasty gossip on the two girls leading the chart-topping podcast that had gone dark. People blamed me for the silence.

Then, after two weeks, the girls released a cryptic statement saying they legally weren't allowed to comment on the developing situation. Which was utter insanity, because it immediately made it seem like I'd somehow muzzled them and we'd already lawyered up to sue the pants off each other. I texted them both to say they were more than allowed to say anything they wanted to the public, to their fans. That's always how I've done it at Barstool—radical transparency. But they left it quiet for their fans to pull their hair out trying to decipher.

To anyone wondering how best to temper a growing PR scandal, invoking a legal gag order is about the worst thing you can do. In one small statement, Alex and Sofia had collaboratively punted the hornet's nest of internet curiosity straight into my lap.

Normally, I don't negotiate with terrorists. But it being COVID, with so little else to talk about, I reasoned it would be better to get one more year out of them than end up in an expensive lawsuit, which is where things were headed if they left. I wouldn't have had a choice but to sue them for breach of contract, and it would have ratcheted the whole sensation up another hundred degrees.

So I came up with the following deal:

- $500,000 salary each.
- 3.5 percent each of all merch they sold. At the end of their term, they would own all their merch sales.
- Cut six months off their contract so they would have to do the podcast with us for only one more year.
- At the end of that year, we would relinquish full ownership of the intellectual property of *Call Her Daddy* to them.
- Barstool would retain the rights to any alcohol brand started by *Call Her Daddy*, but they would get 10–20 percent of that brand, if we launched one.

We get alcohol. They get everything else. After one year, at $500K each.

At the time, this was the most generous offer I'd ever given anyone in Barstool's history. It felt almost out of character. But I knew these girls were leaving no matter what. Alex and Sofia were never Barstool lifers; they were always looking to the future, to the next greener pasture or more successful professional athlete to climb aboard until his elbow gave out for a season-ending Tommy John surgery. Opportunistic, ambitious, and emotionally detached from the chess moves of their career, Sofia and Alex seemed willing to step on any neck and burn any bridge to get ahead.

For the appetite of the national public, the table was set for perhaps the greatest falling-out in the history of podcasting.

After what felt like months (but was really just a few weeks), I finally managed to set up a meeting with Alex and Sofia on the rooftop of my apartment building. It became known in *Call Her Daddy*/Barstool lore as "The Rooftop Meeting."

I thought it was a sweetheart deal. Finish your contractually obligated term (six months early) with us at a solid salary and then go off and be millionaires instantly. Everybody wins! We signed you with the hope that you would become successful, and now you have. You need to honor that risk we took by letting us all be successful together for just one more short year.

I didn't hear a word from them for three days. Then out of nowhere, I got a call from Alex asking if she could meet with me again. Without Sofia. We'd done this dance before, so I said yes and we once again trekked up to my rooftop.

"I love the deal you proposed, and I want to take it. But Sofia is never going to take it. Her boyfriend is running this entire thing. I don't trust him, he wants to be our manager, and he's working a deal with Wondery. There is just no way Sofia will accept your deal."

"Okay," I said. "You guys realize I'll sue you if you take the podcast to another network before your contract is out, right?"

Alex claimed to me that they had a plan to say they were both sexually harassed at Barstool.

That was it. That was their game plan to get out of their contractual obligation to Barstool Sports in the event that I did not relinquish their IP to them and wish them well on their merry way as they jumped ship to a rival podcast network. In April 2020, you may recall that the world was pretty furious with men and their workplace behavior toward women, as story after story was coming out of Hollywood executives and business leaders having leveraged their positions of power for inappropriate sexual relationships. For years, Barstool and I had been pilloried for making sexist jokes, but we'd never been accused of inappropriate workplace conduct. But had they decided to go that route, even though it was patently untrue, it would have been a tough fight for us to win in the court of public opinion. Nobody would have believed my side of the story. The same assholes who have lied or misrepresented things about me would have eaten this story up. Mina Kimes, my ESPN enemy, would have had a field day with it. It would just be added to the never-ending list of Dave Portnoy atrocities. Not to mention, how do you even sexually harass or create a toxic work environment for employees who don't show up to the office in the first place?

By the way, I realize that this is a heavy accusation I just made: how *Call Her Daddy* was allegedly planning to break their contract with us by lying about sexual harassment at Barstool.

But you don't just have to believe my recollection of events, or believe that this is what Alex told me. Just look at the title of the last podcast *Call Her Daddy* ever published before they quit working. It was titled "Kesha . . . The End." The intro song they used for the episode was Kesha's song "Praying." Alex and Sofia said people could interpret that however they wanted. For context, Kesha is a singer who, at that time, was embroiled in a legal fight with her producer, Dr. Luke, where she accused him of sexual assault, harassment, and rape in an attempt to get out of her recording contract with him. Dr. Luke denied the accusations and the legal case was settled without admission of wrongdoing. I mean, by choosing that song, I believe that Alex and Sofia weren't even trying to hide what they planned to do.

In the weeks that followed, *Call Her Daddy* would constantly post captions like "Free the Fathers" or say that they "couldn't speak" about the situation. All 100 percent bullshit obviously. And then Alex came in and claimed that they had concocted this sexual harassment accusation plan. As you'll read later, it wouldn't be the last time Sofia Franklyn and their producer, Muj, would be accused of using sexual harassment accusations as a chess move.

As I was writing this book, it came out that Sofia Franklyn is writing her own memoir of *Call Her Daddy*. I was going to ignore it, but that's not my style. And TikTok is littered with girls being like, "You go girl!" or "Yay, I'm Team Sofia" or "Sophia got done so dirty" or "Any side that Dave is on is the wrong side" blah blah blah.

Listen, I have no idea what she'll write in her book. Maybe it will be 100 percent accurate. But I do know this: In my book, Sofia Franklyn is a fucking liar. Women are going to believe her just because she's a woman, because they feel bad for her or they don't like Alex or they hate my guts or whatever. That's fine. You can say whatever you want about me, but literally nobody has ever said I don't tell the truth 100 percent of the time. So to all these women who think Sofia is some feminist icon, just remember you are propping up a woman who I believe was willing to lie at the drop of a hat about sexual harassment, which sets all women back. Even some of *Call Her Daddy*'s fans were stunned when they found out this was merely a contract dispute and had nothing to do with harassment.

(Quick story time: If anybody harassed or assaulted anybody during *Call Her Daddy*'s time with us, it was Sofia assaulting one of our nicest employees—Spider—the night of our Christmas party. Spider is basically our office manager and jack-of-all-trades. He's like five-eight, 120 pounds soaking wet. Sofia got so drunk that she could barely stand at our Christmas party. Spider tried to escort her into an Uber so she'd get home safe. A full-blown wrestling match broke out on the sidewalk. I think Sofia actually pinned Spider and, like King Kong Bundy, asked for a ten count. The following Monday, Alex came into my office crying that she couldn't work with Sofia anymore; that Sofia had no work ethic and she claimed that Sofia had substance abuse issues to boot. I told Alex that she could obviously do whatever she wanted, but Sofia seemed like the perfect sidekick for her. The podcast was exploding; did she really want to risk breaking it up right now? Alex decided to stick with it, but I knew at that point the dirty little secret nobody else knew about *CHD*: the girls hated each other.)

Thank God it never came to the girls accusing us of sexual harassment. Alex left our meeting saying that she wanted to accept the deal. She also said that Sofia hated my guts, which came as a surprise. The whole time I had believed that Alex was the one who didn't like me, but I thought that I had a solid relationship with Sofia.

"No. I like you and respect you," she claimed. "This whole thing was Sofia's plan from the beginning, it was her and Peter the whole time. I never wanted any of it."

I believed it. But even with that knowledge, I was still willing to make it work with Sofia. So when Alex left, I called her.

"Alex says she's going to take the deal. You should take the deal too. No hard feelings, finish out one more year, then we go our separate ways."

"Okay, let me think about it," she replied, and that was that.

A day went by. Then another. The waiting was infuriating because the stakes were so high, and each day that passed without a new episode of *Call Her Daddy* was costing Barstool tens of thousands of dollars in ad revenue. Keep in mind, they were still under contract this entire time!

Then I got a call from Alex.

"I don't want Sofia, even if she decides to take the deal. Can I get the entire IP for myself if I honor the deal?"

"Sure," I said. Sofia had dragged her feet. You snooze, you lose. Better to have one than none.

Of course, not long after I hung up with Alex, I got the call from Sofia:

"I'll take the deal."

"Too late," I said. "Alex doesn't want you back. She's going to do *Call Her Daddy* by herself. But I'll still honor the other terms of our deal with you—$500,000 salary, start your own new podcast, we'll throw the same promotional weight behind it, and you two can tee off on each other from behind the mics of your respective shows."

It would have been *great*. Just a full-blown podcast war from two shows recorded out of the same studio, in the same building! Former friends become worst enemies. Let's squeeze every last drop we can out of this fracture for as long as possible. People will pick sides, we'll make merch about it . . . Let the hate consume you, Sofia!

She said she'd think about it.

In the meantime, I got a call from a friend of mine in Miami, Dave Grutman. He is the king of Miami nightlife and probably has the most robust rolodex on the planet. He said he had Scooter Braun on the other line, and Scooter wanted to talk to me about *Call Her Daddy*. Yes, the same Scooter Braun who discovered Justin Bieber and feuded with Taylor Swift. I told Dave that I'd talk to him but to let him know everything we said was on the record. To which Grutman replied, "I told him you were a terrorist."

It was one of the nicest things Grutman could have said about me. In his world, it meant I didn't give a fuck who you were or how famous you were. I treated everybody the same exact way. So when Scooter Braun started the conversation saying I had to hire Sofia back on *Call Her Daddy*, I couldn't help but laugh in his face. Who the fuck did this guy think he was? Why in the world would I ever do that? Scooter said he had seen Peter Nelson at the gym or something, and he told him he would smooth out the situation. I have no idea what was in it for Scooter, but after hanging up the phone, the first thing I did was pick up my phone to film a video lampooning Scooter Braun. "Ohhhhh Scooter Braun called . . . Oooooh Scoooooter Braun called . . . Who the fuck is Scooter Braun?"

Needless to say, his call didn't move the needle. The Sofia ship on *Call Her Daddy* had sailed. But her doing her own thing was still an option. That ball was still in her court.

(As a sidenote: During this entire fiasco with *Call Her Daddy*, from the time they started boycotting all the way to them breaking up, the Milfhunter (aka Muj) was constantly in my ear, saying that I should just fire both of them. He kept reminding me that *he* was the actual mastermind behind *Call Her Daddy*. That he wrote all the episodes. That both these girls were a dime a dozen. That he could find two new girls to easily replace both of them and take over the feeds. I think that at the same time, he was talking to both Sofia and Alex, pretending to be a confidant. Keep in mind, this was the guy who was supposedly Alex Cooper's best friend. His treachery was clearly unknown to Alex because at one point she wanted to keep Muj. I recall Alex telling me that all changed when Muj tried to hold Alex hostage and demanded $15K cash from her for him to choose Alex over Sofia. Alex laughed him out of the room.)

I kept waiting to hear from Sofia. But it was just more silence. I started to worry that Alex and Sofia were mending fences, uniting behind one strategy that would leave Barstool up a creek again and back to fighting fake sexual harassment allegations. For me, the worst thing that could happen was for these two girls to see eye to eye again.

So I did what any self-respecting business owner would do: I went to the *New York Post*.

By the middle of May, the *Post* had already written two articles covering *Call Her Daddy*. The Page Six articles were replete with splashy Getty images of the girls dressed up for a photoshoot in schoolgirl outfits, and it was one of those stories that seemed to hook anyone who read it regardless of age, gender, religion, or sexual persuasion.

The writers of these *New York Post* articles had contacted me for each piece they wrote, so I already had their phone numbers. I texted them to say I had some new details about the story they might like to hear, then proceeded to tell them that the girls actually hated each other's guts. Until then, everyone following the story had been assuming that it was Barstool vs. Alex and Sofia. I did the thankless duty of informing the world that in fact, it was now Alex vs. Sofia, and things were quickly shifting toward Barstool and Alex vs. Sofia. Thanks in no small part, in my view, to the meddling fingers of one Peter Nelson—boyfriend to Sofia Franklyn, HBO Sports executive, and public enemy number one as far as the Daddy Gang should be concerned.

They ran the story the next day.

"'Call Her Daddy' podcast hosts have 'turned on each other,' insider says."

"They've completely turned on each other and started arguing over who was the real talent and who did more of the heavy lifting [for the podcast]."

It worked perfectly: Alex and Sofia completely severed all communication. They each believed the other had leaked the story. The friendship, and the podcast as we knew it, would never exist again. They *hated* each other.

The next day, I went into the machinery of the *Call Her Daddy* podcast feed and decided to take her out for a spin. The dusty, dormant warhorse that only a few months earlier had galloped to the front of podcast charts had not been utilized in far too long. And I had the keys.

I recorded an episode of *Call Her Daddy* by myself, telling the entire story as I knew it from start to finish. I called both girls "unprofessional, disloyal, and greedy." I denounced Suitman and told everyone what to expect going forward—that Alex would be running the podcast by herself.

The next day, some two million subscribers of *Call Her Daddy* were hit with a notification on their phone they hadn't seen in forever: a new episode of *Call Her Daddy* was now available for download. As the army of Daddy Gang rushed to listen, many were introduced to me for the first time. As the show had built an audience that wasn't exactly comprised of the typical Stoolie fan base, many of these young women listeners had no idea who I was or even that the show belonged to Barstool.

The response was electric. People flooded to my DM inbox to praise my transparency and handling of the whole situation. I had hundreds of date requests from young women who thought I was hilarious. For the first time in my life, I was suddenly desirable to women.

Growing up, I was never what people would call a ladies' man. I had always been a pretty decent living room guy. Meaning that just like any good college football coach, if I could get into the living room of a recruit, I had a decent chance of winning them over. Personality and humor were always my calling cards; not dashing good looks. The hard part for me was getting into the living room though. I rarely make the first move, and I'm an absolute wallflower when I go out. And I definitely don't have the type of face that causes girls to swoon when they see me.

Well, when I took over the *Call Her Daddy* podcast stream, it was like I had a captive living room of hundreds of thousands of women listening to me be hilarious, charming, and rich. The Daddy Gang couldn't get enough of me.

It was a game-changer for my social life. Suddenly my DMs were inundated with women who were proactively pursuing me: women who wanted to hang out with me, go out on dates with me, or just plain fuck. And lots of them were gorgeous too. Well, not all of them, but I just ignored the ugly ones. It honestly wasn't the worst problem to have. If fat/gross Dave could have seen me then, he would have never believed it.

I was getting enough inbound DMs that when I saw a random TikTok from a girl asking for the best way to slide into a celebrity's DMs, I felt qualified to answer.

Without giving it more than a few seconds of thought, I replied with a video saying that it was easy to get a celeb's attention. All you had to do was follow these three steps:

1. Don't be ugly.
2. Be very hot.
3. Write "I fuck."

I then pressed publish and sent it into the interwebs.

This little video was like pouring gasoline on the *Call Her Daddy* fire. I didn't make that TikTok thinking girls would respond to it, but they ate it up. Every day I woke up to hundreds of DMs saying, "I'm hot and I fuck." What a time to be alive!

In fact, did you know that the gossip website Deuxmoi was basically created by reporting on my dating activities? Like this is such a preposterous thing to even say that I'm sure lots of the people reading this probably just spit out their coffee and weren't even drinking any. I swear to God. Somewhere around this time, this Deuxmoi site was born in NYC. And whenever they posted me on dates or talking to girls, their traffic blew up. Deuxmoi was finding out what lots of websites have found out over the years: Barstool moves the needle. Mention my name and you need to buy ink by the barrel. Again, it's just how the Stoolies are. They are loyal and want to get their hands on anything Barstool related.

Anyway, back to *Call Her Daddy*. The revelation of Alex and Sofia's torpedoed friendship was almost more than the public could handle. Two girls who the world loved to hate now hated each other. All the details swirled into one perfect soap opera tornado: betrayal, alleged contract violations, huge sums of money at stake, and a seemingly controlling boyfriend all worked together to detonate this nuclear sensation of a podcast.

The *New York Times* wrote a long article about it. As did every other newspaper, website, magazine, and gossip rag across the country. The front page of Reddit was filled with fan theories and opinions, refreshing each day with more and more far-fetched conspiracies. It was the most viral story I had ever been a part of in almost twenty years of running Barstool.

Shortly thereafter, Alex came back in to record a new episode of *Call Her Daddy*. I was the featured guest. From there, she took off and never looked back. By honoring her word, Alex and I were able to move past the entire circus. She finished out her year and was immediately offered $60 million over three years from Spotify to take *Call Her Daddy* there. In 2024 when that deal finished, she jumped over to Sirius XM, where she is currently on a three-year contract for $125 million. These days, it's less Gluck Gluck 3000 and more Barbara Walters, as she has veered more toward reflective interviews on mental health and political and social issues. Alex has interviewed presidential candidates and pop stars, bestselling authors and business titans. She started a production company and a beverage company and married a major Hollywood movie producer.

Through it all, Alex Cooper has never forgotten the company that helped launch her. She credits me and Barstool frequently, and I'm genuinely happy for all the success she has found. I'm even hoping she helps me promote this book. I guess we'll see what she thinks of this chapter.

I have no fucking idea what Sofia is doing.

17

The Art of the Deal

Now, while the *Call Her Daddy* drama seemed like the biggest thing going on at Barstool Sports, I was dealing with something far more important—not only for my future but for the future of the company. By 2019, I was fed the fuck up with Barstool Sports. I was nearing the end of the five-year contract I had signed with Chernin when they bought 51 percent of the company in 2016. As a reminder, I was making $400K a year, the same amount I'd been making since I signed the original contract. I hadn't been offered a raise in four years. Given my principles, I wasn't asking for more money. I knew what I had signed up for, and I intended to honor it to the end. But the growing headaches and lack of gratitude that stemmed from both my employees and my "boss" in Peter Chernin had me ready to leave it all behind as soon as my contract was up.

That's right: I was ready to abandon my child. The way I do things is if you're killing it, I renegotiate and pay you more. The Chernin Group never once made any gesture of the sort. It's like they knew they had me on the hook for a bargain bin price, and they wanted to squeeze me dry and run me into the ground. They never once proactively offered me a bonus or more money. I was paying other Barstool talent far more than I was making because that was the price of talent. It was insulting. Anything extra I got, which wasn't much, was because Erika demanded it for me.

I'd devoted the last fifteen years of my life to building, running, and protecting Barstool. It seemed that on a weekly basis, we (and myself in particular) were getting attacked by some new crusader hell-bent on making a name for themself among the sea of white-knight blogger/journalists. The usual suspects were watching our every move, dissecting our every joke, waiting for any slip to pounce on and portray Barstool as an existential threat to humanity. It was truly the golden era of wokeism, and those who trained their pens upon us knew exactly what a furious column about "The History of Misogynistic Humor at Barstool Sports" could do for their publication, and their career.

I was tired. I didn't really want to fight the fight anymore, especially for a parent company that I thought didn't appreciate my efforts. I had a few conversations with Chernin about renewing my contract and their offers were all wildly low. I was no longer the naïve negotiator I was the first time I felt they had swindled me in buying the company for $12.5 million (when it was probably worth like three times that much). I think they offered me roughly two million a year to continue what I was doing. I knew my worth. I didn't even counteroffer; it was that insulting.

It also bothered me that I don't think Peter Chernin had publicly defended us once during the entire time he owned the company. Granted, that wasn't part of our deal and I never asked him to, but I didn't think I should have needed to ask. The way I operate is that if somebody in my family gets attacked, that's an attack on me and I will respond in kind. I knew they knew that all the attacks on Barstool and my character were bullshit. And they'd gladly say that privately but not publicly. It bothered me. Maybe it was a combination of martyrdom and fatigue, but I really was considering laying down the sword once my contract ran out. I just didn't see a way for me to continue at Barstool. I knew I could make a ton more money on my own with far fewer headaches. I could just retrench to the Milton days when I didn't have to give a fuck about anything, and the people who wanted to follow me there could follow me there.

The universe had other plans.

In May 2018, the United States Supreme Court struck down a federal ban against sports gambling. This gave individual states the right to legalize sports gambling if they wanted to, which triggered an arms race for gambling licenses and user acquisition among the major players in the gambling game. The minute gambling was legalized, I walked into Erika's office and told her this was our exit strategy. This was how we were going to sell Barstool Sports for hundreds of millions of dollars.

Now, I know what you're thinking. *Hey hold on, Dave . . . you just said you were ready to quit like two paragraphs ago. Now you're saying you knew this would be your big cash-out moment? Make it make sense.* Well, just because I thought it would be our exit strategy doesn't mean it was easy to accomplish.

In 2019, with the help of the Chernin Group, we hired an investment bank to quietly set the wheels in motion to sell Barstool Sports. The bank was Moelis, which was supposedly the bank of choice in the gambling space. They went out to DraftKings, FanDuel, PokerStars, Flutter . . . anyone who was anyone in the sports gambling industry. We had meeting after meeting with gambling company after gambling company. Moelis and Chernin led each meeting. I don't think we got one offer. It was vaguely reminiscent of the time Dan and I had pitched *The Rundown* to studio execs in LA and got nowhere. It was almost like we were speaking a different language. Eventually, the frustration of not being able to capitalize on the moment spilled over. As Chernin pressed Moelis, who was hired to facilitate the sale, on why they weren't getting anywhere, they decided to blame it all on me. *Nobody wants to work with Barstool Sports because Dave is too toxic.*

Hey, maybe that was true, I don't know. But fuck them for saying it anyways. And fine—if Chernin and Moelis and their fancy suits can't fucking sell this company, I'll do it myself.

Barstool had hired a gambling consultant named David-something who was our internal liaison with Moelis and Chernin. He told me about Jay Snowden over at Penn Gaming. In truth, I'd never even heard of Penn, which is hard to believe given how much I knew about the gambling industry. Penn was the largest regional operator of casinos, with locations in West Virginia, Pennsylvania, Mississippi, and many other states. They had the gambling licenses already but their casinos were under all different names, and there was a lack of brand cohesion under which they could wrap a much-needed sports gambling vertical to enter the full-blown sprint that was now underway among the gambling powerhouses. We had the branding. They had the licenses.

Now, unlike all the prior meetings that were led by Moelis and Chernin,

Barstool handled these meetings. No bankers in the room. No VCs in the room. It was largely just Erika and me. Dan was added to the mix as the conversations progressed.

From the first handshake with Jay Snowden, we were a match made in heaven.

Penn Gaming understood how valuable the stickiness of our audience was. They knew that we had the most loyal fans in the absolute world; that Stoolies would not only go to war for us, but would utilize our sports betting app as their preferred means of locking in bets on Sunday mornings before football began. Jay Snowden was a fan of ours himself. He knew that betting the same bets that Big Cat, Dave, and your other favorite Barstool personalities had made would be a winning strategy. Other major gambling companies were putting gigantic money behind celebrities and athletes to serve as the faces of their apps. But why would anyone take the "LeBron James three-team parlay" when nobody had ever heard LeBron say a word about gambling in his life?

Big Cat and I were battle-tested, trench-warfare-hardened sports gamblers. We'd been talking about it for *years*. Everyone knew we walked the walk as much as we talked the talk. So if people were going to follow our bets, they could trust that we were taking the risks ourselves. That is exactly the type of authenticity that has separated Barstool from every other media company in the game, and it was the winning ingredient that brought Penn to our door with an offer beyond anything I ever dreamed I'd see when I was handing out newspapers in Boston.

The deal came easily. There was a lot of faith and trust on both sides, which was refreshing. Jay Snowden and his crew agreed to pay $136 million for 36 percent of the company in 2020, with a path for Penn to buy the remaining 64 percent in a couple years for $388 million more if we hit certain performance targets. The total valuation was $650 million.

I still owned 34 percent of the company myself. In total, I would personally make about $178 million from the deal. All my early Milton guys, to whom I gave equity during the original Chernin deal, would also become millionaires. But by far the biggest winner of the entire thing was the Chernin Group. They'd net a roughly $250 million profit from their original investment. The valuation of Barstool had gone from $12.5 million to $650 million without any help from them except for staying out of our way. And the best part for those guys is they didn't have to do a damn thing to collect their ransom. They could take their gigantic profit and run. By contrast, Big Cat and I had to sign long-term contracts with Penn to ensure we'd stay with them. Dan signed a four-year deal. I signed a five-year deal. And unlike Chernin, we weren't getting a huge lump sum up front. We had to work for it and would get paid off over the duration of the contract. After taxes, we'd barely get anything in year one. And any delusions I had of retiring or scaling back were gone like dust in the wind.

It was a bittersweet moment. I was going to make more money than I could ever have dreamed of, but I was committing to work my guts out from now until I was close to fifty. But I guess if you're going to work your dick off, it's easier to do it when you have an insane pile of money waiting for you at the end of the rainbow.

The only real hiccup that almost prevented this deal from happening actually had nothing to do with Penn. As I just previously mentioned, this deal didn't instantly produce a huge windfall for any of the Barstool employees because of the way it was structured. We'd receive our money through a combo of cash and Penn stock that would vest over time. Yes, we were all rich . . . but we were delayed rich. So I put myself in Dan's shoes. What number would make me so happy that this deal would be a no-brainer? I knew that Big Cat needed to be taken care of in a big way. If he didn't want to do this deal, he could go sign a huge deal with DraftKings, FanDuel, or ESPN. And without Dan there was no deal. He had busted his absolute ass for years, growing *Pardon My Take* into the behemoth it was, and I knew that he deserved (and needed) a serious bonus to ensure his continued happiness and commitment to our new path forward under Penn—not something promised down the road that he had to work for. He deserved an instant bonus that would change his life immediately.

So with that in mind, I suggested to Chernin that Dan be given an additional $7 million signing bonus on top of his equity. That was the bare minimum he deserved for helping play a gigantic role to get us to this place and close this deal.

Chernin didn't agree. The contract was the contract. The equity was the equity. They didn't want to budge. I told them this was an absolute deal-breaker. I hadn't talked to Dan about the extra signing bonus, but I was just viewing it through his eyes and my eyes as somebody who knew Dan inside and out at this point. I was sort of acting as his de facto agent, and at the same time in the best interest of Barstool. It was just what was fair and I knew it.

What Chernin didn't get at first is that this wasn't a negotiation. It was take it or leave it. You either give Dan the $7 million signing bonus or I walk from the deal. They had no choice. With that ultimatum looming over their heads, Chernin came around to seeing things my way. But even that wasn't without a fight. Initially they wanted me to split Dan's bonus payment with them. Get the fuck out of my face with that shit. That would be my entire bank account at that point. They wanted me to throw in $3.5 million of my own money alongside their $3.5 million? My company had just turned their $12 million investment into $250 million thanks to us busting our fucking asses. We had absolutely killed it for them for five years and they wanted to squabble over $3.5 million. If anything I felt that it was insane they weren't already giving all of us nice signing bonuses from their end as a token of their appreciation—because that's what I would have done.

Nope. These were cutthroat, ruthless businessmen to the very end. As we were staring at the incredible amount of money that we, Barstool, had delivered to them through our hard work, they were cold, calculating, and cutthroat. Peter Chernin actually told me he wasn't sure he could give Dan any extra money because he had to get approval from investors in order to clear any additional bonuses. Like I gave a fuck about his investors. I felt that they should be pretty happy with the 2,080 percent return on investment over five years. Also, I knew they had no leg to stand on. I would have walked from the deal and been done with Barstool if they hadn't agreed to my demands. I told Mike Kerns he was being rude and selfish and I wasn't negotiating. It was either take $243 million profit instead of the $250 million or take nothing. I had them over the barrel. It wouldn't be the last time I used leverage in a negotiation to my advantage. I probably could have demanded more, looking back on it now, but that's not how I operate. I always negotiate in good faith and will stop at what I think is fair. And guess what? Chernin agreed to my terms, even if it was at gunpoint. But as far as my relationship with the Chernin Group went, the damage was done.

We never popped champagne together. We never had that celebratory moment—not a dinner, not a photograph, not a hug, nothing. They moved on to their next feast and that was that. It bums me out a bit, but it was just another teaching moment for me on the frigid temperaments one encounters in the world of big shot businessmen. They're never your friend, no matter how many smiles and dinners you have, no matter how well you do by them. You're just one of many balls they keep in the air, hoping eventually one of you will bring in the bacon.

I can't say that it soured the moment entirely though. After all, I was now worth—on paper—around $200 million. You can't make an omelette without cracking a couple eggs, and I guess you can't make $200 million without realizing that some people you thought were your friends . . . are not. That's not to say the Chernin people are bad people. I'm sure if I met them outside business I would be friendly with them. But I've always mixed those two worlds. I don't separate business and personal like other people do. I expect people to treat me how I'd treat them, but that's rarely the case.

Over the years, the Chernin Group has asked me to be a reference for other companies that they are looking to invest in. I'm always willing to do it. My message is the same: The Chernin guys did what they said. They gave us money. They gave us credibility. They stayed out of our way. But they will run you over if they think it's in their best interests. They aren't your friends. They are your business partners, trying to make the most money humanly possible off you. As long as you know that going in, you could do a lot worse.

And at least they weren't as bad as those investment bankers over at Moelis—the ones who were hired to facilitate the sale of Barstool but who accomplished absolutely nothing. They didn't get one offer. The only thing they did was blame all their failures on me. Meanwhile, I closed the one deal I ran without them. And yep, they still wanted their full commission for doing *nothing*. I can't hear their names without my skin crawling. Just vultures in suits that come in and try to leech off what real hardworking people have built.

A quick sidenote: Last year I had a call with Champions Circle, which runs the University of Michigan NIL (Name Image Likeness) program. There were three guys on the call. One of them introduced himself and said he was from Moelis. I'd never met him before but I quickly interjected that I hated Moelis and had a major issue with them. He was like, "We can discuss that later." Umm, not really. I won't give money to or do business with groups I don't trust. Not even at my beloved University of Michigan.

Anyway, we announced the deal in February 2020. Seventeen years of building Barstool brick by brick, dripping blood and sweat into every blog I wrote, had resulted in a windfall beyond my wildest of wild dreams. I remember calling Renee and being like we're worth $200 million. She was in shock. So was I. It still hadn't sunk in. We'd come a long way from playing PartyPoker to try to win her forty bucks to get her nails done.

Plus, my team was taken care of. From Erika to Gaz, Kevin, Keith, Dan . . . the people who had been with me for a decade or who had done the most to get us here, they all made out with life-changing sums.

It was hard for me not to feel that I was on top of the world that day. Everything truly seemed like it was coming up Pageviews. Jay Snowden and I were scheduled to ring the bell at the New York Stock Exchange on February 27 to celebrate the occasion.

It was a galling fuck-you to every hit piece writer, every KO Barstool protester, every enemy who had fought to tear us down. I had won, against all odds. Was it luck, business savvy, or both? Who knows. Maybe I always thought it *could* happen, but I never dared to dream it would be of the multi-hundred-million-dollar magnitude.

However, before I could relish our victory, the world flipped on its head. The coronavirus had seeped into America and brought the world to a screeching halt. The day we rang the bell on the stock market was the worst-performing day in the history of the Nasdaq. We popped champagne and clinked glass as confetti rained down from the ceiling. Meanwhile, the world was burning around us. It was a perfectly Barstool moment.

18

The King of COVID

What is that old expression? The best-laid plans of mice and men often go awry? Well, I think that certainly applies here. The ink on our shiny new deal with Penn Gaming wasn't even dry and suddenly everything was going to shit. It's tough to promote sports gambling when there are no sports to bet on. It's tough to tell people to visit casinos when all the casinos are closed. Overnight, Barstool Sports employees were forced to stop coming into the office. The world was shutting down around us.

But I was just getting started.

Okay, so I can't bet on sports anymore? Time to do what I do best: pivot, shake, move, and try something else. On one of the last days in the office before the total shutdown, I decided to start fucking around with the stock market—which I view as just another version of gambling. I plopped a couple hundred grand into a few stocks and livestreamed myself watching the ticker go up and down, trying to time it perfectly so I could squeeze out a few bucks. People instantly gravitated toward it. I could tell something was there.

The next day, I installed a bell outside my office, wore a suit to work during a time in which NYC was a virtual ghost town, and declared that the doors to *Davey Daytrader Global* were open for business.

I would go live every day for the opening and closing of the stock market. I asked Glenny Balls if he had any stock advice. He told me to go long on Shake Shack because people get hungry at lunch. So I bought a million dollars of Shake Shack. The stock went up 4 percent that day. That's $40K profit. The Wolf of Ball Street was born.

(A quick sidenote here before I get back into the story of *Davey Daytrader.* Glenny Balls was yet another in the long line of weird brains who somehow meandered their way into our universe. In Glenny's case, he kind of floated in like a manatee. We found him when we moved to our NYC offices and put out an ad for interns. Glenny showed up wearing a Hawaiian shirt and fat. In other words, he was right in my wheelhouse. I asked him if he had a nickname. He said, "Not really . . . well, some people call me Glenny Balls."

Say less, Glenny Balls. This kid clearly had the stuff we were looking for.

Now, what is that so-called stuff that makes you Barstool material, you may ask? What do I look for in a prospective employee? The answer is . . . I really don't have a clue. Some people I hire because of clear talent—your Pat McAfees, your *Bussin' With the Boys,* your *Spittin' Chiclets* of the world, etc.

And then there are others I find that just have a certain something that draws me to them, and them to me. We find employees in the most preposterous or unlikely situations. It's like there is some sort of higher power at work, luring these weird brains into our galaxy.

Here are just a few examples:

Caleb Pressley: we found Caleb when he was running down the sidelines of a North Carolina football game with a headset on and his blond hair flowing. His title was "Professor of Morale" for UNC football. After the broadcast, we had him on *The Rundown* the next day. There was something unique about him that I couldn't quite put my finger on, but we made a strong effort to hire him once he graduated, even though we had no clue what he'd do. Caleb would bounce around from project to project over the years until he hit a home run with *Sundae Conversation*—an interview series that featured the aforementioned Glenny Balls as his sidekick. Caleb left a few years ago after being lured away by a multimillion-dollar offer. Once again, this is a common theme with people who leave Barstool. It's generally not because they want to, but rather because somebody else made an offer they couldn't refuse.

Next up, Brandon Walker. April 8, 2019, was the night of the college basketball national championship. We were flying back from Minnesota, where the Final Four had been held. Minnesota was a state in which sports gambling wasn't yet legal. And I was ranting and raving about how much I loved Texas Tech to win it all, and I had wanted to put $250K on them, but I couldn't get the bet in because Minnesota didn't allow sports gambling.

Well, from the clouds, an incredibly shady offshore gambling website called MyBookie started chirping me, saying that I was full of shit. That I never had any intention of placing a bet that large, and I was just boasting about it to make myself seem tough. Listen, I'd been called just about every name in the book by this point—racist, sexist, homophobic, etc. But I draw the line at being called a fake gambler! How dare you question my degeneracy, good sir!

So naturally, I freaked out on MyBookie. The gloves came off instantly. Again, hit me with a feather, here comes the wrench. Well, the very first human to be affiliated with MyBookie after this blowup was Brandon Walker. Now, Brandon was a simple family man from Mississippi, who just happened to be hosting an online sports show from his basement the morning after the MyBookie controversy. His show was sponsored and advertised by MyBookie. The second he went live, the Stoolies attacked. Walker had no clue what was happening. His show, which normally drew an audience of tens, suddenly had thousands. He went from total confusion to hostility, then back to confusion. People were mocking everything about him, from his haircut to his shirt. To his credit, he handled the entire situation pretty well. Well enough, at least, that I decided—in a petty attempt to piss off MyBookie—I would hire Brandon Walker on the spot and steal him from them. And that's exactly what I did.

I offered Walker a job and told him he had twenty-four hours to decide. It was now or never. He could join Barstool or stay stuck in Mississippi, toiling away in his basement for his rabid audience of six people. After a few moments of hesitation, Walker made the clear and obvious choice: he was joining Barstool. He told me hiring him would be one of the best decisions I ever made. Okay okay, Walker. Nobody cares. You could be a potted plant and I would have hired you. I was doing it out of pure spite. It had nothing to do with you.

But to Brandon Fucking Walker's credit, he's been one of our most dynamic and productive hires in recent memory. He lived up to his word. And I found him all because MyBookie called me a fake gambler.

And last but certainly not least is Frank the Tank. Frank went viral one spring day as he was trying to take New Jersey Transit to watch his beloved Mets play on opening day. There was some sort of delay causing Frank to be late for the game. Naturally, he took it all in stride, as he is prone to do. Just kidding. He threw a tantrum. And in an incredible stroke of luck, the local news caught it all on camera. They had Frank decked out head to toe in Mets gear, ranting and raving about the incompetence of NJ Transit. As we'd come to find out later, he would have acted the same exact way regardless of whether the cameras were rolling. It was straight out of *Seinfeld*, and it was viral gold. I knew I needed to have him.

The next day, we had Frank on Barstool Radio to discuss his viral moment, and he proceeded to tell us he had written a blog called The Sports Encyclopedia, every day, for thirteen years straight, to a grand audience of nobody. Like I'm not exaggerating. His YouTube videos had zero views. Now that is what I'm talking about when I say doing it for the love of the game.

When I hired Frank, I never dreamed he'd become the star he is today, but that can be said about a lot of our weird brains. They are just people who needed a shot to let their star shine through in their own unique way. And for whatever reason, the Barstool Galaxy is the place where all these misfit toys seem to find the exact right settings and circumstances that let them thrive. Who could have dreamed that Frank's viral NJ Transit moment would lead him to starring in videos with Arnold Schwarzenegger about the virtues of staying in shape? Frank has lost close to three hundred pounds since he joined Barstool, and he is a role model to so many people in their weight loss journey. The Barstool Difference indeed.)

Okay, enough about the weird brains. Back to COVID and *DDTG*.

Every day my audience grew. I didn't miss one day of livestreaming. At

9:25 a.m., you could find me ready to trade. At 3:30 p.m., you could find me ready to trade. I was betting millions on different stocks every day. I documented the ups and downs of it all. I was winning and losing seven figures per day. I got kicked off E-Trade for complaining about how much the platform sucked. I kept pressing the wrong buttons by accident. I saw a deer outside my door in the Hamptons when I had COVID. So I bought John Deere stock. I picked three letters out of a Scrabble bag randomly and bought a million of $RTX. I learned how to short stocks and got smushed. Boeing became my archenemy. I started to learn the names of the various CEOs of the companies I invested in, and I would rip them apart when I didn't like what they said or praise them like kings when they moved the market in my favor. I had my team of internet ninjas and seasoned graphic designers creating hype videos as if *DDTG* was a sports team.

Mad Money was revolutionary for the stock market when it hit the airwaves. Nobody had ever seen anything like Jim Cramer before. But there had been no innovation in decades. And out of nowhere, here came *DDTG* from a world none of these Wall Street suits had any clue about.

I decided to go big on Spirit Airlines one day. I theorized that I didn't think they'd go out of business even though the travel industry was totally shut down at the time. Less than thirty minutes after I had yelled *buy buy buy* on Spirit Airlines, the Oracle of Omaha, Warren Buffett, said he was selling all his airline stocks and was totally out. I positioned it as me vs. Buffett. "WE FLY IN THIS COUNTRY! STOCKS ONLY GO UP!"

I had a green hammer of death that I smashed whenever I wanted to buy something big. It was hype video after hype video coming out. Miraculously, Spirit Airlines rebounded and quickly quadrupled in price. People were sending me pictures of Spirit Airlines planes in the sky. I proclaimed myself the new king of the stock market. Warren Buffett was nearing ninety years old and washed-up. I was the new captain. *DDTG* was featured daily everywhere, from the *Wall Street Journal* to the *New York Times* to the *London Times*. I was on every business channel there was. Things that were clearly meant to be tongue-in-cheek from me—insane stock picks, screaming at billionaire CEOs—were being reported as literal. I documented all my wins and losses in real time, just like betting on sports and winning or losing a game at the buzzer.

Most of these publications called me an idiot and said I was dangerous. I was getting in fights with actual Wall Street analysts who cried that I was making a mockery of the stock market. They were right. But more specifically, I was making fun of them and their ivory towers. I countered that they were just mad that the stock market was now accessible to the everyday person. You didn't need to work at a big firm or be a licensed trader to make money anymore; you just needed access to a computer. The barrier to entry was gone and I was exposing all these frauds.

DDTG was everywhere. I was even lampooned in the Showtime series *Billions*. The show that started on a whim with Glenny Balls advising me to buy Shake Shack stock (which had tripled in just a year, by the way) was now routinely getting thirty thousand concurrent viewers every time I went live. People were asking me for stock tips all day long. I had done what Barstool has done so many times over the years: I had disrupted an industry that hadn't seen innovation in forever. And it all culminated with the GameStop fiasco.

Before the GameStop and the whole memestock craze even began, the beloved leader of the whole movement, Roaring Kitty (that was his online alias), had already made a video praising *DDTG* and ripping the established financial community who didn't see the value or humor in what I was doing. So when the Reddit forum r/WallStreetBets helped push GameStop to the moon, I was right there with them. It wasn't a question of whether I was going to make money on GameStop; just how much. And then Robinhood and Vlad Tenev pulled the plug on the entire thing.

It became the biggest story in the world. As a quick reminder of what happened: The internet, led by a Reddit forum called r/WallStreetBets and Roaring Kitty, decided collectively that everybody should buy GameStop stock. Everybody did buy it. And the stock went berserk. It just kept going up and up and up. Normal, everyday people—who had never bought a stock in their lives—were making more money than they'd made in their lifetime. There seemed to be no end in sight to it.

Until the most popular trading platform for bros and everyday traders, Robinhood, shut down all buying of the stock and would only allow sell orders. This immediately tanked the stock. It was unprecedented and egregious.

Robinhood had effectively stepped in and played referee to save the billionaire hedge fund owners who had bet against GameStop. The uproar was immediate, and naturally, I was right smack-dab in the middle of it. I actually secured the first interview with Vlad Tenev, the CEO of Robinhood, for a *DDTG* exclusive and just raked him over the coals about the whole thing.

> **TENEV:** I'm proud of the way the team handled the crisis . . . We were able to protect the firm. We were able to prevent customers from having a bigger issue.

> **DAVE:** How can that be possible? You guys are billed as a firm to retail traders, and you screwed them over.

Now keep in mind, I only knew like 10 percent of how the stock market even worked in the first place, but that made me the same as everybody else who had bought GameStop. Me personally? I lost $700K on it. I was furious. I was the voice of the people—a rich voice, but a voice nonetheless. I chased Steve Cohen, the owner of the Mets, off Twitter. He literally deactivated his account because I was nonstop hounding him about GameStop and whether he was involved. (I have a theory that Cohen would later exact his revenge with Business Insider, but I've never been able to prove it.)

I played such a big role in the entire saga that I was featured in the movie *Dumb Money*. They actually took real video from *DDTG* and just replaced Vlad's face with the actor playing Vlad. But I was in it. They didn't ask me for permission either. They just took the footage from the internet. I didn't even know I was in the movie till it came out and people told me about it. I still don't know how that works. It seems like I should have been paid for that, but I guess they knew it would stroke my ego being in a major motion picture.

I'd continue to dutifully stream *DDTG* every single day during COVID until the country opened back up and I had to go back to my real job.

By the way, this was also when I dabbled with Bitcoin for the first time. I made a video about how I had no clue what it was. Well, it turned out the

Winklevoss twins were staying at the same hotel I was at during COVID, and they owned like 5 percent of all the Bitcoin in the world. They are also six-four and there are two of them, in case you didn't know?

They came over to my room and tried to explain Bitcoin to me. I bought $2 million of it at a price of $11,000. Then they proceeded to tell me that it would explode in value because Elon Musk was going to fly to outer space and mine gold from the stars, and the gold would fall plentiful from the sky, making it worthless, and Bitcoin would replace it. That's literally what they told me. I looked at them like they had nine heads. I quickly sold all the Bitcoin that I had just bought because I thought they were crazy. Naturally, it rocketed to $60,000 within a few months: a nifty $12 million profit down the drain because I thought the Winklevosses were on hallucinogens when they came to my door that fateful morning.

Either way, I had fully broken down the doors of the finance industry and captured a new audience, which was probably worth more than the $12 million I lost. Because as my old friend Warren Buffett once said, the only thing more valuable than money is eyeballs.

(Warren Buffett did not say this but it's a quote that for some reason I attribute to him anyway. In actuality, I think I just made it up.)

While the overall character of Davey Daytrader was basically a satire of the finance industry, I will say that I believed 99 percent of the stuff I was saying about the space during those days—especially in regard to the GameStop saga. Wall Street is filled with crooks and criminals masquerading as superior businessmen. They like to pretend like they are smarter than everybody else, and that the average Joe Schmo can't trade stocks without them. In reality, it's a good old boys club. It's designed to keep the rich rich and the poor poor. And when, for the first time in the history of Wall Street, the little guy was winning, the big guys just pressed pause on the entire game to reset the playing field. It was disgusting. I have no respect for people who build their fortunes through Wall Street. You should have to build something of value to get rich in this country; not just piggyback off the work of others playing a rigged game. There is no honor in that.

Another victim of COVID was my pizza reviews. For five years straight, I had been visiting a local pizzeria every single day and doing my patented one-bite review. COVID brought that to a crashing halt. So once again I pivoted. Instead of doing pizzerias, I moved to frozen pizza reviews. I had every frozen pizza company in the world sending me their frozen pizza to try. Everybody except Jack's Pizza, that is. They were the only one I couldn't get my hands on. So I actually reached out to them and asked if they'd send me one. Their Instagram account replied that they were too busy to fulfill my request. *Okay, that's a bit strange that you can't mail one frozen pizza to me, but if you say so.* Later, I would receive a Jack's Pizza from a random Stoolie. I don't think they froze it correctly. It came out all floppy and disgusting. I gave them a horrible but fair score based on what I ate and ripped them for not sending me a pizza like everybody else. Jack's Pizza instantly became one of my archenemies.

On the brighter side though, I was able to save dozens and dozens of pizzerias from going out of business with my frozen pizza reviews. A good review could land a place thirty to forty thousand orders overnight. You read that correctly. Thirty to forty thousand orders overnight. That's how popular my reviews were. It was insanity. Small businesses that were on the verge of going out of business were suddenly given a lifeline and had to hire more people to fulfill the orders.

This was the genesis of me coming out with my own line of frozen pizza called . . . wait for it . . . One Bite frozen pizza. This concept actually started with our sales group in New York. They did a sales deal—without my knowledge—in which they were going to lease the name to a third-party company to make the pizza, and we'd receive ad dollars to promote it. Umm, no thanks. I stopped the deal in its tracks once I found out about it. Why would I give the IP to somebody else? If I was going to make a frozen pizza, I wanted to own the pizza and the name and not let somebody else get rich off my IP. So we totally restructured the deal. The only problem? The pizza sucked. I mean even for frozen pizza it was bad. There is nothing worse than having to endorse a shitty product and that's exactly what I had. It was so bad that I actually had to edit in a very obvious and preposterous crunch sound to make the crust seem crispy whenever I took a bite.

Despite how bad it was (and as a testament to my marketing power), it was still the largest frozen food launch in the history of Walmart. We sold millions of pizzas the first month. People were driving from the city to Walmarts just to buy the pizza and make their own videos with it.

But I couldn't keep pushing it. I knew it was no good. I refused to continue with it. As it turns out, I should have started an entirely new process to look for a great manufacturer rather than rely on whoever the sales team had found. That was my fault. I didn't do enough due diligence on them. I took whatever they said to me at face value. The manufacturer told me this was the best frozen pizza you could mass-produce on the market with the available technology. It turned out they just didn't have the best or newest equipment. They were using my name and the One Bite pizza to raise more money for their company so they could improve the product. It was ass-backward.

Now, as of the writing of this book, I am gearing up to launch One Bite frozen pizza 2.0. This time I love the pizza. I can promote it and be proud of it. I guess time will tell if you only get one bite at the apple (no pun intended but intended) with the frozen food game. But I know this: the first version sucked and I refused to continue promoting it. The second version I'd happily eat 24/7 and be satisfied. I'll let you know how it goes.

Anyway, back to COVID. One day, when I was reviewing pizza, I heard a buzz at my doorbell. I ran downstairs to get the package and meanwhile, the camera for my pizza review (my cell phone propped up on my kitchen table) was still running. I brought in the package and announced I had another frozen pizza delivery. I didn't think much about it, but my address was clearly visible for the world to see on the package. When I posted the pizza review, the entire world learned exactly where I lived.

The next day, I had half a dozen or so packages at my door. *Hmm, that's weird.* Ever the showman, I decided to open them all on camera at the end of my daily frozen pizza review—kind of like a bonus section of the video. The day after that, there were two dozen packages waiting for me at my apartment. I opened them all again on camera. The next day there were fifty. I no longer could fit opening all the packages into my pizza reviews. This was becoming its own daily segment.

Introducing *The Unboxing.* Every single night at 8 p.m., I would set up my iPhone and unbox whatever was sent to me in the mail. It grew wildly out of control, and fast. I had hundreds and hundreds and hundreds of packages a night. I even think there were days when I had over a thousand packages.

it's a Boy

Every time I did *The Unboxing*, I was basically encouraging the world to send me more shit. And shit they did send me. People started sending me live animals, weapons, drugs, cockroaches, ants, etc. I even got a new pet out of it: Randolph the Goldfish became an instant sensation. We had Randolph necklaces and merch that sold out in a heartbeat. Randolph became part of my *DDTG* hype videos. I had an entire school of koi fish living in my bathtub. I got baby ducklings sent to me. How the fuck do you mail baby ducklings? I had to find a local farm to take them for me. Eventually people would send me stuff to try to scare me, like a dead fish or something. One night my doorbell rang and a fully paid-for prostitute was at my door, ready to fuck me. *Sorry, ma'am, I'm in the middle of* The Unboxing *right now.* I felt bad for her, so I gave her four hundred bucks for her trouble and sent her on her way.

The Unboxing was as close to being depressed as I've ever been in my life. I was absolutely dominating the content game, but my life SUCKED. I don't think people realized how much *The Unboxing* took out of me. I'd start at 8 p.m. every night and finish unboxing around 2 or 3 a.m. My apartment looked like a bomb hit it when it was over, with animals and insects littered everywhere. Then it would take me an hour or two to upload all the footage to my right-hand man, Frankie Borrelli, who would then compile a highlight reel to post the next day. I'd probably get to bed at 4 a.m., barely able to move in my own apartment. Just living in filth. Then I'd wake up at 8 a.m. to let Servpro into my apartment to clean up the mess from the prior night. (Just in case you are wondering what Servpro is, they are an emergency disaster relief company.) They clean up after hurricanes or floods, or in my case, one night of *The Unboxing*. Then, all day while I did *DDTG* and my frozen pizza reviews, I'd make trips to the lobby of my apartment building to bring up the new packages. By the time Servpro was done around 5 p.m., another thousand packages were stacked and ready to be opened. I had somewhere between thirty and forty thousand concurrent viewers for *DDTG* in the mornings and afternoons, and then anywhere between sixty and a hundred thousand concurrents at night for *The Unboxing*. And they were completely different crowds. I didn't have a minute to myself in my own apartment. But I was absolutely dominating COVID.

My next COVID venture was the *BFF* podcast.

This started one day when I was scrolling Twitter and I noticed that Charli D'Amelio and Lil Huddy were the number one trend in the world. If you don't know who either of these people is, don't worry because neither did I at the time. What the hell is a Lil Huddy? But the impressions and virality of it were undeniable. So I quote-tweeted some post about them and asked, "Who the fuck are these people?" To answer that question, I was introduced to Josh Richards, a young guy who was apparently in that world. And when I say in that world I mean he was a TikToker, or as I called them, Wiggle Dickers (guys who dance in front of the mirror, wiggle their dicks, and make videos of it).

Josh and I decided to do an Instagram Live where he could explain who these people were to my audience and why they were fighting. The chemistry between Josh and me was surprisingly good. So good, in fact, that Snapchat pitched us a show together based on that Instagram Live.

I had no interest in that. I was quickly getting up to speed on this new platform called TikTok and the power it held. I had been doing Barstool for almost twenty years at this point. We were getting old. Nobody on TikTok knew who we were and I didn't know who they were. So even though I really had no interest in learning about the gossip of teenagers, I decided that it would be worth doing a show with Josh. *Let's reestablish our connection with the youth of this country.*

Josh gave us access to his world. I gave him credibility beyond just being a TikToker. I remember flying out to LA to visit the Sway House (a house filled with ten or twelve Joshes living together). Each Sway House member had been assigned a podcaster to build a podcast with. I looked around the room and asked Josh, "How'd you end up with me and everybody else got morons?"

I was right, of course. We called our show *BFFs* (best friends forever), and Josh and I were the only podcast that lasted. It took me less than a month to burst onto the TikTok scene. It went from nobody knowing who I was on TikTok to everybody knowing who I was. Eventually we added Brianna Chickenfry to the mix—a breakout TikTok star I'd hired as an intern—and we had a bona fide hit show on our hands.

My mission was accomplished. My personal fan base continued to grow, made up of one of the weirdest mishmashes of people on the planet. I had teenagers from *BFFs*, little kids from pizza reviews, finance bros from *DDTG*, couples from *The Unboxing*, Stoolies from the newspaper days, liberals who hated my guts, and conservatives who loved me from Fox News. During COVID, I started appearing on Fox News shows, where they would call me on to rant about how unfair the COVID restrictions were to small businesses. When clips of my appearances went viral, they'd have me back more and more. The point is, people found me from all different places. And it didn't matter *how* you knew me so long as you knew me.

All of it culminated with what still to this day I am most proud of from my entire journey with Barstool Sports. And that, of course, was the Barstool Fund.

I've had a long-standing policy at Barstool that we don't talk politics. Of course, this has sort of become a farce because I myself can't abide by my own rules. I get so frustrated and fed up with politicians that I can't help but speak my mind sometimes. It just boils up within me and I've got to let it explode. During the COVID lockdowns, this happened a lot. I just didn't understand how the government could lock down entire states and tell businesses they couldn't open their doors, but with no way to compensate them for this situation. There were all these promises of getting money down the road but they were just promises that did no good in the near term. These bars, restaurants, bowling alleys, dry cleaners, and gyms were going out of business *now*, in real time with no end in sight. As somebody who had spent fifteen years building Barstool, I just couldn't fathom getting all the way to the point where I was finally earning a living only to be shut down by the government. It made me sick to my stomach.

So I posted a rant basically saying how ludicrous the entire thing was. I said listen, everybody knows that COVID is a risk. If a person wants to risk getting sick and wants to go to a restaurant, that is up to them—not the government. If you're afraid of catching COVID, stay home.

Well, a guy by the name of Marcus Lemonis tweeted at me to shut up and put my money where my mouth was. That was the prompt I needed to start the Barstool Fund. I put $500K of my own money into it and told any business owners who needed a grant to survive COVID to reach out to me. I would pay all their expenses for as long as COVID continued. Month after month, they would receive a check covering everything from payroll to rent to electricity bills.

We were immediately inundated with submissions. Barstool basically shut down everything else we were doing to run this fund. We would pore through the submissions to find companies that met the criteria, and they would be passed up the ladder to me. I would then call the business to tell them they'd been selected while recording their reactions on FaceTime. It was these little videos that made the Barstool Fund explode. It was a real, unfiltered, authentic, and emotional look into the heartbeat of America. People broke down weeping when they heard my voice on the phone. Family businesses, passed down through generations, were on their last lifeline and about to lose everything when I'd make the call. And while politicians were screaming and yelling at each other and getting nothing done per usual, we were making a real impact.

Courtesy of Fox Archives

When it was all said and done, we had raised close to $50 million and saved over four hundred businesses across America. It took less than forty-eight hours from when I told a recipient that they had been chosen until the funds were in their account. And those funds would be added every single month until the pandemic was over.

One of the beautiful things was that lots of these businesses that received the grants then turned around and gave the money back to the fund so it could help other businesses, once they were able to open their doors again. They wanted to help other companies that needed assistance. Still to this day, one of the most satisfying feelings I get is when I go into a new city and see a Barstool Fund recipient thriving. Not to be sappy, but this is the America I love and would fight for. It's people helping people. No agenda. No politics. Just everybody pitching in to keep the American Dream afloat. It probably makes Zohran Mamdani sick to his stomach.

(A funny sidenote from the Barstool Fund: the success of this movement landed me the cover of *N Magazine*, which is like a bougie Nantucket glossy magazine. They reached out to me and asked if I would be interested. I'm not gonna lie; I was pretty excited about it. It was probably my ego speaking, but I thought it was a huge honor to get featured on the cover of a magazine from my favorite place in the world; a magazine that I knew everybody on the island read. So I flew to Nantucket in the offseason to do a photoshoot, and I spent a bunch of time doing interviews for it. Well, once the magazine came out, all hell broke loose.

Now keep in mind, *N Magazine* is not exactly *Time*, the *New Yorker*, or *The Atlantic*. It's a fluff magazine. It's supposed to be light and breezy summer reading. There should have been absolutely nothing controversial about featuring one of the more famous summer residents who had been coming to the island for over a decade, and who, by the way, had just raised $50 million for small businesses throughout America. But this is me we're talking about. Some angry locals were mortified that the magazine would feature me. It all started with a lunatic crazy liberal lady who worked at a bar called The Gaslight. And yes, if you feel like almost every Dave Portnoy hit piece starts with some lunatic crazy liberal lady, you are probably correct.

Anyway, this lady launched a campaign to get *N Magazine* to retract my cover. How do you retract a cover? I'll never know. She quoted every hit piece ever written about me from the beginning of time to prove her case that *N Magazine* had basically just featured Hitler on their cover. It got so bad that eventually *N Magazine* publicly apologized.

Well, as you can probably imagine by this point in the book, that didn't sit well with me. It was all-out war. I called for a boycott of The Gaslight. I crucified *N Magazine* for having no spine. I named names. I was pissed. Here I was, donating my time to this magazine, and this was how they repaid me? By apologizing for shit that wasn't even real? Get the fuck out of my face with that. I have no time for spineless jellyfish. To this day, I still won't go to Gaslight and I hate *N Magazine* and everybody affiliated with it.

I'm sure lots of people on Nantucket still hate my guts for the uproar I caused. But I also know the first night I was back on the island after the dustup, I had dinner at a restaurant called the SeaGrille (great spot by the way). The waiter calmly came up to me as I was getting ready to leave and whispered in my ear, "Just so you know, all the normal people have your back on this island." It meant a lot and truthfully that's how I view Barstool. All the normal people know who we are and have our backs. Let the lunatic fringe stomp their feet and cry and moan. Life is too short to be that miserable.)

PS: I'm just going to throw this out there. I know Gavin Newsom is going to run for president. I DESPISE him. And my disgust started during COVID. California had just about the strictest lockdown rules in America. I mean they were arresting people for going to the beach. If you were a business owner and tried to open your doors, it was straight to jail. You had to mask up at all times. As a result, we were flooded with Barstool Fund applications from California in particular. People were losing their entire livelihoods and nobody was helping. And in the middle of all this, Gavin Newsom went to the fanciest restaurant in the country—the French Laundry—and was photographed with no mask on, having the time of his life. It infuriated me beyond belief. Rules for thee but not for me. I just couldn't imagine being the one who was responsible for all these hard lockdown rules and then openly flouting them in people's faces with such reckless abandon. Like it's one thing if you issue these lockdown orders and then you abide by your own rules. I don't agree with it but I can live with it. But I just can't handle the blatant hypocrisy, especially when I was seeing firsthand the damage it was doing to the people of his state. It still disgusts me to this day.

PPS: One last paragraph in this COVID chapter. I don't want to suck my own dick too much here, but something that I feel gets overlooked with me is that not only am I one of the biggest personalities at Barstool, I'm still involved in the day-to-day running of the business. That balancing act—of prioritizing making content and creating headlines while dealing with behind-the-scenes shit—is something I have constantly juggled for two decades. I've had to deal with a ton of big personalities, negotiate contracts, and make sure everything is running smoothly.

COVID eliminated most of this for me. Everybody was working at home. There wasn't much going on besides making content. It was the first time I was able to focus solely on that since I had sold the company to Chernin. I think COVID proved that when content is all I have to focus on, I can still jam a 103 mph fastball right down your cock.

19
Politics

Trigger Warning! This chapter talks a lot about politics and how I came to view the world as I do today, in case you've been too stupid to figure it out by now. Lots of Donald Trump talk. Lots of politics. If this is going to drive you insane, I suggest you just skip ahead. No need to give yourself an ulcer. Proceed at your own risk.

Donald Trump ran for president in 2016. Up to that point I would say I rarely, if ever, talked about politics. I pretty much hated all politicians—Republicans, Democrats, whatever. It didn't matter; I thought they were all slimebags. Hillary Clinton was the epitome of slimy politicians to me at that point: somebody who seemingly would stoop to any level to become president. If you told me she had murdered somebody in her political career, I would have believed it. So I wasn't surprised when I believed the DNC rigged the election for her against Bernie Sanders to help her get the nomination. She was everything I despised about traditional politics.

Meanwhile, Donald Trump was different. He was the most unpresidential presidential candidate I'd ever seen, hurling insults and one-liners like he was a blogger at Barstool. I thought he was hilarious and a much-needed breath of fresh air. I had long thought our two-party political system was broken and needed a total reset, or somebody who could disrupt and break the system. To me, Donald Trump was that guy. Not because of any of his policies. He was just making a mockery of the entire political system and I was here for it. So I publicly supported his run for president and I said exactly that. I thought he could break politics as we knew them. Little did I know at the time that he would, in fact, shock the world and become the president of the United States.

His election flat-out broke people's brains. A new disease riddled America called Trump Derangement Syndrome. My dad suffered from it. Deadspin suffered from it. Every Democrat on the planet seemingly suffered from it. Toxic masculinity became all the rage. I'm pretty sure the pussies at Deadspin literally deleted their entire Twitter/social footprint and apologized for every joke they'd ever made over the past century. Jokes were now off-limits. Nothing was funny anymore. If you didn't rush to condemn Trump, you were a ghoul and a disgusting human. If you were in a frat, you were a rapist. Forget the fact that more than half the country voted Trump into office. Nope, nuance was gone. Trump was Hitler and if you supported him, you were a Nazi. End of story.

I thought the entire thing was insane. I didn't apologize. I didn't delete my social media history. I stood by every joke I'd ever made in my twenty years of being online. For all the people who hated my guts over the years, my vote for Trump was confirmation bias of every preconceived notion they had of me. They didn't have to say any of the prior allegations. All the left had to say was "Dave Portnoy is a Trump supporter" and then that somehow automatically meant I was a racist, sexist, homophobic piece of shit. The country was tipping over sideways. There was no space for reason, no room for moderate thought. Trump Derangement Syndrome was more contagious than COVID ever was.

And all that was before I interviewed Trump.

Fast-forward to 2020, and Trump ran again. And one day, while I was lounging by my pool on Nantucket, I got a call from Washington. They wanted me to interview Donald Trump in the Rose Garden at the White House . . . tomorrow.

Wait, what? It was so out of left field that I wondered if it was even real at first. Like yes, I had supported Trump four years earlier when he ran for president. But I wasn't overly vocal about him during his presidency. I kind of followed my own advice and stayed away from politics. It was so toxic that you were going to piss off half the country no matter what you said. And I was a firm believer in that old Michael Jordan quote: both red and blue states buy sneakers. Or in our case, both red and blue states buy T-shirts.

But this was the president of the United States summoning me to the Oval Office. I couldn't say no.

Now, I'm not an interviewer. I don't mean I'm not a good interviewer. I mean I don't think I had ever formally interviewed anybody about anything, ever, prior to Trump. People ask me all the time—was I nervous? Fuck yeah I was nervous. You've got to remember, this was long before Trump made googly eyes at every Tom, Dick, and Harry on social media. This was before he did major podcasts like Joe Rogan, Theo Von, and the *NELK* Boys; and even before he did nondescript podcasts like *Bussin' With the Boys*. This was revolutionary for the time: a blogger getting to interview the sitting president of the United States.

I knew I had to do it. My only requirement was that his team wasn't allowed to screen my questions beforehand. I was going to ask whatever I wanted to ask. The White House agreed and the interview was on. It was probably the biggest thing I'd ever done up to that point. Now, I also knew it would bring a firestorm because of what a lightning rod Trump was. I knew the same people who already hated me would hate me even more for doing the interview. But who fucking cared? I could cure cancer and they'd still hate me. And hell, if Kim Jong Un had invited me to North Korea to interview him, I'd probably do it. I'm Davey Pageviews; not Davey Switzerland.

So on July 22 I was relaxing at my pool on Nantucket, working on my golden chocolate chip cookie tan, probably sexting some girls; and the next day I was in Washington, interviewing the president of the United States. Just an insane turn of events in twenty-four hours. When I arrived in DC, I got a tour of the White House, which was supercool because I'd never been in the White House before. I don't care what your stance on this country is; it's hard not to be moved by all the history there. The patriotism was coursing through my veins to the point where I thought I might transform into a bald eagle right on the spot.

Then they brought me into a waiting room where various members of Trump's cabinet or family came up to me and said they were fans of Barstool. The legendary Yankees closer Mariano Rivera was there. He said he was a big fan. The whole thing was surreal. The only person I had with me was my camera guy Frankie Borrelli. But when they led me out to interview the president, Borrelli wasn't allowed to come with me. So out I went, surrounded by seemingly twenty of the president's men. All by myself. It was intimidating to say the least.

Now, when the president came out, it became fairly obvious he didn't really know much about me or Barstool. There was no "Hey Dave, great to see you" moment. His handlers brought him over, we shook hands, and the interview began. Right off the bat, I hit him with an icebreaker. I asked him about his appearance on *Da Ali G Show* years earlier, when he quickly saw through the comedian's setup and knew he was being trolled. Honestly, Trump's the only guy I saw on that show who was able to pick up on it that fast. Trump loved it, loved that I gave him credit for that, and said nobody had ever mentioned that before. Instantly, he let his guard down as he realized this wasn't going to be a gotcha interview.

I didn't want to ask overly political questions because I knew I didn't have the depth of knowledge to push back on his answers if they weren't true or had major flaws in them. But I didn't want to just go and be a fanboy and suck his dick either.

In the end, I did ask him about Black Lives Matter, Colin Kaepernick kneeling during the anthem, and a few other questions that I didn't think were exactly softball questions. And I thought Trump answered them honestly. I also think I may be the first and only interviewer in the history of interviewing Donald Trump to get him to admit he made a mistake about something. I asked him if he ever regretted some of his crazy tweets the morning after posting them because I knew I sometimes regretted mine.

DAVE: Because I follow you on Twitter . . . do you ever tweet out and wake up like, "Oh man, I wish I didn't send that one out."

TRUMP: Too often. In the old days, before this, you'd write a letter and you'd say, "This letter is really bad," you put it on your desk, and then you go back tomorrow and you say, "Oh, I'm glad I didn't send it," right? But we don't do that with Twitter. We put it out instantaneously. We feel great, and then you start getting phone calls, "Did you really say this?" I say, "What's wrong with that?" And you find a lot of things. You know what I find? It's not the tweets, it's the retweets that get you in trouble.

Maybe I was a professional interviewer after all? It certainly wasn't the most hard-hitting interview of all time, but I don't think it was strictly fluff either.

After the interview was over, Trump told me to follow him into a room. No cameras, just the two of us. It was a little closet/gift shop room and he told me, "This is the Monica Lewinsky room." We both shared a laugh. I also told Trump that my father absolutely despised him. Like when you look up Trump Derangement Syndrome in the dictionary, there is probably a picture of my dad's face there. I purposely didn't tell my dad that I was interviewing Trump because I wanted to surprise FaceTime him when I was there. I had no clue whether Trump would let me do it, but he was all for it. So that's exactly what I did. I FaceTimed my dad and when he picked up, it was me and the president of the United States.

I asked him if he had anything to say to President Trump after killing him all these years. My dad froze up in his big moment. I guess you can't really blame him. He was probably in a state of shock. It still yielded an iconic photo of both me and Trump laughing as my dad fumbled over his words.

Photo by Mallory Blount Jaspers, WH 45 Staff

Now, I knew there would be backlash with the Trump interview. But I don't think I was prepared for how apeshit Big Cat went. I didn't realize how much he despised Trump at this point. He hated him even more than my dad did. He felt that by me interviewing Trump, I was basically saying all of Barstool was pro-Trump, including him. And I get his point. When I speak on politics or any bigger issues, the world assumes that I speak on behalf of Barstool. I don't. My employees know they're absolutely allowed to say whatever they want from their personal social media channels; they're allowed to have differing opinions from mine; and they're even allowed to publicly criticize me, even if their criticisms are moronic.

This is a nuance that isn't grasped by the audience or the broader public. Nobody takes the time to look under the hood and see that Barstool is a wildly varied company with wildly different political viewpoints.

So Dan legitimately worried that because I was associating myself with Trump, everyone would assume that *he* was a Trump guy too; that this interview would make it seem that Barstool had signed off on this and endorsed Trump as their president of choice. Furthermore, we had a long-standing policy of not doing politics, and not only had I interviewed the most polarizing president ever, but I hadn't even told anyone about it. He took it as a slap in the face that he wasn't in the loop after everything he had done for the company. Oh, and he really, really hated Trump.

I'd actually never seen Dan this upset. And all his points were valid. It's also why I consciously hadn't told him. Like I was going to do this interview no matter what. What would have happened if I had alerted him before the interview and he had threatened to quit if I went through with it? Then Barstool and I would have been fucked. It would have put all of us in an unwinnable situation. At least by keeping him in the dark, he could honestly say he had no clue and was totally caught off guard and hated it. I figured it was better to do it and beg for forgiveness afterward. I stand by the decision, and to this day it's the only major decision I've made regarding the company where I kept Dan completely in the dark. It's also the only disagreement he and I have had since the ESPN saga. We've pretty much been in lockstep with everything since then. It just shows how divisive Trump can actually be, given that it caused this big of a ripple between Dan and me when, for the most part, we see the world the same way.

People ask me all the time: Do I like Donald Trump? Well, I absolutely liked him from that interview six years ago. I found him funny, personable, engaging, etc. And to be honest, every time I've seen him since that interview, I've found him to be the same way. He always remembers me, makes small talk, and makes me feel seen. That's a pretty impressive trait for the leader of the free world. And maybe how I view Trump is shaped by my own life experiences. I've been dragged through the coals by the woke left media, lied about, have had things ripped out of context over and over and over again. If I read and believed all the hit pieces written about me over the years, *I* would think I'm Hitler. And I know these "journalists" do it on purpose. They are intentionally misleading people and leaving out context and facts. It drives me bonkers. My knee-jerk reaction whenever this happens is to attack the writer and publication. So when Trump coined the phrase "Fake News," I could certainly appreciate it. When Trump is rude and mean to a *New York Times* or *Washington Post* reporter, I get it. That's how I would be and act if I were him. If I think you are being fair to me, I'll be fair to you. But when I know you have an agenda, the gloves come off. Granted, I'm a blogger and not the president, but I do sympathize with him.

That's why when people attack Trump, I take most of it with a grain of salt until I can research what they are talking about myself. Because all these people who proclaim Trump to be the worst human in the world literally say the same exact thing about me. I've tried to have this conversation with my dad and say, "If I wasn't your son and you didn't know me, you'd hate me because you believe everything the media says." If all you do is read and listen to media outlets who hate Trump, you are just going to reinforce your own bias. My dad really has no answer to this except to say Trump is bad and I'm his son, so I'm good.

There is no doubt that me supporting Trump in 2016, along with my interview with him, has shaped how the world perceives me. Or maybe it just confirmed it. If you hate Trump, you hate Dave Portnoy. There is nothing I could ever do or say to change your opinion of me, or the way the left covers me. I could save a dying puppy on the side of the road. *Fuck him, he likes Trump!* I could save a village of women from drowning in a flood. *Fuck him, he voted for Trump!*

On the flip side, if you love Trump then you think I'm the biggest Trump guy on the planet and you love me. There is no in-between, and frankly it's what I despise most about politics. People sometimes make fun of me for always saying I hate both extremes but I do. The world would be a better place if they both were just erased from the face of the earth. I hate how when you know how somebody will answer every single question before you even ask it just based on their political affiliation. The facts are that I don't fit into a box.

Despite what social media says about me, I'm not some crazy Trump guy. Before the 2024 election, I was on the record as saying I'd vote for Nikki Haley in the Republican primary. I went on the *NELK* podcast—which is basically a Trump fan club—saying I wouldn't vote for him again because I thought he was too divisive for the country. Meaning that he had already broken so many people's brains that there was just no way the country could move forward in harmony with him as president, no matter what he did. Plus, I knew Trump would continue to antagonize all his enemies exactly like how I do, but he's the president. Like I want this country to get along. I hated how toxic and divided it was then. And even though I don't think Trump has been treated fairly by the media, I just didn't think he'd be the best thing for us to move forward in 2024. The seeds of hatred had already been planted so deep and people's brains were so broken in this country that we just needed a fresh start. I said all this before the election. In fact, I turned down countless opportunities to interview Trump before the election because I didn't want to just be a shill for his campaign. But I'm still portrayed as some MAGA yes-man.

More than anything, the Trump era has just reconfirmed to me how little I trust the media and how much I hate the left. Because all the people who continually attack me now look and sound and talk the same exact way as the people who have attacked me for decades. If it was the right attacking me instead of the left, I'd probably hate them more. From the early days of KO Barstool to the No Fun Squad to Occupy Wall Street to Deadspin to the Daily Beast to the extremes of the #MeToo movement or BLM or Free Palestine—

it's the same group of serial protesters who hate America and move from cause to cause, complaining about how awful this country is. Or how evil white men are. They talk about how morally superior they are to everybody else. They lecture the rest of the country on what jokes are okay to laugh at and who it is acceptable to vote for. These are the people I fucking hate. And the ironic thing is, I'm probably closer to their political views than I am to the right, but they are so damn insufferable that they've pushed me to Trump. And they probably got him elected. Twice.

PS: Since I'm ranting about the absurdity of politics, can I say one more thing that drives me crazy? I guess I can since it's my book. I hate how so many people in this country proclaim to hate it. All they do is criticize it. They don't want to celebrate the Fourth of July. They don't want to root for America in the Olympics. When was the last time AOC or Ilhan Omar or Rashida Tlaib said something positive about the United States? It's always about how awful it is here. How racist, how unfair, how sexist. How bad capitalism is. Yet all anybody wants to do is come to this country. All anybody wants to do is migrate here. I'm not saying the United States is perfect by any stretch of the imagination, but where else would you want to live? Who is doing it better than we are? If it's so fucking bad, you can leave. But nobody ever does. They just complain about it. People wave flags of other countries in the street and say death to America while not wanting to be within miles and miles of the place they came from. In half these countries, if you tried to protest in the streets, you'd be thrown in prison or killed. This is all stuff that made the Donald Trump movement grow. At some point you are just sick of hearing how shitty your country is when it's still the best country in the world.

Anyway, toward the end of COVID, I fled down to Florida. I was sick of all the bullshit in the world. I would snicker from afar whenever I'd see mass BLM protests with no social distancing and no masks while Democratic leaders were still shutting down states and arresting business owners for having their stores or restaurants open. I'd laugh when Democratic leaders all flocked to

DC for Biden's inauguration, openly defying their own COVID rules about travel restrictions and large gatherings. It was just another vivid case of rules for thee but not for me.

I was fed up with pretty much everything at that point. If I hadn't just signed the Penn deal, I probably would have left Barstool right then. Alas, I was barely into year one of a five-year contract. And even though I was mad at my own company, I had made a promise to Penn to work my ass off for them, and a Lannister/Portnoy always pays his debts.

But if I thought I was fed up then, I hadn't seen anything yet.

20

Business Insider

Business Fucking Insider. I've been thinking about how to write this chapter ever since I agreed to do this book. Just the mere mention of this publication still takes me to a pretty dark place and makes my blood boil to the point where I should probably see a doctor. All the emotions and all the hate start flooding back to me like it's all happening all over again. There are still massive unpaid debts for everybody who was involved in this hatchet job on my life. There are still engraved champagne bottles sitting on my shelf waiting to be popped.

I'm never above dancing on people's graves. A trademark of mine is to pop bottles of champagne when my enemies fail. I actually get them personalized in advance, with the names of my enemies engraved onto the bottle, and I stow them away for the day when they fall. I've had the good fortune of popping a lot of bottles of champagne in my time. And there are plenty left sitting on the shelf.

I've written and talked about this so much in the past that I'm sure some longtime Stoolies will skip over this chapter because they're sick of hearing me rant and rave about it. But I'm pretty sure if you were ever the victim of such a seemingly fabricated smear campaign in your life, you'd stay pretty fucking mad too. If you had to call your parents and warn them that their son was basically about to be accused of rape, you'd be pretty pissed. If your girlfriends' parents had to read that you were a rapist before you even got a chance to meet them, you'd be pretty fucking angry too.

Now, for those who may not be overly familiar with every detail of my life, I guess I should do a quick recap. In November 2021 and then again in February 2022, I was the victim of two Business Insider hit pieces that basically accused me of rape without calling it rape. What do I mean by that? Well, this was the headline of the article:

> "I was literally screaming in pain": Young women say they met Barstool Sports founder Dave Portnoy for sex and it turned violent and humiliating

Umm, that sounds like rape to me, doesn't it? What is crazy is that if you actually read the article, you'd realize that all the accusers said it was 100 percent consensual sex at all times. So what are we even talking about here? Well, Business Insider was just using the most salacious and made-up headlines possible to get people to buy these articles that were hidden behind a paywall. *Hey we never said he raped anybody . . . we just made it sound that way so you'd pay for the article and we can't be sued.* Unfortunately, this technique is par for the course with Business Insider. This was a publication started by notorious scumbag Henry Blodget—a man so vile that he was literally kicked off Wall Street for lying and cheating. He would privately send emails about how shitty certain stocks were to coworkers while simultaneously telling his unsuspecting clients to buy them. Just the worst type of human alive. I mean do you know what type of absolute lowlife dirtbag you need to be to be kicked off Wall Street, an industry filled with scoundrels, thieves, and crooks? But Blodget was the worst of the worst. There seemed to be no line he wouldn't cross to make a buck. This is who owned Business Insider.

I guess it shouldn't be surprising then that a publication, owned by a guy who was kicked off Wall Street for lying, cheating, and stealing, dropped both hit pieces on the day before Penn Gaming announced their earnings. That's right: both articles miraculously were published less than twenty-four hours before Penn's earning calls. Not only that but somebody had shorted Penn stock both times right before the hit pieces dropped because they had inside information. They knew what was coming and they knew how to profit from it. It appeared that someone may have been up to his old Wall Street tricks again.

(For those non-savvy Wall Street people, shorting a stock is like betting on a team to lose a game. And knowing that a hit piece about me was about to go viral, and would tank Penn's stock, would be like knowing the starting QB is injured when nobody else knows that. It's inside information and it's illegal.)

As I sit here today, I still don't know how Business Insider got away with it. When I say there wasn't an ounce of truth to any of the allegations, I mean there wasn't an ounce of truth to any of the allegations. Not .00001 percent truth. Like I went back and read my old blogs from this time period to refresh my memory of it all, and my jaw still hits the floor every time because of how shocking and blatant the lies are. I was pretty much instantly able to publish a mountain of evidence unequivocally proving my innocence, and Business Insider has never once been forced to apologize or retract a word.

A "journalist" named Julia Black spent almost two years trying to dig up dirt on me and reached out to every single woman I was connected to on social media. She spent months and months researching this story. And once the story was done, they sent me a gigantic list of questions to confirm or deny and only gave me a day to respond before they were going to publish it. I had basically no time at all to provide my side of the story. (I put journalist in quotes because prior to this hit piece on me, Julia's most compelling investigative journalism pieces were "This Roasted Squash Recipe Is the Ultimate Vegetarian Main" and "How Hannah Bronfman Stays Healthy While Eating Out a Ton." How she went from that hard-hitting journalism to a two-year hit piece on me, I'll never know.) Either way, Julia Black was never willing to sit down with me and let me present any of my evidence.

Imagine spending that long working on a feature story about one person, and that person is not only willing to speak to you but actively wants to go on the record with you, and you provide such a short time? Insane. Not surprisingly, she also never reached out to my ex-wife Renee or Erika Nardini or my current girlfriend at the time or any female who she knew would defend me and contradict her made-up narrative. She did somehow get in touch with my best friend Elio though. Elio called me one day and was like, "YOU OWE ME BIG TIME." I asked him what for. He said, "I JUST TALKED TO SOME REPORTER JULIA BLACK FOR AN HOUR FOR YOU!" Buddy, that's a hit piece! She just talked to you so she could pretend that she was interested in both sides of the story. You were a patsy! I think Elio was quoted in the article as saying, "Dave is a nice guy." Fucking Elio.

(As a sidenote, Renee was probably my number one confidante during this entire mess. She knew me better than anybody and was equally outraged at the accusations. She was the only person who wanted Julia Black dead more than I did. [My editor wanted me to clarify that I would never actually kill Julia Black. So I'll just say that if she were to die of natural causes, I'd be happy.] Renee and I had been separated for years by then, and I'm sure reading those stories was not easy for her. But she did it and she didn't judge me at all; she just wanted revenge. That's a real ride-or-die.)

Now, I debated relitigating my entire case here in this book and posting all the text messages and screenshots again. But what's the point? I've already proven my innocence beyond a shadow of a doubt. I've already posted all the hard evidence and it's readily available on the internet if you want to check it out. Anybody with a brain (even my dumbest employee Mintzy, more on him in a bit) who looked at this bullshit for more than two seconds could clearly see that all the accusations were bullshit. The stories are filled with outright lies and contradictions.

The question I've always had is, why did they lie? How did this entire thing start?

Here is what I do know for a fact. I know that at one point prior to this Business Insider story being published, my old friend Sofia Franklyn from *Call Her Daddy* was putting up posts on her Instagram story every single day asking if any girls had stories of hooking up with me, then deleting her story posts to cover it up. Now, at this time, she was recording her own solo podcast, *Sofia with an F,* and her producer was Muj, aka the Milfhunter. Yes, the same guy I was forced to hire for *Call Her Daddy*. A guy who publicly quit Barstool with a nonsensical Twitter rant about how I was racist and Barstool was the worst company in the world. There isn't a ton of context that you are missing behind this guy. He was with us for less than a year and quit out of left field, saying his morals couldn't let him work for us anymore.

The *Milfhunter* said that.

Yes, the same guy who was constantly maneuvering behind the scenes to stab both Alex and Sofia in the back. The guy who tried to pressure Alex Cooper for money. The guy who actually told me at one point there was never a person he'd met in his life who he hadn't tried to con prior to his arrival at Barstool. Yes, that Milfhunter took a moral stand against a place he had worked at for ten minutes. And now he and Sofia were working together. Two people who hated my guts and seemingly blamed all their problems on me.

Oh, and did I mention the fact that Muj was *dating* the star witness from the Business Insider article? A girl who, after the BI article blew up, instantly became an OnlyFans porn star? A girl who openly confessed to being a pathological liar on camera?

How did I know that? Because this girl went on a podcast and literally said she was dating Muj, and that Muj and Sofia were the ones who connected her to Business Insider.

Gee, you don't say.

So you had Sofia (who hates my guts, Alex had claimed she was willing to lie about sexual harassment charges, and was actively begging for dirt on me) and Muj (who was now dating one of Business Insider's star witnesses). This is who Julia Black trusted as her key sources? Hmm, maybe this should have been mentioned somewhere? Because it would not only seem possible but overwhelmingly probable that Sofia and Muj put this plan in motion as revenge for the way *Call Her Daddy* ended for them. And by the way, I respect a grudge revenge plan as much as the next guy. But to just blatantly make up sexual assault charges? Disgusting on all levels.

So I'm pretty sure Sofia and Muj concocted this entire plan. But I still don't get how they got connected to Business Insider. Why would Julia Black ever believe these two losers when their stories were so flimsy? Why would she publish such clear and obvious lies? How was it possible she had access to all the girls' DMs and text messages before they hooked up with me, but no access to the messages that came *after* they hooked up with me? How did Julia ignore or withhold every single piece of evidence that would have exonerated me? I still had all the receipts and they all showed that nothing bad had happened. To me, this selective omission of evidence was clear and obvious malice, which is exactly why I sued Business Insider. I was willing to literally spend as much money as was necessary to get answers to these questions.

Who had ordered this hit piece? Who had connected Sofia and Muj to Business Insider? Why did the articles keep dropping right before the Penn earnings calls, when they could have the strongest impact on Penn stock? Was Steve Cohen from the GameStop saga somehow involved with insider trading, manipulating Penn stock to crash so he could collect billions for his firm? Who was lying the most? Where did it all start? I just wanted Business Insider to have to answer these basic questions and turn over their email communications because I knew it would vindicate me and possibly land them in jail.

Unfortunately, the American justice system is fucked. From day one, every lawyer I spoke with told me I was fighting an uphill battle. They said that unless Business Insider had said something like "Dave Portnoy was arrested and spent two days in jail" (when I clearly didn't), it would be almost impossible to prove defamation. Julia Black could always hide behind the fact that she was a shitty reporter. And that's pretty much exactly what the judge said before throwing out my case. The judge said that shoddy, negligent reporting did not qualify as malice required for public-figure libel cases. In other words, being a complete idiot and not doing your job right didn't meet the standard needed to prove defamation.

It all seemed insane to me. Like wasn't it Julia Black's job to verify these girls' stories or pick holes in them instead of just blindly believing their lies and trying to ruin my life? Nope. She seemed to want them to make shit up because it helped her preconceived narrative, and she could always plead ignorance of all the evidence that she didn't know existed.

I'd like to believe you can live in a world where people can't blatantly make up rape accusations about you and get away with it, but Business Insider did. I often wonder what would have happened if I hadn't kept all those texts and screenshots that proved my innocence. Would people have believed me? I'd like to believe they would have. After all, one of the reasons I've never been successfully canceled is because I've been brutally honest with our readers over two decades. They've seen the good, the bad, and the ugly. I'm an open book. Even when this article broke, the Penn lawyers were telling me not to say anything. My own lawyers were telling me to stay silent. I ignored their advice and responded to the allegations head-on and immediately, the same way I always do. I wasn't worried about incriminating myself or causing more problems because I had nothing to hide. That's the reason I've been able to survive and thrive through all this madness. It's because I always tell the truth and I'm willing to go to the end of the earth to defend it.

But it's not enough for me to survive each attack. I need revenge. I need to see my enemies suffer. And unfortunately, not all of them have yet.

Example number one of that is Mina Kimes. Yes, the woman who is omnipresent on ESPN. I think she's one of the great frauds and hypocrites of our generation. A true cancer to society. She has earned herself a champagne bottle that I can't wait to pop open one day. Why do I hate her so much? Well, she retweeted the original article about me ten minutes after it was published, saying it was "disturbing reporting." It was almost like she knew the article from BI was coming. Up to that point I had never interacted with Mina Kimes and actually thought she was rational. So I DM'd her and told her to read my rebuttal to the accusations before passing judgment. Because anybody who looks at the facts of this case would clearly see I was 100 percent innocent.

Well, instead of doing that, Mina blocked me. Then, when Business Insider wrote their follow-up hit piece, she once again retweeted it to her hundreds of thousands of followers, again just ten minutes after it was published. I'm not exaggerating the timeframe. Literally ten minutes after it was published both times. Honestly, I think she should be in jail for this. Think about how mad you would be if this were you. Somebody makes up a totally fabricated story calling you a rapist, and a well-known media personality is retweeting them and spreading these lies before she even has time to read the actual articles. It's insanity and she should be held responsible for it.

A few years ago, Business Insider held a strike against management. Basically, Blodget and his cronies were accused of stealing healthcare and other benefits from their employees. The biggest loser in the world, Nick Carlson, who was the editor of Business Insider, was literally filmed riding his bike around town ripping down protest signs.

So what did I do? Well naturally, I showed up outside Business Insider

HQ to join the picket line. What is that old expression, the enemy of my enemy is my friend? Needless to say, the Business Insider employees didn't know what to do. They couldn't decide who they hated more: Boss Blodget or me? In the end, they just ran and hid inside the building so they didn't have to deal with me. It was basically the same cowardly behavior Business Insider has shown whenever I try to confront them about their lies.

If you thought I was through the woods once the Business Insider scandal ended, you'd be wrong. A few months later, the *New York Times* came calling. All of a sudden I started getting the same random messages and calls from women I hadn't talked to in years, or in some cases from girls I had never even met, saying the *New York Times* contacted them for comment on me. It all sounded so eerily familiar: the reporters asking if I ever did anything inappropriate with them, etc. This went on for roughly eight months or so. Every day a new girl would randomly DM me being like, "I thought you should know that a weird, creepy reporter reached out to me." There were actually two reporters working on the case at the time. One was Emily Steel, who won a fucking Pulitzer in 2018 for her work uncovering sexual misconduct during the #MeToo movement. More specifically, she won for uncovering secret settlements and a toxic culture in the media industry, including reports on Bill O'Reilly and Vice Media. Her reporting led to $45 million in settlements.

Well, this ace reporter spent a year digging through all my skeletons and my past history, trying to win her second Pulitzer. You know what she found on me? NOTHING. A big fat zero. There were no secret deals. No secret accusations or lawsuits. She wasted a year of her life on me and got jack shit. Essentially, that's what should have happened with Julia Black too. But my guess is that the *New York Times* holds their reporting to a higher journalistic standard than Business Insider. In other words, they don't print completely disproven lies.

Emily Steel's lack of a story was a ringing endorsement of my character. One of the most famous bulldog-feminist-#MeToo reporters of the generation had me in her crosshairs and found nothing. After a year of wasting her time trying to build a nonexistent case against me, she gave up and pivoted the story into a big nothing-burger about legalized gambling in the United States. Once again, Emily managed to contact every single female in my life except Renee. It was so transparent what she was trying to do.

PS: A funny little anecdote. There were originally two reporters assigned to the *New York Times* article about me, Emily Steel and Liz Day. Well, Liz happened to live in Coral Gables, which was pretty close to me in Miami. I tried reaching out to them via email and phone many, many times to offer my own comments for their article. Naturally, I assumed any real journalist would be thrilled to interview the very subject they were writing their article about. But they kept stonewalling me, kicking the can down the road. By now, I knew how these things went: they'd wait until the night before they published to finally ask you for comment, catching you off guard with no time to craft a real response so they could just say, "We reached out for comment and Portnoy didn't reply."

Well, I wasn't going to let that happen. Since both Emily Steel and Liz Day refused to talk to me about the article, I took it upon myself to talk to them. After being denied every opportunity to share my side of the story, as a last resort, Bald Paul and I decided we'd drive to Liz Day's house.

I had tried to reach out to Liz at least five times asking her to sit down with me, and she had ignored me every time. Instead, I got an email back from the *New York Times* demanding that I stop harassing their reporters. Harassing? Who is harassing who here? I am the one who has been under constant surveillance for three years. I've had to live in constant fear that a reporter is making up lies about me, and I have no chance of a rebuttal. The *New York Times* seemed to believe that only their journalists could dig for information. Only their journalists can ambush people. That I had to sit idly by and let them dig through my trash and tarnish my name.

But no fucking way was I playing by their rules. I had been through enough wars and had been the victim of enough hit pieces to know these people had zero interest in the truth.

That's why I went to Liz Day's house. It was a scene straight out of *Point Break*. We were just sitting in the car, eating snacks with Paul chewing as disgustingly as possible for like five hours. Finally, Liz and her husband came home and we stepped out to talk to her. I asked her why she was calling women and claiming she wanted to talk to them about Miami nightlife, only to then quickly pivot the conversation to whether they had had any negative interactions with me. Why was she trying to coerce them into lying about me? I said if she had any questions, she could ask them to my face. I was happy to answer anything she wanted to know. I was not only an open book, but I had facts and evidence to back up everything I said.

The next day, Liz dropped off the article.

By the way—I never published the video of me ambushing her. It's a hilarious video that the Stoolies would have loved, and if she had stayed on the Dave Portnoy beat, I probably would have. But I had proven my point. Also, luckily her husband was somehow like four feet tall. He was quite literally the least intimidating guy of all time, and that's coming from one of the least intimidating guys of all time. I'm not sure what I would have done if he was some six-foot giant who threatened to pummel me for ambushing his wife like that in their front yard. Luckily, I didn't have to cross that bridge. Once again, the Barstool Gods were shining on me.

(Funny note: The editor of the book read this last Liz Day story and suggested that I delete it. She was actually trying to protect me. She was like, "You've built up all this goodwill and sympathy and then you kind of come across a jerk at the end. Like what about all the people who only know you from pizza reviews? They may be shocked to see this side of you."

Umm, news flash: I can be a jerk. Nobody has ever accused me of taking the high road. When they go low, I go lower. If somebody fucks with me or my life, yes, I take the gloves off. Hate is my Gatorade. Maybe it's an East Coast personality trait or maybe it's just a Dave Portnoy personality trait. Either way, I think it's why I've accumulated so many fans and so many haters along the way. But I'll never change, and who am I trying to fool anyway? If you don't like the guy you are reading about in this book, I probably don't like you either.

In every single house that I own, I have a flag hanging that says "Don't Give Up the Ship." It's an old Navy slogan that I adopted somewhere along the way. I try to live by it. Essentially, what this slogan means to me is that when things are bleakest, and when the easiest option would be to capitulate or give up, that is the exact time when you need to stick to your guns. The flag is a reminder to myself to keep fighting for what I believe is right. And if that means I go down with the ship, so be it.

Don't give up the ship.)

21
Under New Management

By 2022, I had done the impossible. I had been attacked by everybody, from the Daily Beast to Deadspin to Business Insider to the *Washington Post* to the *New York Times*. On and on and on it went. I had been called racist, sexist, homophobic, etc. I had lived through Occupy Wall Street, #MeToo, BLM, COVID, and Trump Derangement Syndrome. And not only was I still standing, but I was seemingly coming out of it at the height of my powers. What is that old expression? Whatever doesn't kill you only makes you stronger? That seemed to be what always happened with me and Barstool. Every time we survived an attack, we found more fans and notoriety. We were appreciated for our straightforward, no-bullshit, it-is-what-it-is attitude. We didn't let the winds of public pressure affect us. We stayed true to our guns and held our convictions.

So many other publications and personalities had fallen by the wayside during my twenty-year rise to the top. So many influencers or celebs had blinked and gotten crushed. We never took a step back. We never apologized for being us. The Pirate Ship had somehow navigated the Seven Seas, plundering and pillaging everywhere we went. And I was still at the wheel, and our flag was still flying.

But like any good story, there was one final battle coming.

In theory, our deal with Penn Gaming should have worked. In a perfect world it would have worked. When we signed the deal with them, I 100 percent thought it would work. They had the sports gambling licenses; we had the brand. It should have been a match made in heaven. And maybe if not for an early decision that we collectively made as a group, it would have been successful.

One of the first discussions we had when Penn acquired Barstool was whether we should name our soon-to-be-launched gambling app the Barstool Sports Sportsbook, or if we should come up with an entirely new name that we could direct all our marketing efforts and traffic toward. I was in favor of keeping the name Barstool in it. I felt like that's what Penn had paid all those millions of dollars for: our name and brand awareness. The counterpoint was that while we clearly had a well-established and rabid fan base, we also had a loud, vocal minority who hated our guts. Putting our name on a gambling app would be like waving red meat in front of them. In the end, we decided the name was too powerful to ignore and we'd just deal with the headaches. That . . . may have been a mistake.

Right from the jump, we had problems. The thing with sports gambling is that it's regulated by the states. And each state can pretty much make up their own rules on how to regulate the thing. Well, surprise, surprise, the liberal states hated my guts and hated Barstool's guts. States like Massachusetts made it nearly impossible for us to do business. We were seemingly operating under a totally different set of rules and regulations from our competitors. They could get away with saying and doing stuff that we couldn't dream of doing. There was literally a Massachusetts Gaming Commission meeting where one of the committee members stood up and openly asked another committee member why she was holding the Barstool Sportsbook to a different standard than everybody else. In New York, we were denied a gambling license because they said our technology wasn't good enough. The only problem with that logic was that we were using the same exact third-party technology as the rest of our competitors. Erika would have to appear before state committee after state committee, fending off a barrage of questions on why we did this or why we said that. The bottom line was that there were liberals on these committees who believed every hit piece ever written about me and recited them like they were reading some unbiased, factual account of my life as opposed to seeing it for the made-up bullshit it was.

Despite all this, we still came out of the gates pretty good. Our crowd showed up and we were making a dent in the industry, with tons of Stoolies signing up and using the Barstool Sportsbook as their sports betting app of choice. So despite all the headaches, I think Penn and I were still pretty positive we were going to navigate our way through all this crap. After all, I'd been dealing with these lunatics for nearly two decades and they hadn't gotten me yet.

Of course, what made this situation far different than anything we had dealt with in the past was that our fortunes were held in the hands of a few people in each state, with no oversight. Usually if you didn't like us, I could tell you to just go fuck yourself. But here we had to play by their rules or lose our licenses.

Then one by one, the dominos began to fall. Things or incidents that would have been laughed at or shrugged off in the past were now far more serious in our new, regulated environment. In April 2021, I had my first sex tape leak. Yes, I said my first sex tape. Now don't go searching for any of them because they are all taken down and it's a federal crime to watch it in the first place. But lots of people committed federal crimes the day it leaked. It felt like maybe the whole country should have been arrested. I remember I was lying in bed with my girlfriend at the time when my phone started blowing up around midnight. I looked at a few texts and was like . . . *wtf?* My girlfriend asked to see my phone because she thought I was talking to another girl. I told her that I'd prefer not to show it to her. She demanded to look at it. Fine, okay, here you go. No big deal. It's just a sex tape of me that just hit the internet streets.

Needless to say, she got up and left. I had tried to tell her she didn't want to look at my phone. Just a classic case of damned if you do, damned if you don't.

Now, I've had a lot of viral moments during my career at Barstool. But still to this day, they all pale in comparison to Sex Tape Leak #1. I couldn't go anywhere without people mentioning it. Walking down the street, total strangers would yell, "Hey Pres, way to fuck her, buddy!" Going to CVS to get ice cream, I'd hear, "Nice stance, Bagwell!" People thought my fucking stance looked like Jeff Bagwell's batting stance, and to be honest, it kind of did. Everywhere I went, people were talking about it.

To this day, I have no idea who leaked it or how. I honestly didn't care. I thought I looked pretty good in it and the girl was hot. I certainly could have had worse angles. I did feel horrible for the girl in it though because she definitely didn't sign up for that and it was a very old video. She had a boyfriend when the leak happened and I'm sure that's the last thing in the world she wanted.

Over the years, people had always come out of the woodwork to try to blackmail me with X-rated content that had leaked somehow. At one point, I suggested to Erika that I just create an OnlyFans with all my explicit content in one spot, and I'd donate all the money to charity. I doubt anybody would have bought it, but at least that would have put an end to the blackmail attempts pretty quickly. Sadly, Erika didn't think Penn would go for it.

Oh yeah, back to Penn. My sex tape caused Penn stock to instantly tank 5 percent. I released a public statement that was on brand for me:

> Somebody committing a crime by leaking an old video of sex between two consenting adults seems like a dumb reason for a stock to go down. As far as I know, nobody would exist on earth without intercourse. And anybody who shared or watched it committed a federal crime. It was never meant for public consumption. Either way, it presents a good buying opportunity in my mind.

Hey Penn Gaming, welcome to the Dave Portnoy experience. Obviously I felt bad about it, but at the same time this had happened long before I did the deal with Penn. There was nothing that I could have done differently to stop it.

The next shoe to drop was the Business Insider hit pieces, which I discussed in the last chapter. As a reminder, both hit pieces dropped the day before Penn earnings calls and caused the stock to drop close to 20 percent. Again, I felt awful about it, but what could I have done differently? I was the victim of a vicious smear campaign, and somebody was shorting Penn stock and making a boatload of money off this entire thing by knowing when the hit pieces were coming out and exactly how they would affect the stock price. It felt like an episode of *Billions* on Showtime. Oh by the way, was that show based on a real person? I forget.

Anyway, Penn stuck with me and publicly defended me through each ordeal, which I'm sure wasn't easy. It was also more than the Chernin Group ever did, which I appreciated. I will say that I remember Jay Snowden and me having one very uncomfortable conversation after the Business Insider articles. He wanted me to promise that I wouldn't date any women under twenty-four years old. Now keep in mind, I was in a fully committed, long-term relationship at this point. But I still refused to make that concession. To me that would have been a win for Business Insider. Why should I have to abide by a totally different set of rules from the rest of society? Because people made up lies about me? I will never break any laws, but I also won't agree not to do things that every other citizen of the United States is allowed to do. It was a principle thing for me.

Weirdly, I feel like the Business Insider debacle brought Jay Snowden and me closer together. And we were already pretty close. He trusted me and went to bat for me and defended me to his board. Then, as the facts played out, everything I told him was 100 percent the truth. If he didn't trust me before, he did then. He had a partner in me who, through the good, the bad, and the ugly, would never lie to him. So even though the entire thing sucked, life at Barstool continued as usual. Nonsense, controversy, conflict . . . the freakshow rolled on. That is, until the dumbest employee I've ever hired rapped the N-word on a livestream.

Enter Ben "Mintzy" Mintz. Bearing the face and brain of an infant, Mintzy is forever stumbling through life on the way to his next colossal mistake. He then bows his head and apologizes profusely for his idiocy, promises to be better going forward, and gets himself off the hook because if the fault lies with anyone, it's me. I am to blame for keeping this bumbling fool aboard our ship, because I know full well that he will continue to break things and fuck up on a scale that seems cosmically impossible. We all know that age-old definition of insanity: repeating the same thing and expecting different results. In this case, I guess I'm a little insane for continuing to allow Mintzy his airtime while expecting that he won't say or do something that brings down a horde of ferocious wasps on our necks.

In 2023, Mintzy started a live morning show called *Wake Up Mintzy*—some half-hearted effort to prove to me that he did, in fact, do work around here. The show was never going to be a hit, never going to bring in ad revenue, but it was my equivalent of handing the football to the youngest kid in the family at Thanksgiving and letting him run for a touchdown.

Somehow, his show was livestreamed. Somehow, his producers had not worked in a ten-second dump button. Somehow, nobody thought to install any sort of safety precaution to guard against the utterly inevitable moment when Mintzy would do something that the world should not see, causing gigantic ramifications for the company that produced his show.

That moment came one fine morning when Mintzy decided to rap the lyrics to Bone Thugs-N-Harmony's "1st of tha Month." No beat, simply reading the lyrics off a screen, lost in the lyrics of one of the nineties' greatest rap groups, Mintzy stomped the landing on an N-word lyric. He immediately looked up in shock, realizing what he'd said out loud, knowing he'd uttered the one word you really can never say online. (Yes, I know I did the same thing years earlier, before the BLM movement. That's what made this one twice as bad. *Oh, there goes Barstool being Barstool again . . .*)

If you watch the video, it's clear he's not being racist or mean in any way. It's a true Ron Burgundy moment when he cannot self-censor and will read any words that are put in front of him. It would have been hilarious had it not caused such a problem for Penn.

They called me that day to tell me I had to fire him. Do not pass go, do not collect $200, Mintzy must leave the building.

I was stunned. I pushed back against Penn's firing directive. I tried to explain that if we fired Mintzy for this, it would go against so much of what I had defined as our company culture for so many years. Barstool cancels one of its own? Really? That went against every fiber of my being. I hated the idea that we would fall in line with the masses of protesters, the crusaders, the woke liberators who held humans to an impossible standard of perfection—a standard where any human error, however accidental, should result in someone losing their job, their healthcare, and possibly their future.

Where would Ben Mintz go if I fired him? I felt an obligation to protect him, because he was one of my guys, part of my flock. If we fired him, it's not as though other media companies would rush in to scoop him up. He's a moron, remember?

But Penn felt differently. This was a word that every single employee knew was a deal-breaker beforehand. This was a line that Penn had promised regulators would never be crossed. And if it was, there would be immediate repercussions. They had no choice but to act on their promise to the regulators.

I called Mintzy to let him know, and I told him I tried hard to convince them otherwise and I wasn't happy with their decision at all. He understood, apologized profusely, and thanked me for his time with us. It was devastating.

Later that day, I issued an Emergency Press Conference on Twitter. Here was my exact statement:

> I hate the decision. I disagree with the decision. I would not have made the decision. But I don't deal with the things Penn deals with in terms of state regulators, etc. Penn paid a lot of money for Barstool and they have to make the best decisions to protect their business. I trust and respect that Jay Snowden makes what he thinks are the right moves, and that's all you can ask for. Doesn't mean I'll always agree, but again, he deals with things I don't have to think or deal with. Penn believes there's a legitimate chance lots of states could pull their licenses because of this. Penn's a multibillion-dollar company. Without their

> licenses, they are a zero-dollar company. Investors, families, employees, thousands of people they believe it's their job to protect all this for, and the only answer is to fire Ben Mintz.

I still disagreed with it and maybe I'm naïve, but I thought, *There is just no way anybody can look at that clip and think the punishment fits the crime.* It makes my skin crawl thinking a guy could lose his job on an innocent mistake. Yes, horrible, but clearly no intent. It's everything I had stood against for twenty years.

As predicted, our fans were disgusted by the move. Twitter and Reddit ran riot through the streets, disavowing Penn as the dark corporate overlords of their once-beloved Barstool, and they destroyed me for selling my soul to the devil. There was nothing I could do. Barstool was Penn now. I had to eat it, no matter how much I hated the taste. Wall Street hated it too. Penn stock plummeted 13 percent. Just an absolutely miserable day all the way around. The worst part was that I think Jay agreed with everything I was saying. In no world did he think Mintzy deserved to be fired or did he want me to fire him. But his hands were tied by the regulators. Would you risk a billion-dollar business to save Mintzy?

I had to accept that I could no longer protect the circus of goofballs, weirdos, and freaks I had come to love. My people, my oddballs, were no longer mine to keep if they stepped too far out-of-bounds. Granted, it shouldn't have been hard to stay within the lines, but again . . . Mintzy.

Now, about the same time that the Mintzy incident happened, Penn was in the process of doing a major tech overhaul of our gambling app to hopefully put it on a more even playing field with our competitors. The big question was whether our fans would continue to support it after the Mintzy incident now that they viewed Penn as the corporate bad guy. Well, this was a question we never had the chance to answer.

One day in the summer of 2023, Jay Snowden hit me up to meet with him in New York for lunch. We met in an empty Italian restaurant that had the feel of a *Godfather* movie. I literally said to Jay as we walked to our table that this felt like a restaurant where somebody would get whacked. It's still maybe the best call I've ever made in my life.

After exchanging pleasantries for a few minutes, Jay proceeded to tell me that over the past couple weeks, he had brokered an exclusive deal with ESPN to promote the Penn sportsbook. At first, I didn't even process what he was saying. I thought this was good news. I said, "Oh man, that's awesome. Are McAfee and Van Pelt going to promote it for us too?" Then he went on to tell me that there was one sticking point in the deal that ESPN said was nonnegotiable. Disney (the owner of ESPN) specifically said that I couldn't be part of this transaction in any form.

Wait, what? What does that mean? Am I getting whacked here? What is going on? But yes, I had heard Jay right. The Barstool Sportsbook was becoming ESPN Bet. Penn had formed a partnership with ESPN, and the only way ESPN would agree to it was with the understanding that I wasn't a part of Barstool anymore.

Jay then told me that all my stock options would vest instantly, which would make me a very rich man. I could finally quit the grind and go buy an even bigger dream home in Nantucket and not have to deal with any of the bullshit anymore.

Needless to say, I was stunned. Walking out of that restaurant, I didn't even know how I felt. Was I happy I was done? Was I mad that ESPN, of all places, had just fired me from my own company? What would happen to all the idiots at Barstool once I left?

I called Renee and told her what had happened. She was speechless. Then I spoke with Dan and Erika, who had each separately met with Jay. I asked them what they wanted to do. Did they want to work for ESPN?

It wasn't a long discussion. Dan still hated ESPN from the *Barstool Van Talk* days. Erika had no interest in working for them. I also knew that 80 percent of our employees would probably get laid off if I was gone. There would be no need for the circus anymore with ESPN taking over.

So I made a decision: I was going to get my idiotic company back.

The next day, I called Jay and told him that I wasn't going to go quietly into the night. I wasn't leaving Barstool. Bob Iger could go fuck himself, for all I cared.

It was an impossible situation for Penn. Over the years it had become painfully obvious that Barstool—and specifically me—couldn't thrive in a regulated environment. Jay had stuck with us, defended us, and tried everything in his power to make it work. But it was just one regulatory setback after another, one scandal after another. So I certainly understood why the ESPN opportunity was so tempting for him.

But Jay also knew me pretty well. There was just no way I was going to let ESPN fire me from my own company, the company I had spent two decades building.

So Jay and I sat down and hashed out a deal. We had always had a good relationship and we both agreed that Barstool should remain in my hands. At the time, Barstool was losing close to $12 million a year. I would buy the entire company back for one dollar, taking us off Penn's books and inheriting all the expenses. In exchange, I agreed that I would never disparage ESPN Bet, and I signed a ten-year NDA promising as much. And yes, keeping my mouth shut, knowing what those fucks at ESPN had tried to do to me, has been one of the hardest things I've had to do in my career.

Now, who knows: maybe the Penn/ESPN/Barstool deal would have worked if ESPN hadn't demanded that I get fired. Maybe Barstool could have promoted ESPN Bet and made a huge impact together, but I guess we'll never know. Disney/ESPN refused to allow it. Instead, ESPN's app delivered worse numbers than ours had, and we hadn't even tried to promote with the new-and-improved app yet.

ESPN Bet's performance was so dismal that at the end of 2025, Penn exercised their exit clause to get out of the deal. You know what that means, right? I don't have to keep my mouth shut anymore. I can tell the world what actually happened.

People always ask, "Hey Dave, how did you get Barstool back?" Well, it's all thanks to those morons at ESPN who tried to fire me from my own company. Instead, they gave me the greatest gift possible. Not only did I get my company back for one dollar, but they also gave me the perfect ending to this twenty-three-year fairy tale. After delivering all those newspapers, after all the hit pieces, after all the scandals, after selling the company twice, I bought it all back for one dollar. I mean, the best scriptwriter in Hollywood couldn't write a better ending than this.

You don't cancel me; I cancel you.

Epilogue

The final section of a book, play, or movie that comes after the main story ends. It usually shows what happens to the characters later or gives closure to the story.

My editor said I need this part, so here goes:

So I've had Barstool back for about three years now. Shortly after I got full control of the company back, Erika decided that it was time for her to part ways. She offered to stay as long as I needed her, but I think she knew that the goals of the company were no longer to grow at warp speed anymore. These days, I just want Barstool to be a place where people enjoy working and we don't lose money. And Erika had accomplished everything she set out to accomplish and then some. We still stay in touch and I know if I need her for anything, she'd be there in a flash.

Once I took over, my first order of business was to hire back that idiot Mintzy and right the wrong of being forced to fire him for an honest mistake. The second order of business was to make us profitable again. That took me about five minutes to do.

Almost all of us early guys from the Milton days are still here. We're all a bit older, a bit richer, and a bit grayer. Bald Paul is still bald and chewing his gum as loudly as ever. All these years later, Barstool is still an absolute content machine that operates best when unburdened by the rules of traditional media. We still have the biggest mishmash of weird brains ever assembled under one roof. Rico Bosco is as crazy as ever. Frank the Tank still rants about the Mets. We continue to lose some stars, like *Bussin' With the Boys* and Caleb Pressley, but we replace them with new stars like Jon Gruden and Ryen Russillo.

Pardon My Take is still a machine. I'd say Dan has taken over as the acting day-to-day CEO in many respects. He now gets to deal with lots of the headaches and issues that I had to deal with over the decades. Every now and again, I'll get a call from him being like, "You'll never believe this happened." I think he has a newfound respect for how difficult it can be to balance being in content and managing content.

As for me, I still have final say on all major decisions and I still obviously do lots of content. Deals and opportunities get thrown my way that are just too big to pass up. But my next birthday will be my fiftieth. I'll have been at the helm of the Pirate Ship for nearly half my life and a quarter of a century. I've always said that one day I'd like to just disappear on a beach and never be heard from again. Well, I live in the Florida Keys in the winter and Nantucket in the summer, so I'm getting closer and closer to that point. That would be the dream ending for me—to actually become the lyric from one of my favorite Jimmy Buffett songs:

But now he's incommunicado
Leavin' such a hole in a world that believed
That a life with such bravado
Was takin' the right way home

But then again, buying horses ain't cheap. So who knows? Maybe I'll never stop working. Go Go Greys Stables ain't gonna pay for itself.

Where's our chapter?